Praise for *Bobos in Paradise*

"An absolute sparkler of a book, which should establish David Brooks—not that he needs establishing—as *the* smart, fun-to-read social critic of his generation."

—Christopher Buckley

"In his briskly written, clever *Bobos in Paradise,* David Brooks astutely describes a new-ish American elite. . . . An enormously accomplished and perceptive reporter."

—Benjamin Schwarz, *Los Angeles Times*

"David Brooks has written a smart, funny book about the new meritocracy, the information-age elite whose members . . . set the tone of our time."

—Diane White, *The Boston Globe*

"A mixture of heartfelt fondness and dead-on ridicule, animated by an energetic glass-half-full ambivalence. The book is a pleasure, simultaneously bracing and comforting."

—Kurt Andersen, *The New York Times Book Review*

"A breezy, well-argued explanation for why affluent, well-educated people crave sub-zero refrigerators. Clever observations . . . and gentle fun."

—Deirdre Donahue, *USA Today*

"As both comedy and sociology, *Bobos in Paradise* succeeds nicely. A terrifically entertaining read, it is fundamentally correct in its premise."

—Alan Wolfe, *The New Republic*

"Insightful and entertaining. The book abounds in perfectly rendered vignettes about the folkways of the educated class of the 1990s, a number of them laugh-out-loud funny."

—Gary Rosen, *Commentary*

"Written with compelling insight, extraordinary felic-itous language, cunning wit, and great affection. . . . Explains numerous paradoxes of the late 20th and embryonic 21st centuries."

—Carlo Wolff, *Fort Worth Star-Telegram*

"A serious social critic wittily dissects an American elite that blends Woodstock hedonism with corporate values."

—Chris Waddington, *Star Tribune* (Minneapolis)

"A thoroughly entertaining shellacking of our most upwardly mobile friends and neighbors."

—Arthur McMaster, *The Tampa Tribune*

"Erudite and readable. Delivers densely packed cultural history and observation sprinkled with gut-busting passages. Brooks's eye is superb."

—Frank Bentayou, *The Plain Dealer* (Cleveland)

"I tried to resist *Bobos in Paradise* . . . but once I started, I was reading big chunks of it out loud to passersby."

—Marta Salij, *Detroit Free Press*

Bobos

SIMON & SCHUSTER PAPERBACKS

NEW YORK   LONDON   TORONTO   SYDNEY

in Paradise

*The New Upper Class
and How They Got There*

David Brooks

TO JANE

Simon & Schuster Paperbacks
Rockefeller Center
1230 Avenue of the Americas
New York, NY 10020

For information about special discounts for bulk purchases,
please contact Simon & Schuster Special Sales at
1-800-456-6798 or business@simonandschuster.com

Designed by Edith Fowler
Manufactured in the United States of America

20 19

The Library of Congress has cataloged the hardcover
edition as follows:
Brooks, David [date].
   Bobos in paradise : the new upper class and how
they got there / David Brooks.
      p.   cm.
   Includes index.
      1. Elite (Social sciences)—United States.
2. Upper class—United States   3. United
States—Social conditions—1980–   4. United
States—Social life and customs—1971–   I. Title.
HN90.E4 B76 2000
305.5'2'0973—dc21   99-88094

ISBN-13: 978-0-684-85377-2
ISBN-10:   0-684-85377-9
ISBN-13: 978-0-684-85378-9 (Pbk)
ISBN-10:   0-684-85378-7 (Pbk)

Contents

Introduction

THIS BOOK started with a series of observations. After four and a half years abroad, I returned to the United States with fresh eyes and was confronted by a series of peculiar juxtapositions. WASPy upscale suburbs were suddenly dotted with arty coffeehouses where people drank little European coffees and listened to alternative music. Meanwhile, the bohemian downtown neighborhoods were packed with multimillion-dollar lofts and those upscale gardening stores where you can buy a faux-authentic trowel for $35.99. Suddenly massive corporations like Microsoft and the Gap were on the scene, citing Gandhi and Jack Kerouac in their advertisements. And the status rules seemed to be turned upside down. Hip lawyers were wearing those teeny tiny steel-framed glasses because now it was apparently more prestigious to look like Franz Kafka than Paul Newman.

The thing that struck me as oddest was the way the

old categories no longer made sense. Throughout the twentieth century it's been pretty easy to distinguish between the bourgeois world of capitalism and the bohemian counterculture. The bourgeoisie were the square, practical ones. They defended tradition and middle-class morality. They worked for corporations, lived in suburbs, and went to church. Meanwhile, the bohemians were the free spirits who flouted convention. They were the artists and the intellectuals—the hippies and the Beats. In the old schema the bohemians championed the values of the radical 1960s and the bourgeois were the enterprising yuppies of the 1980s.

But I returned to an America in which the bohemian and the bourgeois were all mixed up. It was now impossible to tell an espresso-sipping artist from a cappuccino-gulping banker. And this wasn't just a matter of fashion accessories. I found that if you investigated people's attitudes toward sex, morality, leisure time, and work, it was getting harder and harder to separate the antiestablishment renegade from the pro-establishment company man. Most people, at least among the college-educated set, seemed to have rebel attitudes and social-climbing attitudes all scrambled together. Defying expectations and maybe logic, people seemed to have combined the countercultural sixties and the achieving eighties into one social ethos.

After a lot of further reporting and reading, it became clear that what I was observing is a cultural consequence of the information age. In this era ideas and knowledge are at least as vital to economic success as natural resources and finance capital. The intangible world of information merges with the material world of money, and new phrases that combine the two, such as "intellectual capital" and "the culture industry," come into vogue. So the people who thrive in this period are the ones who can turn ideas and emotions into products. These are highly educated folk who have one foot in the bohemian world of creativity and another foot in the bourgeois realm of ambition and worldly success. The members of the new information age elite are bourgeois bohemians. Or, to take the first two letters of each word, they are Bobos.

These Bobos define our age. They are the new establishment. Their hybrid culture is the atmosphere we all breathe. Their status codes now govern social life. Their moral codes give structure to our personal lives. When I use the word *establishment,* it sounds sinister and elitist. Let me say first, I'm a member of this class, as, I suspect, are most readers of this book. We're not so bad. All societies have elites, and our educated elite is a lot more enlightened than some of the older elites, which were based on blood or wealth or military valor. Wherever we educated elites settle, we make life more interesting, diverse, and edifying.

This book is a description of the ideology, manners, and morals of this elite. I start with the superficial things and work my way to the more profound. After a chapter tracing the origins of the affluent educated class, I describe its shopping habits, its business culture, its intellectual, social, and spiritual life. Finally, I try to figure out where the Bobo elite is headed. Where will we turn our attention next? Throughout the book I often go back to the world and ideas of the mid-1950s. That's because the fifties were the final decade of the industrial age, and the contrast between the upscale culture of that time and the upscale culture of today is stark and illuminating. Furthermore, I found that many of the books that really helped me understand the current educated class were written between 1955 and 1965, when the explosion in college enrollments, so crucial to many of these trends, was just beginning. Books like *The Organization Man, The Death and Life of Great American Cities, The Affluent Society, The Status Seekers,* and *The Protestant Establishment* were the first expressions of the new educated class ethos, and while the fever and froth of the 1960s have largely burned away, the ideas of these 1950s intellectuals continue to resonate.

Finally, a word about the tone of this book. There aren't a lot of statistics in these pages. There's not much theory. Max Weber has nothing to worry about from me. I just went out and tried to describe how people are living, using a method that might best be described as comic sociology. The idea is to get at the essence of cultural patterns, getting the flavor of the times without trying to pin it down with meticulous exactitude. Often I make fun of the social manners of my class (I sometimes think I've made a whole career out of self-loathing), but on balance I emerge as a defender of the Bobo culture. In any case, this new establishment is going to be setting the tone for a long time to come, so we might as well understand it and deal with it.

1

The Rise of the Educated Class

I'M NOT SURE I'd like to be one of the people featured on the *New York Times* weddings page, but I know I'd like to be the father of one of them. Imagine how happy Stanley J. Kogan must have been, for example, when his daughter Jamie was admitted to Yale. Then imagine his pride when Jamie made Phi Beta Kappa and graduated summa cum laude. Stanley himself is no slouch in the brains department: he's a pediatric urologist in Croton-on-Hudson, with teaching positions at the Cornell Medical Center and the New York Medical College. Still, he must have enjoyed a gloat or two when his daughter put on that cap and gown.

And things only got better. Jamie breezed through Stanford Law School. And then she met a man—Thomas Arena—who appeared to be exactly the sort of son-in-law that pediatric urologists dream about. He did his undergraduate work at Princeton, where he, too, made Phi Beta

Kappa and graduated summa cum laude. And he, too,
went to law school, at Yale. After school they both went
to work as assistant U.S. attorneys for the mighty Southern District of New York.

These two awesome résumés collided at a wedding
ceremony in Manhattan, and given all the school chums
who must have attended, the combined tuition bills in that
room must have been staggering. The rest of us got to read
about it on the New York Times weddings page. The page
is a weekly obsession for hundreds of thousands of Times
readers and aspiring Balzacs. Unabashedly elitist, secretive,
and totally honest, the "mergers and acquisitions page"
(as some of its devotees call it) has always provided an accurate look at at least a chunk of the American ruling
class. And over the years it has reflected the changing ingredients of elite status.

When America had a pedigreed elite, the page emphasized noble birth and breeding. But in America today it's
genius and geniality that enable you to join the elect. And
when you look at the Times weddings page, you can almost feel the force of the mingling SAT scores. It's Dartmouth marries Berkeley, MBA weds Ph.D., Fulbright
hitches with Rhodes, Lazard Frères joins with CBS, and
summa cum laude embraces summa cum laude (you rarely
see a summa settling for a magna—the tension in such a
marriage would be too great). The Times emphasizes four
things about a person—college degrees, graduate degrees,
career path, and parents' profession—for these are the
markers of upscale Americans today.

Even though you want to hate them, it's hard not to
feel a small tug of approval at the sight of these Résumé
Gods. Their expressions are so open and confident; their
teeth are a tribute to the magnificence of American ortho-
donture; and since the Times will only print photographs
in which the eyebrows of the bride and groom are at the
same level, the couples always look so evenly matched.

These are the kids who spent the crucial years between ages 16 and 24 winning the approval of their elders. Others may have been rebelling at that age or feeling alienated or just basically exploring their baser natures. But the people who made it to this page controlled their hormonal urges and spent their adolescence impressing teachers, preparing for the next debate tournament, committing themselves to hours of extracurricular and volunteer work, and doing everything else that we as a society want teenagers to do. The admissions officer deep down in all of us wants to reward these mentor magnets with bright futures, and the real admissions officers did, accepting them into the right colleges and graduate schools and thus turbocharging them into adulthood.

The overwhelming majority of them were born into upper-middle-class households. In 84 percent of the weddings, both the bride and the groom have a parent who is a business executive, professor, lawyer, or who otherwise belongs to the professional class. You've heard of old money; now we see old brains. And they tend to marry late—the average age for brides is 29 and for grooms is 32. They also divide pretty neatly into two large subgroups: nurturers and predators. Predators are the lawyers, traders, marketers—the folk who deal with money or who spend their professional lives negotiating or competing or otherwise being tough and screwing others. Nurturers tend to be liberal arts majors. They become academics, foundation officials, journalists, activists, and artists—people who deal with ideas or who spend their time cooperating with others or facilitating something. About half the marriages consist of two predators marrying each other: a Duke MBA who works at NationsBank marrying a Michigan Law grad who works at Winston & Strawn. About a fifth of the marriages on the page consist of two nurturers marrying each other: a Fulbright scholar who teaches humanities at Stanford marrying a Rhodes scholar who teaches philosophy there. The remaining marriages on the page are mixed marriages in which a predator marries a nurturer. In this group the predator is usually the groom. A male financial consultant with an MBA from Chicago may marry an elementary school teacher at a progressive school who received her master's in social work from Columbia.

These meritocrats devote monstrous hours to their career and derive enormous satisfaction from their success, but the *Times* wants you to know they are actually not consumed by ambition. Each week the paper describes a particular wedding in great detail, and the subtext of each of these reports is that all this humongous accomplishment is a mere fluke of chance. These people are actually spunky free spirits who just like to have fun. The weekly "Vows" column lovingly details each of the wedding's quirky elements: a bride took her bridesmaids to get drunk at a Russian bathhouse; a couple hired a former member of the band Devo to play the *Jeopardy* theme song at the reception; another read A. A. Milne's Christopher Robin poems at a ceremony in a former du Pont mansion. The *Times* article is inevitably studded with quotations from friends who describe the bride and groom as enchanting paradoxes: they are said to be grounded but berserk, daring yet traditional, high-flying yet down to earth, disheveled yet elegant, sensible yet spontaneous. Either only paradoxical people get married these days, or people in this class like to see themselves and their friends as balancing opposites.

The couples tell a little of their own story in these articles. An amazing number of them seem to have first met while recovering from marathons or searching for the remnants of Pleistocene man while on archeological digs in Eritrea. They usually enjoyed a long and careful romance, including joint vacations in obscure but educational places like Myanmar and Minsk. But many of the

couples broke up for a time, as one or both partners pan-
icked at the thought of losing his or her independence.
Then there was a lonely period apart while one member,
say, arranged the largest merger in Wall Street history
while the other settled for neurosurgery after dropping out
of sommelier school. But they finally got back together
again (sometimes while taking a beach vacation at a group
home with a bunch of people with cheekbones similar to
their own). And eventually they decided to share an apartment. We don't know what their sex lives are like because
the *Times* does not yet have a fornication page ("John
Grind, a lawyer at Skadden Arps with a degree from
Northwestern, has begun copulating with Sarah Smith, a
cardiologist at Sloan-Kettering with an undergraduate degree from Emory"). But we presume intimate relations are
suitably paradoxical: rough yet soft, adventurous yet intimate. Sometimes we get to read about modern couples
who propose to each other simultaneously, but most of
the time the groom does it the old-fashioned way—often,
it seems, while hot-air ballooning above the Napa Valley
or by letting the woman find a diamond engagement ring
in her scuba mask while they are exploring endangered
coral reefs near the Seychelles.

Many of these are trans-conference marriages—an
Ivy League graduate will be marrying a Big Ten graduate—so the ceremony has to be designed to respect everybody's sensibilities. Subdued innovation is the rule. If you
are a member of an elite based on blood and breeding, you
don't need to carefully design a marriage ceremony that
expresses your individual self. Your high status is made
impervious by your ancestry, so you can just repeat the
same ceremony generation after generation. But if you are
in an elite based on brainpower, like today's elite, you
need to come up with the subtle signifiers that will display
your own spiritual and intellectual identity—your qualifi-
cation for being in the elite in the first place. You need in-

vitations on handmade paper but with a traditional type-
face. Selecting music, you need Patsy Cline songs mixed in
with the Mendelssohn. You need a 1950s gown, but done
up so retro it has invisible quotation marks around it. You
need a wedding cake designed to look like a baroque
church. You need to exchange meaningful objects with
each other, like a snowboard engraved with your favorite
Schiller quotation or the childhood rubber ducky that you
used to cradle during the first dark days of your Supreme
Court clerkship. It's difficult to come up with your own
nuptial wrinkle, which will be distinctive without being
daring. But self-actualization is what educated existence is
all about. For members of the educated class, life is one
long graduate school. When they die, God meets them at
the gates of heaven, totes up how many fields of self-
expression they have mastered, and then hands them a divine diploma and lets them in.

The Fifties

The *Times* weddings page didn't always pulse with
the accomplishments of the Résumé Gods. In the late
1950s, the page projected a calm and more stately ethos.
The wedding accounts of that era didn't emphasize jobs or
advanced degrees. The profession of the groom was only
sometimes mentioned, while the profession of the bride
was almost never listed (and on the rare occasions when
the bride's profession was noted, it was in the past tense,
as if the marriage would obviously end her career). Instead, the *Times* listed pedigree and connections. Ancestors were frequently mentioned. The ushers were listed, as
were the bridesmaids. Prep schools were invariably mentioned, along with colleges. The *Times* was also careful to
list the groom's clubs—the Union League, the Cosmopolitan Club. It also ran down the bride's debutante history,

where she came out, and whatever women's clubs she might be a member of, such as the Junior League. In short, the page was a galaxy of restricted organizations. A description of the gown took up a good portion of the article, and the description of the floral arrangements was also exhaustive.

As you read through the weddings page of that time, sentences jump out at you that would never be found on today's weddings page: "She is descended from Richard Warren, who came to Brookhaven in 1664. Her husband, a descendant of Dr. Benjamin Treadwell, who settled in Old Westbury in 1767, is an alumnus of Gunnery School and a senior at Colgate University." Or "Mrs. Williams is an alumna of Ashley Hall and Smith College. A provisional member of the Junior League of New York, she was presented to society in 1952 at the Debutante Cotillion and Christmas Ball." Even the captions would be unthinkable today: "Mrs. Peter J. Belton, who was Nancy Stevens." (The *Times* would only use that past tense caption today for people who have had sex change operations.)

The paper, more reticent, did not list ages in those days, but the couples were clearly much younger; many of the grooms were still in college. A significant portion of the men had attended West Point or Annapolis, for this was a time when the military academies were still enmeshed in the East Coast establishment, and military service was still something that elite young men did. The section itself was huge in the late fifties. On a June Sunday it could stretch over 28 pages and cover 158 weddings. The ceremonies were much more likely then than now to have taken place in old-line suburbs—such towns as Bryn Mawr on Philadelphia's Main Line or Greenwich in Connecticut, Princeton in New Jersey, or the haughtier towns around Chicago, Atlanta, San Francisco, and elsewhere across the nation. The section was also, predictably, WASPier. About half the couples who were featured in the late fifties were married in an Episcopal ceremony. Today fewer than one in five of the marriages on the *Times* page are Episcopalian, while around 40 percent are Jewish, and there are many more Asian names. It's hard to directly measure the rise of different religious groups, because in the 1950s Jewish weddings were listed separately on Mondays, but it's pretty clear the trends of the last 40 years have been bad for the Episcopalians and good for the Jews.

Looking at the faces and the descriptions of the wedding section of the 1950s is like looking into a different world, and yet it's not really been so long—most of the people on those yellowing pages are still alive, and a sizable portion of the brides on those pages are young enough that they haven't yet been dumped for trophy spouses. The section from the late fifties evokes an entire milieu that was then so powerful and is now so dated: the network of men's clubs, country clubs, white-shoe law firms, oak-paneled Wall Street firms, and WASP patriarchs. Everybody has his or her own mental images of the old Protestant Establishment: lockjaw accents, the Social Register, fraternity jocks passing through Ivy League schools, constant rounds of martinis and highballs, bankers' hours, starched old men like Averell Harriman, Dean Acheson, and John J. McCloy, the local bigwigs that appear in John Cheever and John O'Hara stories. Of course, no era is as simple as its clichés—John J. McCloy, the quintessential East Coast patrician, was actually a self-made man—but the sociological evidence from the period does generally support the stereotypes.

There was a strong sense of inherited European culture. "Have John learn Greek," McCloy's father rasped on his deathbed. Young girls still cared about the aristocratic Coming Out rituals, which were measured by gradations that are now long forgotten. Christmas season was the busiest time to debut, while the Thanksgiving period was the briefer but more socially select time. Main-line Protestant denominations were thriving in those days. Three-quarters of the political, business, and military elites were Protestant, according to studies done at the time. It really was possible to talk about an aristocratic ruling class in the fifties and early sixties, a national elite populated by men who had gone to northeastern prep schools like Groton, Andover, Exeter, and St. Paul's and then ascended through old-line firms on Wall Street into the boardrooms of the Fortune 500 corporations and into the halls of Washington power. The WASPs didn't have total control of the country or anything like it, but they did have the hypnotic magic of prestige. As Richard Rovere wrote in a famous 1962 essay entitled "The American Establishment," "It has very nearly unchallenged power in deciding what is and what is not respectable opinion in this country." If you look at the news photographs from *Time* or *Newsweek* in those days, you see one sixtyish white male after another. Among other things, this elite had the power to drive the ambitious climbers who lacked the proper breeding—like Lyndon Johnson and Richard Nixon—nearly crazy with resentment.

Meanwhile, every affluent town in America had its own establishment that aped the manners and attitudes of the national one. There were local clubs where town fathers gathered to exchange ethnic jokes and dine on lamb chops topped with canned sauces—cream of mushroom, cream of asparagus, cream of leek. (People didn't worry about cholesterol then, since it had not yet become unfashionable to get sick and die.) The WASP aesthetic sense was generally lamentable—Mencken said Protestant elites had a "libido for the ugly"—and their conversation, by all accounts, did not sparkle with wit and intelligence. They tortured their young girls by allowing them to take horseback riding lessons but then forcing them to compete in dressage competitions, where they mastered all the virtues that were characteristic of the WASP elite and that are so uncharacteristic of today's educated elite: good posture, genteel manners, extreme personal hygiene, pointless discipline, the ability to sit still for long periods of time.

This was the last great age of socially acceptable boozing. It was still an era when fox hunting and polo didn't seem antiquarian. But the two characteristics of that world that strike us forcefully today are its unabashed elitism and its segregation. Though this elite was nowhere near as restrictive as earlier elites—World War II had exerted its leveling influence—the 1950s establishment was still based on casual anti-Semitism, racism, sexism, and a thousand other silent barriers that blocked entry for those without the correct pedigree. Wealthy Jewish and Protestant boys who had been playing together from childhood were forced to endure "The Great Division" at age 17, when Jewish and Gentile society parted into two entirely separate orbits, with separate debutante seasons, dance schools, and social secretaries. A Protestant business executive may have spent his professional hours working intimately with his Jewish colleague, but he never would have dreamed of putting him up for membership in his club. When Senator Barry Goldwater attempted to play golf at the restricted Chevy Chase Club, he was told the club was restricted. "I'm only half Jewish, so can't I play nine holes?" he is said to have replied.

The WASP elite was also genially anti-intellectual. Its members often spoke of "eggheads" and "highbrows" with polite disdain. Instead, their status, as F. Scott Fitzgerald had pointed out a few decades before, derived from "animal magnetism and money." By contrast with today's ruling class, they had relatively uncomplicated attitudes about their wealth. They knew it was vulgar to be gaudy, they tended toward thriftiness, but they seem not to have seen their own money as an affront to American principles of equality. On the contrary, most took their elite status for granted, assuming that such position was simply part of the natural and beneficent order of the universe. There was always going to be an aristocracy, and so for the people who happened to be born into it, the task was to accept the duties that came along with its privileges. At their best they lived up to the aristocratic code. They believed in duty, service, and honor, and more than just as words. The best of them still subscribed to the code of the natural aristocracy that one of their heroes, Edmund Burke, had included in *An Appeal from the New to the Old Whigs*. Burke's sentence is worth quoting in full because it captures a set of ideals that serve as an interesting foil to those of our own age:

> To be bred in a place of estimation; to see nothing low and sordid from one's infancy; to be taught to respect one's self; to be habituated to the censorial inspection of the public eye; to look early to public opinion; to stand upon such elevated ground as to be enabled to take a large view of the widespread and infinitely diversified combinations of men and affairs in a large society; to have leisure to read, to reflect, to converse; to be enabled to draw the court and attention of the wise and learned, wherever they are to be found; to be habituated in armies to command and to obey; to be taught to despise danger in the pursuit of honor and duty; to be formed to the greatest degree of vigilance, foresight, and circumspection, in a state of things in which no fault is committed with impunity and the slightest mistakes draw on the most ruinous consequences; to be led to a guarded and regulated conduct, from a sense that you are considered as an instructor of your fellow citizens in their highest concerns, and that you act as a reconciler between God and man; to be employed as an administrator of law and justice, and to be thereby among the first benefactors to mankind; to be a

professor of high science, or of liberal and ingenu-
ous art; to be amongst rich traders, who from their
success are presumed to have sharp and vigorous
understandings, and to possess the virtues of dili-
gence, order, constancy, and regularity, and to have
cultivated an habitual regard to commutative justice: these are the circumstances of men that form
what I should call a *natural* aristocracy, without
which there is no nation.

There are parts of this code that barely touch our
own—the emphasis on the military virtues, the sense that
one is an elevated instructor to one's fellow men, the sense
that one should act as a reconciler between God and man.
And while nobody has written to lament the decline of the
WASP as beautifully as Giuseppe Tomasi di Lampedusa
lamented the declining of the old Sicilian aristocracy in
The Leopard, or as elegantly as Evelyn Waugh lamented
the British aristocracy in *Brideshead Revisited,* it is still
possible to look back with some admiration at the Protestant elite, despite the racism, anti-Semitism, and rigidity
that were its fatal flaws.

At its best, the WASP establishment had a public service ethic that remains unmatched. Its members may have
been uncomfortable with ambition, but they were acutely
aware of obligation. They cared about good manners and
self-control, and looking back on them, they sometimes
seem weightier than we who have succeeded them, perhaps because they sacrificed more. Young gentlemen like
George Bush volunteered to fight in World War II without
a second thought, and a disproportionate number of
young men from the privileged WASP families lost their
lives in the world wars. They were a reticent bunch, without the restless rebelliousness of later generations. Com-
paratively, they had little weakness for narcissism. "You're
talking about yourself too much, George," Bush's mother

told him amidst the 1988 presidential campaign. Most important, of course, they led America during the American Century, and they built many of the institutions that the educated elites now happily occupy.

The Hinge Years

But even as those Episcopal brides with early settler ancestors, cotillion memories, and upper-class husbands were staring out from the pages of the 1959 weddings page, their world had already been fatally undermined. The earth-shaking decisions had been made, as many crucial decisions are made, by a college admissions committee. Without much fuss or public discussion, the admissions officers wrecked the WASP establishment. The story at Harvard, told by Richard Herrnstein and Charles Murray in the relatively uncontroversial first chapter of *The Bell Curve*, epitomizes the tale. In 1952 most freshmen at Harvard were products of the same WASP bastions that popped up on the *Times* weddings page: the prep schools in New England (Andover and Exeter alone contributed 10 percent of the class), the East Side of Manhattan, the Main Line of Philadelphia, Shaker Heights in Ohio, the Gold Coast of Chicago, Grosse Pointe of Detroit, Nob Hill in San Francisco, and so on. Two-thirds of all applicants were admitted. Applicants whose fathers had gone to Harvard had a 90 percent admission rate. The average verbal SAT score for the incoming men was 583, good but not stratospheric. The average score across the Ivy League was closer to 500 at the time.

Then came the change. By 1960 the average verbal SAT score for incoming freshmen at Harvard was 678, and the math score was 695—these are stratospheric scores. The average Harvard freshman in 1952 would have placed in the bottom 10 percent of the Harvard freshman class of 1960. Moreover, the 1960 class was drawn from a much wider socioeconomic pool. Smart kids from Queens or Iowa or California, who wouldn't have thought of applying to Harvard a decade earlier, were applying and getting accepted. Harvard had transformed itself from a school catering mostly to the northeastern social elite to a high-powered school reaching more of the brightest kids around the country. And this transformation was replicated in almost all elite schools. At Princeton in 1962, for example, only 10 members of the 62-man football team had attended private prep schools. Three decades earlier every member of the Princeton team was a prep school boy.

Why did this happen? Nicholas Lemann provides the guts of the answer in his book *The Big Test*. It's a remarkable story, because in many ways the WASP elite destroyed itself, and did so for the highest of motives. James Bryant Conant was president of Harvard after World War II, and so sat at the pinnacle of the Protestant Establishment. Nonetheless, Conant was alarmed by the thought that America might develop a hereditary aristocracy consisting of exactly the sort of well-bred young men he was training in Cambridge. Conant dreamed of replacing this elite with a new elite, which would be based on merit. He didn't envision a broad educated populace making democratic decisions. Rather, he hoped to select out a small class of Platonic guardians who would be trained at elite universities and who would then devote themselves selflessly to public service.

To help find these new guardians, Conant enlisted Henry Chauncey, a graduate of Groton and Harvard, an Episcopalian, a descendant of Puritan stock. Chauncey didn't have Conant's grand vision of what society should look like, but he did have a more distilled passion—for standardized tests and the glorious promise of social science. Chauncey was an enthusiast for tests the way other technoenthusiasts have fallen in love with the railroad, or nuclear power, or the Internet. He believed tests were a magnificent tool that would enable experts to measure people's abilities and manage society on a more just and rational basis. Chauncey went on to become the head of the Educational Testing Service, which created the Scholastic Aptitude Test. And so to a degree rare among social engineers, he was actually able to put his enthusiasm into practice. As Lemann observes, we are now living in a world created by Conant and Chauncey's campaign to replace their own elite with an elite based on merit, at least as measured by aptitude tests.

Conant and Chauncey came along during an era uniquely receptive to their message. The American intellectual class has probably never been so sure of itself, before or since. Sociologists, psychologists, and macroeconomists thought they had discovered the tools to solve personal and social problems. Freud's writings, which promised to explain the inner workings of the human mind, were at their peak of his influence. The McCarthy controversy mobilized segments of the intellectual class. The launching of Sputnik made educational rigor seem vital to the national interest. Finally, John F. Kennedy brought intellectuals into the White House, elevating intellectuals into the social stratosphere (at least many of them thought so). As we'll see in Chapter 4, intellectuals began to take themselves (even) more seriously in these years, often with good reason.

Conant and Chauncey were not the only academics who rose up to assert intellectual values against those of the WASP Establishment. In 1956 C. Wright Mills wrote *The Power Elite,* a direct assault on the establishment if ever there was one. In 1959 Jacques Barzun wrote *The House of Intellect.* In 1963 Richard Hofstadter wrote *Anti-Intellectualism in American Life,* a sprawling, confident broadside by an academic superstar against the "practical" classes, both rich and poor. In 1964 Digby Baltzell, of the University of Pennsylvania, wrote *The Protestant Establishment,* a book that introduced the term *WASP* and detailed the establishment's intellectual and moral failings. Though largely sympathetic to WASP ideals, he argued that the WASP elite had become a self-satisfied caste that was unwilling to bring in enough new talent to replenish the ranks. By and large, these academics wanted the universities to serve as meritocratic and intellectual hothouses, not as finishing schools for the social elite. Faculty members demanded that admissions officers look at the legacy applications more critically.

The WASPs had fended off challenges to their cultural hegemony before, either by simply ignoring them or by counterattacking. The first half of the century brought what historian Michael Knox Beran calls the "risorgimento of the well-to-do." Families like the Roosevelts adopted a tough, manly ethos in order to restore vigor and self-confidence to the East Coast elite and so preserve its place atop the power structure. In the 1920s, sensing a threat to the "character" of their institutions, Ivy League administrators tightened their official or unofficial Jewish quotas. Nicholas Murray Butler at Columbia reduced the proportion of Jews at his school from 40 to 20 percent in two years. At Harvard, President A. Lawrence Lowell diagnosed a "Jewish Problem" and also enforced quotas to help solve it. But by the late fifties and early sixties, the WASPs could no longer justify such discrimination to others or to themselves. John F. Kennedy's chief of protocol, Angier Biddle Duke, was forced to resign from his favorite men's club, the Metropolitan Club in Washington, because it was restricted.

History, as Pareto once remarked, is the graveyard of aristocracies, and by the late fifties and early sixties the WASP Establishment had no faith in the code—and the social restrictions—that had sustained it. Maybe its members just lost the will to fight for their privileges. As the writer David Frum theorizes, it had been half a century since the last great age of fortune making. The great families were into at least their third genteel generation. Perhaps by then there wasn't much vigor left. Or perhaps it was the Holocaust that altered the landscape by discrediting the sort of racial restrictions that the Protestant Establishment was built on.

In any case, in 1964 Digby Baltzell astutely perceived the crucial trends. "What seems to be happening," he wrote in *The Protestant Establishment,* "is that a scholarly hierarchy of campus communities governed by the values of admissions committees is gradually supplanting the class hierarchies of local communities which are still governed by the values of parents. . . . Just as the hierarchy of the Church was the main avenue of advancement for the talented and ambitious youth from the lower orders during the medieval period, and just as the business enterprise was responsible for the nineteenth century rags-to-riches dream (when we were predominantly an Anglo-Saxon country), so the campus community has now become the principal guardian of our traditional opportunitarian ideals."

The campus gates were thus thrown open on the basis of brains rather than blood, and within a few short years the university landscape was transformed. Harvard, as we've seen, was changed from a school for the well-connected to a school for brainy strivers. The remaining top schools eliminated their Jewish quotas and eventually dropped their restrictions on women. Furthermore, the sheer numbers of educated Americans exploded. The portion of Americans going to college had been rising steadily throughout the 20th century, but between 1955 and 1974 the growth rate was off the charts. Many of the new students were women. Between 1950 and 1960 the number of female students increased by 47 percent. It then jumped by an additional 168 percent between 1960 and 1970. Over the following decades the student population kept growing and growing. In 1960 there were about 2,000 institutions of higher learning. By 1980 there were 3,200. In 1960 there were 235,000 professors in the United States. By 1980 there were 685,000.

Before this period, in other words, the WASP elites dominated prestige education and made up a significant chunk of all the college-educated population. By the end of this period, the well-bred WASPs no longer dominated the prestige schools and they made up just an infinitesimal slice of the educated class. The elite schools had preserved their status. The proportion of Ivy League graduates in *Who's Who* has remained virtually constant throughout the past 40 years. But the schools maintained their dominance by throwing over the mediocrities from the old WASP families and bringing in less well connected meritocrats.

The rapid expansion of the educated class was bound to have as profound an impact on America as rapid urbanization has had on other countries at other moments in history. By the mid-1960s the middle-aged WASPs still wielded some authority in the corporate world. They still possessed enormous social and political prestige, not to mention financial capital. But on campus they had been overrun. Imagine now you are a young meritocrat, the child of, say, a pharmacist and an elementary school teacher, accepted to a prestigious university in the mid-sixties. You are part of a huge cohort of education arrivistes. Your campus still has some of the aristocratic trappings of the WASP culture, though it is by now a little embarrassed by them. And as you look out into the world, you see the last generation of the Old Guard—the people we recognize from the 1950s weddings pages—still holding key jobs and social authority. They are in the positions of power and prestige you hope to occupy. But they are still living by an ethos you consider obsolete, stifling, and prejudiced. Among other things, that ethos, which emphasizes birth and connections, blocks your ascent. Naturally, you and your many peers, even if you do not think about it deliberately, are going to try to finish off the old regime. You are going to try to destroy what is left of the WASP ethos and replace it with your own ethos, which is based on individual merit.

More broadly, you are going to try to change the social character of the nation. The rise of the meritocrats produced a classic revolution of rising expectations. Tocqueville's principle of revolutions proved true: as social success seems more possible for a rising group, the remaining hindrances seem more and more intolerable. The social revolution of the late sixties was not a miracle or a natural disaster, the way it is sometimes treated by writers on the left and right. It was a logical response to the trends of the crucial years between 1955 and 1965. The components of elite status were due to change. The culture of upscale America was due for a revolution.

The Sixties

"How's our award-winning scholar?" one of the overbearing adults asks the Dustin Hoffman character, Ben, as he comes downstairs in the first scene in *The Graduate*. Mike Nichols's movie, which was the top money-making film of 1968, is about an introspective college graduate who has just come back to a rich white suburb in California after finishing a lavishly successful stint at an East Coast school. He realizes, to his horror, the immense cultural gulf between his parents and himself. As Baltzell had anticipated, campus values displaced parental values. In that famous first scene, Ben is cooed over and passed around like a conquering hero by a group of glad-

handing, loud-talking WASP elders. Hoffman's face is an
oasis of calm amid a riot of Dale Carnegie bonhomie.
There's plenty of cocktail party jollity. His mother starts
reading out his college accomplishments from the class
yearbook. And one of the smug moguls pulls him out to
the pool, extends a cloak of self-importance, and tells him
that the future is in plastics—a scene that brutally exemplifies the cultural decay of the old order. Millionaire
moviemakers tend to be merciless when depicting millionaire businessmen and lawyers, and *The Graduate* casts an
unpitying eye on the life of the Protestant elite: the lavish
wet bars, the monogrammed golf clothes, the gold
watches, the white furniture against white walls, the shal-
lowness and hypocrisy, and in the form of Mrs. Robinson,
their lives of cocktail-soaked desperation. Ben doesn't
know what he wants out of life, but he is certain he
doesn't want *that*.

In Charles Webb's original novel, the character of Ben
Braddock is a six-foot-tall, blue-eyed blond. Mike Nichols
first imagined Robert Redford in the role. That casting
would have better explained why Mrs. Robinson is sexually attracted to Ben, but it probably would have ruined
the picture's prospects. Who wants to identify with a
mopey, blue-eyed, blond Adonis? But Hoffman is a sensitive soul, not a Aryan Dick Diver type. So he perfectly represented all the new ethnic strivers who were suddenly
pouring through the colleges, facing life in the affluent
suburbs, and finding it arid and stifling.

The educated-class rebellion we call "the sixties" was
about many things, some of them important and related
to the Civil Rights movement and Vietnam, some of them
entirely silly, and others, like the sexual revolution, over-
blown (actual sexual behavior was affected far more by
the world wars than by the Woodstock era). But at its core
the cultural radicalism of the sixties was a challenge to
conventional notions of success. It was not only a political

effort to dislodge the establishment from the seats of power. It was a cultural effort by the rising members of the privileged classes to destroy whatever prestige still attached to the WASP lifestyle and the WASP moral code, and to replace the old order with a new social code that would celebrate spiritual and intellectual ideals. The sixties radicals rejected the prevailing definition of accomplishment, the desire to keep up with the Joneses, the prevailing idea of social respectability, the idea that a successful life could be measured by income, manners, and possessions. The educated baby boomers of the 1960s wanted to take the things the Protestant elite regarded as high status and make them low status. The demographic shifts of the 1950s led to the cultural conflicts of the 1960s. Or, as the endlessly impressive Digby Baltzell prophesied in *The Protestant Establishment:* "The economic reforms of one generation tend to produce status conflicts in the next."

What exactly would the sixties student leaders hate about the *New York Times* weddings page of 1959? The specific cultural changes the educated class heralded will be treated in later chapters. But it's worth making a short list here because the habits of thought that were established when the educated class was in its radical stage continue to influence its thinking now in its hour of supremacy. The student radicals would have detested the couples displayed on the weddings page for what was *perceived* to be their conformity, their formality, their traditionalism, their carefully defined gender roles, their ancestor worship, their privilege, their unabashed elitism, their unreflective lives, their self-satisfaction, their reticence, their contented affluence, their coldness.

We'll go into greater detail about all these cultural shifts in the pages that follow, but to put it bluntly, the radicals of the 1960s favored bohemian self-expression and despised the earlier elite for its arid self-control. And their effort to tear down the old customs and habits of the previous elite was not achieved without social cost. Old authorities and restraints were delegitimized. There was a real, and to millions of people catastrophic, breakdown in social order, which can be measured in the stunning rise in divorce, crime, drug use, and illegitimacy rates.

The *New York Times* weddings pages of the late sixties and early seventies reflect the conflicts and contrasts of that confrontational age. The section was smaller, to start with. While there might be 158 marriages listed in the typical June section in 1959, there were closer to 35 in a typical June section in the late sixties and early seventies. Hip couples didn't want to post their nuptials on a page that was a bastion of ritual and elitism. Among the couples who did send in their announcements, there is a striking dichotomy. Some couples seem oblivious to the turmoil all around them. Their entries are still loaded down with Junior League memberships, prep school affiliations, ancestor name-dropping, and debutante histories. These marriages are seemingly indistinguishable from the 1950s ones. But a few columns over there will be a wedding in which everybody is barefoot and in which the ceremony was performed in the manner of a pagan spring ritual. Another announcement will describe a couple that dispensed with traditional language, wrote their own vows, and hired a rock band for the reception. The new practice of writing your own vows really did mark a historic turning point. The people who used the traditional vows were making a connection to the generations that had come before, taking their place in a great chain of custom. The people who wrote their own vows were expressing their individuality and their desire to shape institutions to meet individual needs. They were more interested in seeing themselves as creators rather than inheritors. They were adopting the prime directive of the educated class: Thou shalt construct thine own identity.

The most famous wedding moment of the period, of course, was the one that took place in the last scene of *The Graduate*. Elaine, the Katharine Ross character, is going through a conventional, if rushed, wedding ceremony in a modern Presbyterian church in Santa Barbara, with a starched blond doctor of the WASP variety. We know he's retrograde because he proposed by suggesting, "We'd make a great team"—a phrase that captures the supposed emotional coldness of the WASP culture, as well as its insistent sportiness. Disheveled Ben rushes into the church just as the ceremony is ending, pounds on the glass on the balcony overlooking the nave, and calls out Elaine's name. Elaine looks up, sees the vicious expressions on her parents' and her husband's faces, and decides to run off with Ben. Elaine's mother, Mrs. Robinson, hisses, "It's too late," and Elaine shouts back, "Not for me." Ben and Elaine ward off the family and the rest of the crowd and dash onto a public bus. The long final scene shows them sitting side by side on that bus, Elaine in her torn wedding dress. At first they look elated, but then they become more and more sober, and finally they look a little terrified. They've emancipated themselves from a certain sort of WASP success, but it dawns on them that they haven't figured out what sort of successful life they would like to lead instead.

And Then Comes Money

The hardest of the hard-core sixties radicals believed the only honest way out was to reject the notion of success altogether: drop out of the rat race, retreat to small communities where real human relationships would flourish. But that sort of utopianism was never going to be very popular, especially among college grads. Members of the educated class prize human relationships and social equality, but as for so many generations of Americans before them, achievement was really at the core of the sixties grads' value system. They were meritocrats, after all, and so tended to define themselves by their accomplishments. Most of them were never going to drop out or sit around in communes smelling flowers, raising pigs, and contemplating poetry. Moreover, as time went by, they discovered that the riches of the universe were lying at their feet.

At first, when the great hump of baby boom college graduates entered the workforce, having a college degree brought few financial rewards or dramatic life changes. As late as 1976, the labor economist Richard Freeman could write a book called *The Overeducated American,* arguing that higher education didn't seem to be paying off in the marketplace. But the information age kicked in, and the rewards for education grew and grew. In 1980, according to labor market specialist Kevin Murphy of the University of Chicago, college graduates earned roughly 35 percent more than high school graduates. But by the mid-1990s, college graduates were earning 70 percent more than high school graduates, and those with graduate degrees were earning 90 percent more. The wage value of a college degree had doubled in 15 years.

The rewards for intellectual capital have increased while the rewards for physical capital have not. That means that even liberal arts majors can wake up one day and find themselves suddenly members of the top-income brackets. A full professor at Yale who renounced the capitalist rat race finds himself making, as of 1999, $113,100, while a professor at Rutgers pulls in $103,700 and superstar professors, who become the object of academic bidding wars, now can rake in more than $300,000 a year. Congressional and presidential staffers top out at $125,000 (before quintupling that when they enter the private sector), and the journalists at national publications can now count on six-figure salaries when they hit middle age, not including lecture fees. Philosophy and math majors head for Wall Street and can make tens of millions of dollars from their quantitative models. America has always had a lot of lawyers, and now the median income for that burgeoning group is $72,500, while income for the big-city legal grinds can reach seven figures. And superstudents still flood into medicine—three-quarters of private practitioners net more than $100,000. Meanwhile, in Silicon Valley there are more millionaires than people. In Hollywood television scriptwriters make $11,000 to $13,000 a week. And in New York top magazine editors, like Anna Wintour of *Vogue,* make $1 million a year, which is slightly more than the head of the Ford Foundation. And these dazzling incomes flow not only to the baby boomers, who might still find them surprising, but to all the subsequent generations of college graduates as well, most of whom have never known a world without $4 million artists' lofts, $350-a-night edgy hotels, avant-garde summer homes, and the rest of the accoutrements of the countercultural plutocracy.

The information age has produced entirely new job categories, some of which seem like practical jokes, though you wouldn't know it from the salaries: creativity officer, chief knowledge officer, team spirit coordinator. Then there are the jobs that nobody dreamed of in high school: Web page designer, patent agent, continuity writer, foundation program officer, talk show booker, and on and on. The economy in this era is such that oddballs like Oliver Stone become multimillionaire moguls and slouchy dropouts like Bill Gates get to run the world. Needless to say, there are still gypsy scholars scraping by while looking for a tenure-track position, and there are still poor saps in the publishing industry parlaying their intelligence into obscenely small paychecks. But the whole thrust of the information age has been to reward education and widen the income gap between the educated and the uneducated. Moreover, the upper middle class has grown from

a small appendage of the middle class into a distinct demographic hump populated largely by people with fancy
degrees. Within a few years, barring a severe economic
downturn, there will be 10 million American households
with incomes over $100,000 a year, up from only 2 mil-
lion in 1982. Consider the cultural and financial capital of
that large group, and you begin to appreciate the social
power of the upper middle class. Many of the members of
the educated elite didn't go out hungry for money. But
money found them. And subtly, against their will, it began
to work its way into their mentality.

The members of the educated elite find they must
change their entire attitude first toward money itself.
When they were poor students, money was a solid. It
came in a chunk with every paycheck, and they would
gradually chip little bits off to pay the bills. They could
sort of feel how much money they had in their bank account, the way you can feel a pile of change in your
pocket. But as they became more affluent, money turned
into a liquid. It flows into the bank account in a prodi-
gious stream. And it flows out just as quickly. The earner
is reduced to spectator status and is vaguely horrified by
how quickly the money is flowing through. He or she may
try to stem the outward flow in order to do more saving.
But it's hard to know where to erect the dam. The money
just flows on its own. And after a while one's ability to
stay afloat through all the ebbs and flows becomes a sign
of accomplishment in itself. The big money stream is another aptitude test. Far from being a source of corruption,
money turns into a sign of mastery. It begins to seem de-
served, natural. So even former student radicals begin to
twist the old left-wing slogan so that it becomes: From
each according to his abilities, to each according to his
abilities.

The educated elites not only earn far more money
than they ever thought they would but now occupy posi-

tions of enormous responsibility. We're by now all familiar with modern-day executives who have moved from
SDS to CEO, from LSD to IPO. Indeed, sometimes you get
the impression the Free Speech movement produced more
corporate executives than Harvard Business School.

What's more amazing is the growth of lucrative industries in which everybody involved is a member of the
educated class. Only about 20 percent of the adult population of America possesses a college degree, but in many
large cities and suburban office parks, you can walk from
office to office, for mile upon mile, and almost everybody
in the place will have a sheepskin in the drawer. Educated
elites have taken over much of the power that used to ac-
crue to sedate old WASPs with dominating chins. Economists at the International Monetary Fund jet around the
world reshaping macroeconomic policies. Brainiacs at
McKinsey & Company swoop down on corporate offices
run by former college quarterbacks and issue reports on
how to merge or restructure.

The educated elites have even taken over professions
that used to be working class. The days of the hard-
drinking blue-collar journalist, for example, are gone
forever. Now if you cast your eye down a row at a Washington press conference, it's: Yale, Yale, Stanford, Emory,
Yale, and Harvard. Political parties, which were once run
by immigrant hacks, are now dominated by communica-
tions analysts with Ph.D.s. If you drive around the old suburbs and follow the collarless-shirt bohemians home from
their organic fruit stands, you notice they have literally
moved into the houses of the old stockbroker elite. They
are sleeping in the old elite's beds. They are swamping the
old elite's institutions. As the novelist Louis Auchincloss
summarized it, "The old society has given way to the society of accomplishment." Dumb good-looking people with
great parents have been displaced by smart, ambitious, educated, and antiestablishment people with scuffed shoes.

The Anxieties of Abundance

Over the past 30 years, in short, the educated class has gone from triumph to triumph. They have crushed the old WASP elite culture, thrived in an economy that lavishly rewards their particular skills, and now sit atop many of the same institutions they once railed against. But all this has created a gnawing problem. How do they make sure they haven't themselves become self-satisfied replicas of the WASP elite they still so forcefully denounce?

Those who want to win educated-class approval must confront the anxieties of abundance: how to show—not least to themselves—that even while climbing toward the top of the ladder they have not become all the things they still profess to hold in contempt. How to navigate the shoals between their affluence and their self-respect. How to reconcile their success with their spirituality, their elite status with their egalitarian ideals. Socially enlightened members of the educated elite tend to be disturbed by the widening gap between rich and poor and are therefore made somewhat uncomfortable by the fact that their own family income now tops $80,000. Some of them dream of social justice yet went to a college where the tuition costs could feed an entire village in Rwanda for a year. Some once had "Question Authority" bumper stickers on their cars but now find themselves heading start-up software companies with 200 people reporting to them. The sociologists they read in college taught that consumerism is a disease, and yet now they find themselves shopping for $3,000 refrigerators. They took to heart the lessons of *Death of a Salesman,* yet now find themselves directing a sales force. They laughed at the plastics scene in *The Graduate* but now they work for a company that manufactures . . . plastic. Suddenly they find themselves moving into a suburban house with a pool and uncomfortable about admitting it to their bohemian friends still living downtown.

Though they admire art and intellect, they find themselves living amidst commerce, or at least in that weird hybrid zone where creativity and commerce intersect. This class is responsible for more yards of built-in bookshelf space than any group in history. And yet sometimes you look at their shelves and notice deluxe leather-bound editions of all those books arguing that success and affluence is a sham: *Babbitt, The Great Gatsby, The Power Elite, The Theory of the Leisure Class.* This is an elite that has been raised to oppose elites. They are affluent yet opposed to materialism. They may spend their lives selling yet worry about selling out. They are by instinct antiestablishmentarian yet somehow sense they have become a new establishment.

The members of this class are divided against themselves, and one is struck by how much of their time is spent earnestly wrestling with the conflict between their reality and their ideals. They grapple with the trade-offs between equality and privilege ("I believe in public schooling, but the private school just seems better for my kids"), between convenience and social responsibility ("These disposable diapers are an incredible waste of resources, but they are so easy"), between rebellion and convention ("I know I did plenty of drugs in high school, but I tell my kids to Just Say No").

But the biggest tension, to put it in the grandest terms, is between worldly success and inner virtue. How do you move ahead in life without letting ambition wither your soul? How do you accumulate the resources you need to do the things you want without becoming a slave to material things? How do you build a comfortable and stable life for your family without getting bogged down in stultifying routine? How do you live at the top of society without becoming an insufferable snob?

The Reconcilers

These educated elites don't despair in the face of such challenges. They are the Résumé Gods. They're the ones who aced their SATs and succeeded in giving up Merlot during pregnancy. If they are not well equipped to handle the big challenges, no one is. When faced with a tension between competing values, they do what any smart privileged person bursting with cultural capital would do. They find a way to have both. They reconcile opposites.

The grand achievement of the educated elites in the 1990s was to create a way of living that lets you be an affluent success and at the same time a free-spirit rebel. Founding design firms, they find a way to be an artist and still qualify for stock options. Building gourmet companies like Ben & Jerry's or Nantucket Nectars, they've found a way to be dippy hippies and multinational corporate fat cats. Using William S. Burroughs in ads for Nike sneakers and incorporating Rolling Stones anthems into their marketing campaigns, they've reconciled the antiestablishment style with the corporate imperative. Listening to management gurus who tell them to thrive on chaos and unleash their creative potential, they've reconciled the spirit of the imagination with service to the bottom line. Turning university towns like Princeton and Palo Alto into entrepreneurial centers, they have reconciled the highbrow with the high tax bracket. Dressing like Bill Gates in worn chinos on his way to a stockholders' meeting, they've reconciled undergraduate fashion with upper-crust occupations. Going on eco-adventure vacations, they've reconciled aristocratic thrill-seeking with social concern. Shopping at Benetton or the Body Shop, they've brought together consciousness-raising and cost control.

When you are amidst the educated upscalers, you can never be sure if you're living in a world of hippies or stockbrokers. In reality you have entered the hybrid world in which everybody is a little of both.

Marx told us that classes inevitably conflict, but sometimes they just blur. The values of the bourgeois mainstream culture and the values of the 1960s counterculture have merged. That culture war has ended, at least within the educated class. In its place that class has created a third culture, which is a reconciliation between the previous two. The educated elites didn't set out to create this reconciliation. It is the product of millions of individual efforts to have things both ways. But it is now the dominant tone of our age. In the resolution between the culture and the counterculture, it is impossible to tell who co-opted whom, because in reality the bohemians and the bourgeois co-opted each other. They emerge from this process as bourgeois bohemians, or Bobos.

The New Establishment

Today the *New York Times* weddings section is huge once again. In the early 1970s the young rebels didn't want to appear there, but now that their own kids are in college and getting married, they are proud to see their offspring in the Sunday paper. For a fee the *Times* will send you a reproduction of your listing, suitable for framing.

And the young people, the second-generation Bobos, are willing to see their nuptials recorded. Look at the newlyweds on any given Sunday morning, beaming out at you from the pages of the *Times*. Their smiles seem so genuine. They all look so nice and approachable, not dignified or fearsome, the way some of the brides on the 1950s pages did. Things are different but somehow similar. For example, a reader opening the weddings section on May 23, 1999, would have learned that Stuart Anthony Kingsley was getting married. Mr. Kingsley graduated magna cum laude from Dartmouth and got an MBA at Harvard before going on to become a partner at McKinsey & Company. His father is a trustee of the National Trust for Historic Preservation, and his mother is an overseer of the Boston Symphony Orchestra and a trustee of the Society for the Preservation of New England Antiquities. Those sorts of affiliations would have set off approving nods from the old WASP dowagers of the 1950s era. But look who Mr. Kingsley is marrying—Sara Perry, whose father is coordinator of Judaic Studies at Southern Connecticut State University and whose mother is associate executive director of the New Haven Jewish Federation, which might not have met with approving nods from the dowagers.

But nowadays such an alliance blends right in. We don't even raise an eyebrow when Mr. New England Antiquities marries Ms. Judaic Studies because we know how much the bride and groom have in common: Ms. Perry graduated from her college magna cum laude, just as her husband did (except hers was Yale, not Dartmouth). She, too, got her MBA from Harvard (and she earned a master's degree in public administration besides). She, too, has become a financial consultant (except she is a senior vice president at Community Wealth Ventures, which works with foundations). The ancient enmities between class and ethnic groups have been overcome by the common bond of meritocratic ascent. They were married by the mayor of New Haven, John DeStefano, Jr., in the home of Ms. Perry's maternal grandparents, Lucille and Arnold Alderman.

Today's establishment is structured differently. It is not a small conspiracy of well-bred men with interlocking family and school ties who have enormous influence on the levers of power. Instead, this establishment is a large, amorphous group of meritocrats who share a consciousness and who unself-consciously reshape institutions to accord with their values. They are not confined to a few

East Coast institutions. In 1962, Richard Rovere could write, "Nor has the Establishment ever made much headway in such fields as advertising, television or motion pictures." Today's establishment is everywhere. It exercises its power subtly, over ideas and concepts, and therefore pervasively. There are no sure-fire demographic markers to tell who is a member of this establishment. Members tend to have gone to competitive colleges, but not all have. They tend to live in upscale neighborhoods, such as Los Altos, California, and Bloomfield, Michigan, and Lincoln Park, Illinois, but not all do. What unites them is their shared commitment to the Bobo reconciliation. People gain entry into the establishment by performing a series of delicate cultural tasks: they are prosperous without seeming greedy; they have pleased their elders without seeming conformist; they have risen toward the top without too obviously looking down on those below; they have achieved success without committing certain socially sanctioned affronts to the ideal of social equality; they have constructed a prosperous lifestyle while avoiding the old clichés of conspicuous consumption (it's OK to hew to the new clichés).

Obviously, none of this is to suggest that all members of the new Bobo establishment think alike, any more than it's true to say that all members of any establishment think alike. Some of the bourgeois bohemians are more on the bourgeois side; they are stockbrokers who happen to like artists' lofts. Some are on the bohemian side; they are art professors who dabble in the market. Nonetheless, if you look at some quintessential figures of the new establishment—such as Henry Louis Gates, Charlie Rose, Steven Jobs, Doris Kearns Goodwin, David Geffen, Tina Brown, Maureen Dowd, Jerry Seinfeld, Stephen Jay Gould, Lou Reed, Tim Russert, Steve Case, Ken Burns, Al Gore, Bill Bradley, John McCain, George W. Bush—you can begin to sense a common ethos that mingles 1960s rebellion with

1980s achievement. You can feel the Bobo ethos, too, in the old institutions that have been taken over by the new establishment, such as the *New Yorker*, Yale University, the American Academy of Arts and Letters (which now includes people like Toni Morrison, Jules Feiffer, and Kurt Vonnegut among its members), or the *New York Times* (which now runs editorials entitled "In Praise of the Counterculture"). You can sense the ethos with special force in the new establishment institutions that would have been alien to the old elite: NPR, DreamWorks, Microsoft, AOL, Starbucks, Yahoo, Barnes & Noble, Amazon, and Borders.

And over the past few years, this new educated establishment has begun to assume the necessary role of an establishment. That is to say, it has begun to create a set of social codes that give coherent structure to national life. Today, America once again has a dominant class that defines the parameters of respectable opinion and taste—a class that determines conventional wisdom, that promulgates a code of good manners, that establishes a pecking order to give shape to society, that excludes those who violate its codes, that transmits its moral and etiquette codes down to its children, that imposes social discipline on the rest of society so as to improve the "quality of life," to use the contemporary phrase.

The new establishment has assumed this role hesitantly. It hasn't become a technocratic elite with a strong sense of public service, as many of the early champions of the meritocracy envisioned. It hasn't established clear lines of authority, since it still has trouble coming to terms with authority. Instead, it has exercised its influence through a million and one private channels, reforming society through culture more than through politics. Its efforts to establish order have been spotty and often clumsy—all the political correctness codes, the speech codes on campuses, the sexual harassment rules. But gradually a shared set of understandings and practices has cohered into a widely accepted set of social norms. Thirty years ago, when tearing down the established structure was the order of the day, civility was not a cherished value, especially on campuses. But now that a new civil order has come into being, the word *civility* is again heard on nearly every educated person's tongue. And somehow some sort of looser social peace is in the process of being restored. Many of the social indicators that skyrocketed during the age of transition, the 1960s and 1970s, have begun to drop: crime rates, abortion rates, teen births, illegitimacy, divorce rates, teenage drinking.

Most of this book is a description of these new codes of etiquette and morality. If you do not share the ethos of the Bobo class, you will probably not get hired by establishment institutions. You will probably not get promoted. For example, early in this century it was perfectly acceptable to be racist and anti-Semitic or homophobic. Today those beliefs automatically banish a person from educated circles. Earlier this century social climbers built ornate castles, aping the manners of the European aristocracy. Today a vice president at Microsoft might build a huge modern mansion, but if he built a house like J. P. Morgan's he'd be regarded as a pompous crank. Forty years ago grandees could still hang the pelts of the wild animals they had killed upon their walls. In today's educated class that would be considered an affront to humane values.

Today's educated elites tend not to bar entire groups, but like any establishment, they do have their boundary markers. You will be shunned if you embrace glitzy materialism. You will be shunned if you are overtly snobbish. You will be shunned if you are anti-intellectual. For one reason or another the following people and institutions fall outside the ranks of Bobo respectability: Donald Trump, Pat Robertson, Louis Farrakhan, Bob Guccione, Wayne Newton, Nancy Reagan, Adnan Khashoggi, Jesse Helms,

Jerry Springer, Mike Tyson, Rush Limbaugh, Philip Morris, developers, loggers, Hallmark greeting cards, the National Rifle Association, Hooters.

The New Pecking Order

So when the Protestant Establishment collapsed, it is not as if America became a magical place without elites, without hierarchies, without etiquette and social distinctions. That may have been true during the age of transition. In the 1970s and through part of the 1980s, it really was difficult to pick out a coherent social order. But that fluidity couldn't last—and it's probably a good thing too. Countries need to achieve new states of social equilibrium, and that has now happened to America. New codes are in place that are different from the old codes but serve many of the same social functions of giving order and coherence to life.

American social life, for example, is just as hierarchical as it was in the 1950s, maybe more so. Hierarchies based on connections have given way. Under the code of the meritocrats, people are more likely to be judged by their posts. Invitations to Renaissance weekends, Aspen Institute seminars, Esther Dyson technology conferences, and exclusive private dinners are all determined by what job you have. If you have a prestigious position, your social life is secure. You will find constant validation by surrounding yourself with people as accomplished as or even more accomplished than you are, and you will come to relish what might be called the joy of summits. If you do not, your social life will always have those awkward moments when someone next to you at dinner turns and asks, "What do you do?"

If you are a visiting name professor from Yale freshly arrived on a small campus to give a guest lecture, you will be taken to dinner at the finest restaurant the town has to offer. But if you are a faculty member at Colgate invited to be a guest lecturer, you'll be dining at the home of your host with her kids. If you are an undersecretary in the Justice Department, you will be the keynote lunchtime speaker at various bar association conferences, but if you move on to some lucrative law firm, you will be lucky to serve on one of the end-of-the-day panel discussions. According to the *New York Observer*, former *New Yorker* editor Tina Brown used to throw parties at which top-rank writers and editors were invited to arrive at eight and lower-ranked writers and editors were told to show up at nine-thirty.

Of course, this does not mean those with the biggest offices automatically earn the highest rank. Your career choice has to reflect the twisting demands of the Bobo ethos. In the 1950s the best kind of money to have was inherited money. Today in the Bobo establishment the best kind of money is incidental money. It's the kind of money you just happen to earn while you are pursuing your creative vision. That means the most prestigious professions involve artistic self-expression as well as big bucks. A novelist who makes $1 million a year is far more prestigious than a banker who makes $50 million. A software designer who has stock options in the millions is more prestigious than a real estate developer with holdings in the tens of millions. A newspaper columnist who makes $150,000 a year will get his calls returned more quickly than a lawyer who makes six times that. A restaurant owner with one successful nightspot will be on the receiving end of more cocktail party fawning than a shopping center owner with six huge malls.

This is the age of discretionary income. People are supposed to forgo earnings opportunities in order to lead richer lives. If you have not forgone any earnings, you just can't expect your status to be very high, no matter how much money you've got in the bank. Professors who are good-looking enough to have become newscasters but chose not to are admired and envied more than professors who had no alternative but to go into the academy. People who have made $100 million with purportedly anticommercial independent movies are more prestigious than people who have made $150 million studio movies. A rock star who goes platinum with a sensitive acoustic album is more admired (and in the long run therefore more bankable) than a rock star who goes double platinum with a regular headbanging album. Media people like Christiane Amanpour and James Rubin will have their wedding featured at the top spot of the *New York Times* weddings page, whereas ordinary financial analysts will be reduced to paragraph status down below. The guy who dropped out of Harvard to start a software company is asked to give the dinner speech at a grand affair, and sitting next to him will be the Vanderbilt heir who eagerly solicits his attention and has to pay for the dinner.

To calculate a person's status, you take his net worth and multiply it by his antimaterialistic attitudes. A zero in either column means no prestige, but high numbers in both rocket you to the top of the heap. Thus, to be treated well in this world, not only do you have to show some income results; you have to perform a series of feints to show how little your worldly success means to you. You always want to dress one notch lower than those around you. You may want to wear a tattoo or drive a pickup truck or somehow perform some other socially approved act of antistatus deviance. You will devote your conversational time to mocking your own success in a manner that simultaneously displays your accomplishments and your ironic distance from them. You will ceaselessly bash yuppies in order to show that you yourself have not become one. You will talk about your nanny as if she were your close personal friend, as if it were just a weird triviality that you happen to live in a $900,000 Santa Monica house and she takes the bus two hours each day to the barrio. You will want to perfect a code to subtly downplay your academic credentials. If asked where you went to school, you will reply "Harvard?" with a little upward lilt at the end of your pronunciation, as if to imply, "Have you ever heard of it?" When referring to your stint as a Rhodes scholar, you will say, "While I was in England on a program . . ." In Washington I once asked a transplanted Englishman where he went to school and he replied, "A little school near Slough." The village of Slough is a modest little place west of London. The next town over is called Eton.

Class Rank

Nor is it true that the decline of the old WASP code of morality has left America in a moral vacuum. Some people see the decline of the old Protestant Establishment and mourn our losses: no more chivalry, no more of that keen sense of duty and public service, no more gravitas and deference to authority, no more reticence and self-effacement, no more chastity or decorum, no more gentlemen, no more ladies, no more honor and valor. They see the codes and rules that have fallen away and too quickly assume that we have entered a nihilistic age.

In fact, our morals have followed the same cycle of decay and regeneration as our manners. The old Protestant Establishment and its ethical system faded. There was a period of anarchy. But more recently the new educated establishment has imposed its one set of rules. And as we shall see in Chapter 5, it is not clear, especially at first glance, which moral framework is more restrictive, the old WASP ethos or the new Bobo one.

These topics are all in front of us. Suffice it to say, this has got to be one of the most anxious social elites ever. We Bobos are not anxious because there is an angry mob outside the gates threatening to send us to the guillotine. There isn't. The educated elite is anxious because its members are torn between their drive to succeed and their fear of turning into sellouts. Furthermore, we are anxious because we do not award ourselves status sinecures. Previous establishments erected social institutions that would give their members security. In the first part of the 20th century, once your family made it into the upper echelons of society, it was relatively easy to stay there. You were invited on the basis of your connections to the right affairs. You were admitted, nearly automatically, to the right schools and considered appropriate for the right spouses. The pertinent question in those circles was not what do you do, but who are you. Once you were established as a Biddle or an Auchincloss or a Venderlip, your way was clear. But members of today's educated class can never be secure about their own future. A career crash could be just around the corner. In the educated class even social life is a series of aptitude tests; we all must perpetually perform in accordance with the shifting norms of propriety, ever advancing signals of cultivation. Reputations can be destroyed by a disgraceful sentence, a lewd act, a run of bad press, or a terrible speech at the financial summit at Davos.

And more important, members of the educated class can never be secure about their children's future. The kids have some domestic and educational advantages—all those tutors and developmental toys—but they still have to work through school and ace the SATs just to achieve the same social rank as their parents. Compared to past elites, little is guaranteed.

The irony is that all this status insecurity only makes the educated class stronger. Its members and their children must constantly be alert, working and achieving. Moreover, the educated class is in no danger of becoming a self-contained caste. Anybody with the right degree, job, and cultural competencies can join. Marx warned that "the more a ruling class is able to assimilate the most prominent men [or women] of the dominated classes, the more stable and dangerous its rule." And in truth it is hard to see how the rule of the meritocrats could ever come to an end. The WASP Establishment fell pretty easily in the 1960s. It surrendered almost without a shot. But the meritocratic Bobo class is rich with the spirit of self-criticism. It is flexible and amorphous enough to co-opt that which it does not already command. The Bobo meritocracy will not be easily toppled, even if some group of people were to rise up and conclude that it should be. So let's go off and survey the manners and mores of today's dominant social class.

2

Consumption

Wayne, Pennsylvania, used to be such a square town. It's 13 miles west of Philadelphia, and while other Main Line communities, like Bryn Mawr and Haverford, have always had a little cosmopolitan flair to go with their dense concentrations of country club grandees, Wayne was strictly a white bread kind of place. *Mary Poppins* played in the town cinema for an entire summer when it was rereleased a few years ago. Dusty apothecaries lingered on the main shopping street, delivering remedies to the old Main Line widows who owned mansions at the southern end of the township. *The Philadelphia Story* was set here; *The Preppy Handbook* might as well have been. Of all the zip codes in the country, Wayne ranked eighth in the United States in total number of families listed in the Social Register (the local St. David's Episcopal Church figured prominently in the *New York Times* weddings page of the 1950s). The women called each other by those weird nicknames WASPs used to go for, like Skimmy and Binky, and competed for choice volunteering assignments at the annual Devon Horse Show. The men could be seen emerging from the train station at about six in their un-memorable suits. Occasionally one would sport a tie showing a flock of ducks, or if he was thinking of having dinner at the Merion Cricket Club, he might browse on his way home at the Tiger Shop men's clothiers for a pair of green golf pants. For decades the local newspaper, cre-atively named the *Suburban,* reassured its serene com-muter readers that nothing was happening in Wayne and nothing was ever likely to happen.

But over the past six years or so, all that has changed. A new culture has swept into town and overlaid itself onto the Paisley Shop, the Neighborhood League Shop, and the other traditional Main Line establishments. The town, once an espresso desert, now has six gourmet coffee-houses. The Gryphon draws a sallow-eyed crowd of teenage sophisticates and hosts poetry readings. Cafe Pro-copio is the one across from the train station, where hand-some middle-aged couples come on Sunday morning, swapping newspaper sections and comparing notes across the tables on their kids' college admissions prospects. Up-scale gathering places like this are filled with texts, and on the side of the take-out coffee cups is a text that informs you that Cafe Procopio is named after a left bank Parisian cafe, founded in 1689, that became "a gathering place where throughout the centuries intellectuals and artists would meet for a good cup of coffee. At Cafe Procopio we carry on the tradition of a true cafe, a natural meeting place with a spirit all its own." There probably still aren't a lot of artists and intellectuals in Wayne, but suddenly there are a lot of people who want to drink coffee like one.

A fabulous independent bookstore named the Reader's Forum has moved into town where the old drug-store used to be (it features literary biographies in the front window), and there's a mammoth new Borders nearby where people can go and feel guilty that they are not patronizing the independent place. The artsy set can now go to a Made By You—one of those places where you pay six times more to decorate your own mugs and dishes than it would cost to buy flatware that other people have decorated—and to Studio B, a gift emporium that hosts creative birthday parties to ensure that self-esteeming kids get even more self-esteeming. There are several new food places in town. Sweet Daddy's sells gourmet jelly beans, spiced apple cider sorbet, and gelato in such flavors as Zuppa Inglese. There are now two stores that specialize in discriminating picnic baskets, in case you want to dine al fresco on sun-dried tomato cheese sticks and Marin County's Best Black Bean Dip, which is fat-free. For lunch Your Gourmet Kitchen sells crab panini and herb-grilled chicken breasts with sprouts on sourdough, and on Saturday mornings it hosts an omelet bar. Near the center of town, there's a new Los Angeles–style restaurant named Teresa's Cafe, which gets crowded and noisy at night, a little enclave of Santa Monica bustle in the midst of the Philadelphia suburbs.

In the old Wayne there weren't any interesting food stores. And there certainly weren't any restaurants with casual-sounding names like Teresa's; instead, they had imposing French names like L'Auberge. But now it is the formidable French places that have had to adjust. The restaurant La Fourchette has changed its name to the less pretentious Fourchette 110. It's traded in its French haute cuisine for more casual food. The menu looks like it was designed by a friendly Gérard Depardieu, not an imposing snob like Charles de Gaulle.

The Great Harvest Bread Company has opened up a franchise in town, one of those gourmet bread stores where they sell apricot almond or spinach feta loaf for $4.75 a pop. This particular store is owned by Ed and

Lori Kerpius. Ed got his MBA in 1987 and moved to Chicago, where he was a currency trader. Then, as if driven by the ineluctable winds of the zeitgeist, he gave up on the Decade of Greed stuff so he could spend more time with his family and community. So he and his wife opened this shop.

They greet you warmly as you walk in the door and hand you a sample slice (I chose Savannah dill) about the size of a coffee table book. A short lecture commences on the naturalness of the ingredients and the authenticity of the baking process, which, in fact, is being carried out right there in front of you. The store is spare so you won't think there is any salesmanship going on. Instead, there are teddy bears and children's books for the kids who hang around, and there's Starbucks coffee on sale for the adults. The Kerpiuses sponsor local arts activities—each kid who sends a drawing to the store gets a free loaf—so the walls of the store are covered with children's colorings alongside tokens of the store's generous participation in the local soccer league. If you ask them to slice the bread in the store, they look at you compassionately as one who has not yet risen to the higher realm of bread consciousness. But they hand you an information sheet for those who might want to slice the bread at home when it is at a more appropriate temperature (cut it in a herringbone pattern). The pamphlet lets you know that the integrity of the bread will not be damaged by freezing and reheating ("On ski trips we've wrapped ours in foil and put it on our engine").

To the west of town there is a Zany Brainy, one of those toy stores that pretends to be an educational institution. It sells lifelike figurines of endangered animals, and it's driven the old Wayne Toytown, which carried toys that didn't improve developmental skills, out of business. Farther down Lancaster Pike there is now a Fresh Fields supermarket. When the shoppers push a cart through the

entrance, they are standing in an epicenter of the Upscale
Suburban Hippiedom that is so characteristic of the new
Wayne and so foreign to the old one. The visitor to Fresh
Fields is confronted with a big sign that says "Organic
Items today: 130." This is like a barometer of virtue. If
you came in on a day when only 60 items were organic,
you'd feel cheated. But when the number hits the three figures, you can walk through the aisles with moral confidence, glancing at an infinite variety of cabbage, like kale
and bok choy, that the scions of the old Main Line families would never even have heard of.

Like so much else in this new cultural wave, Fresh
Fields has taken the ethos of California in the 1960s and
selectively updated it. Gone are the sixties-era things that
were fun and of interest to teenagers, like Free Love, and
retained are all the things that might be of interest to middle-aged hypochondriacs, like whole grains. So in the information age, suburban customers can stroll amidst the
radish sprouts, the bins of brown and basmati rice, the
jars of powdered fo-ti root, the Mayan Fungus Soap,
the Light Mountain All Natural hair coloring, the tree-oil
mouthwashes, and the vegetarian dog biscuits, basking in
their reflected wholesomeness.

Finally, there is a batch of new home furnishings
stores in Wayne. Within a few hundred feet of each other
on Lancaster Pike there are three stores that make new
furniture look old and another store that takes old lumber
to make furniture that is actually new. They sort of meet
in the middle to produce never-before-owned hand-me-
downs.

These stores seem to be competing to see who can
most enthusiastically produce the distressed look, and
they've gone so far that sometimes the furniture doesn't
look distressed; it looks like it's decomposing, with draw-
ers scraped and hanging off, paint chipping on the floor. A
store called the Painted Past sells hand-painted TV ar-

moires, fat smelly candles, and a dented metal bedroom dresser on wheels. A store called Domicile sells hand-painted TV armoires, fat smelly candles, and a Provençal spaghetti strainer. The short-lived Somogyi Collection sold hand-painted TV armoires, no fat smelly candles, but it did have plenty of scratched dining room hutches made from excessively grained gourmet wood.

The apotheosis of this look is a company called Anthropologie, which has placed its flagship store in an old car dealership. It's odd enough for Wayne to have a store named after an academic discipline. The old crowd would have been deeply suspicious of such eggheadism (not to mention the French spelling). But the people in the forefront of this new culture seem to turn life into one long stint of graduate school. What's inside would really shock the old scions of the nearby riding clubs. For a while, there was a coffee shop within Anthropologie, so the shopper in Wayne was never more than 50 yards from a cappuccino and a French magazine to browse through. Second, the store always seems to have Louis Armstrong's "What a Wonderful World" playing on the sound system, not genteel Bach. But more surprisingly, there's not a Hepplewhite chair in sight. No eagle-clawed settees are featured in Anthropologie's showroom (George Washington would not feel at home). Furthermore, there is no Louis XIV furniture or Second Empire stuff. The old Wayne took its furniture cues from the European aristocrats. But the new Wayne, from the look of Anthropologie and its competitors, takes its cues from the European peasantry. The store—a vast open area under exposed beams—is a symphony of what fashion types call Bruise Tones—subdued blues, browns, blacks, and greens.

There are broad chinked floor planks and raw exposed trunks to support the ceiling. There is a section devoted to Provençal and another to Tuscan furnishings. In fact, the whole range of equatorial peasantry is represented. There are nooks that feature Moroccan crafts, Peruvian fabrics, and Indian chests. For the dining room there is an array of harvest tables, unvarnished and worn, so that the country table that was designed for the slaughtering of pigs now serves to show off delicate squash ravioli in $25 earthenware bowls.

Even the iconography is different. The old Wayne preferred images of hunt animals, like stags, hounds, ducks, and horses. The new-style Wayne consumer seems to prefer carvings and images of pacifistic or whimsical animals, like penguins, cows, cats, and frogs. The old-style Wayne matrons went in for floral prints, so when a bunch of them walked together down the street, they looked like a moving copse of hydrangea bushes. But the blouses and sweaters for sale at Anthropologie are monochromatic and muted. Taken in its entirety, the feel of the store says *A Year in Provence*, while the prices say Six Years out of Medical School.

The New Elite in the Old Ones' Beds

The fancy bread store, the artsy coffee shops, and the earthy furniture stores may seem like surface epiphenomena. But these institutions are not just arbitrary shifts in fashion—hemlines were up last decade, so they will probably be down the next. Rather, the kind of transformation we've seen in Wayne and in the rest of America's upscale neighborhoods is a symptom of a profound cultural shift. The demographic changes described in the last chapter have come to Wayne. The educated-class meritocrats have taken over the old Main Line suburb, just as they took over the elite colleges and the *New York Times* weddings page. The manor grounds have been broken up, and developers have put up $600,000 homes for the multidegreed professionals. The lawyers who bought five-bedroom Victorians in the 1990s have different attitudes than the lawyers who bought five-bedroom Victorians in the early sixties. And even the scions of the old WASP families have adapted to the new mode.

And so suddenly the streets of Wayne are dominated by the PBS-NPR cohort: vineyard-touring doctors, novel-writing lawyers, tenured gardening buffs, unusually literary realtors, dangly-earringed psychologists, and the rest of us information age burghers. These people have different aspirations than the old country club and martini suburban crowd, and naturally enough want their ideals reflected in the sort of things they buy and images they project. Shopping may not be the most intellectual exercise on earth, but it is one of the more culturally revealing. Indeed, one of the upshots of the new era is that Karl Marx may have had it exactly backward. He argued that classes are defined by their means of production. But it could be true that, in the information age at least, classes define themselves by their means of consumption.

The Historical Roots of Bobo Culture

The story of the educated class really begins in the first third of the 18th century. It's necessary to go that far back because, while demographically the educated class has only exploded in the past few decades, the values this class embodies are the culmination of a cultural struggle that began with the first glimmerings of the industrial age. It's necessary to revisit the birth of bourgeois ethos, to grasp the essence of that way of living. Then it's important to look back to the early bohemian rebellions, to understand the central bohemian ideals. It's only after reviewing these two rival cultural movements that we can grasp how different strains of the bourgeois and the bohemian world-views were woven together by the squads of biscotti-nibbling Bobos.

The first flowering of bourgeois tastes took place, in America at least, around 1720. That was the period when significant numbers of affluent Americans discovered gentility. After a few decades of struggle, many colonists could afford to live in a more comfortable style than the rough pioneers. American society had stabilized, and the successful merchants wanted their homes to reflect their interests in taste and culture. So they started building new houses and renovating old ones. They began raising the ceilings in their living rooms and covering over the exposed beams. They chose dainty, narrow floorboards instead of the broad sturdy ones of the pioneer era. They added cornices, paneling, plasterwork, and pediments to the walls to create an atmosphere of refined grace. They moved the kitchen and other utilitarian rooms to the back of the house, where visitors would not see them. They reduced the size of the fireplace openings in the front rooms so that what had become a gaping stove and furnace turned into a delicate warming area.

Most important, they began building parlors into their homes. The parlor was a room set apart from the functional uses of the house. It was used to entertain important guests or to conduct such genteel activities as reading, needlepoint, or music appreciation. Families kept their best furniture and most precious belongings in the parlor: brass andirons, gilt mirrors and clocks, the plushest rugs, upright-backed, claw-footed cherry chairs. Armies of craftsmen were employed to create the delicate porcelains, the dainty tea services, and the other gewgaws that the affluent colonials displayed in these salons. The idea was to create an elevated environment where people could cultivate delicate sensibilities and higher interests. It was also a place where people could show off their genteel manners and demonstrate their elite status. "Parlor people claimed to live on a higher plane than the vulgar and coarse populace, to excel them in their inner beings," writes Columbia historian Richard Bushman in *The Refinement of America,* his superb survey of this culture shift.

Most of America, Bushman emphasizes, was rugged and plain; "only a few privileged locales were properly adorned for the society of polished people who knew how to conduct themselves with genteel ease and grace." The new upper middle classes were building a social hierarchy that would allow them to distinguish themselves from the coarse masses. In parlor society, women were praised for having tiny hands and feet and for landing on the carpet like butterflies. Men in the 18th century were expected to wear snug waistcoats, which restricted movement and demanded formal posture. And while the rest of society had to be content with wooden boards for dining room tables and thick stools to sit on, the parlor aesthetic prized polish and smoothness. It was Edmund Burke who later articulated the general principles of this aesthetic: "I do not now recall any thing beautiful that is not smooth. . . . Take a beautiful object, and give it a broken rugged surface, and however well formed it may be in other respects, it pleases no longer."

The American elites may have been guided by European styles and manners, but they were not European aristocrats. Like their middle-class counterparts across the Atlantic, they were merchants, not lords. When courtly etiquette books were adopted by the merchant classes, some of the aristocratic theatrics were dropped, and wholesome manners came to the fore. And gradually the social ethic of the merchant class found its quintessential expression in the writings of Benjamin Franklin.

Franklin celebrated wholesome ambition. The central goal of life, he seemed to imply, is to improve yourself and thereby improve your station in life. Franklin celebrated a characteristically bourgeois set of virtues: frugality, honesty, order, moderation, prudence, industry, perseverance, temperance, chastity, cleanliness, tranquillity, punctuality, and humility. These are not heroic virtues. They don't fire the imagination or arouse the passions like the aristocratic love of honor. They are not particularly spiritual virtues. But they are practical and they are democratic. Anybody with the right work ethic can adopt them. "How little origin is to happiness, virtue or greatness," Franklin observed.

Franklin's ethos doesn't celebrate intellectual acrobatics: "Cunning proceeds from want of capacity." It doesn't endorse long periods of introspection or metaphysical contemplation: "I approved for my part the amusing one's self with poetry now and then, so far as to improve one's language, but no farther," he wrote. And Franklin's religious utterances tend to link the transcendent to the everyday: "God helps those who help themselves," he preached, watering down the Puritan concept that each person has two connected callings, one in this world and one in the next. It's impossible to imagine Franklin renouncing worldly achievement so he could go retire to a monastery to contemplate the eternal. Instead, he managed to place worldly ambition in a low but sturdy moral framework. Be honest. Work hard. Be straightforward. Focus on the concrete and immediate interests rather than the abstract and utopian visions. And he set the tone for a plain-talking style of American wisdom: "Fish and visitors stink in three days" was one of his characteristic sayings, which, like so many of his utterances, has become a truism.

And while Franklin was personally more flamboyant than any large group of people could ever be, his writings do capture the bourgeois values of parlor society. This was a class of people who believed in cultivation and self-improvement, at least so far as was socially or commercially useful. They went in for clean, classical styles, not gaudy baroque ones. Their manners were respectable, not decadent or florid. They were smart but not overly intellectual. Their clothes were well made, but they tended to favor modest hues. They believed in making money, but also in using wealth for self-improvement, not self-indulgence. They savored refinement, but were put off by grandeur and by the extravagant gesture. They wanted to appear more refined than the working masses, but not as flamboyant as the spendthrift and amoral European aristocrats. They were not called the middle classes for nothing. They were comfortable with prudent moderation and loathed extremes.

The Bohemian Revolt

Within half a century of Franklin's death in 1790, writers, artists, intellectuals, and radicals were in open rebellion against the growing dominance of the bourgeoisie and bourgeois tastes. The rebels congregated in the town that Franklin had conquered just a few decades before, Paris. In a world dominated by the merchant classes, these artists no longer had aristocratic sponsors to flatter, which was emancipating, but they had to fend for themselves in the marketplace, which brought its own traumas. To succeed, artists and writers had to appeal to an impersonalized audience, and many of these creative types came to resent their dependence on disembodied middle-class patrons, who never seemed to pay sufficient homage to genius. And as writers and artists felt more and more detached from the rest of society, they developed heroic images of their own importance.

One of the books that wonderfully captures the artistic revolt against the merchant class is César Graña's 1964 work, *Bohemian versus Bourgeois*. In the 1830s, Graña notes, pained abhorrence of the bourgeoisie became the official emotion of most writers and intellectuals. Flaubert, the most virulent of the rebels, signed some of his letters with the title "Bourgeoisophobus" and railed against the "stupid grocers and their ilk." Hatred of the bourgeoisie, he concluded, was "the beginning of all virtue." Stendhal dismissed Benjamin Franklin, "the Philadelphia artisan," as a pious bore. Poet and playwright Alfred de Musset hurled himself against the sacred institutions of the parlor crowd: "Damned Be the Family and Society. Cursed Be the Home and Cursed Be the City. Damnation upon the Motherland."

What, exactly, did the French literati find so appalling about the middle classes? In a word, their materialism. The bourgeois definition of success seemed all wrapped up with money and productivity. The artists, conversely, admired creativity, imagination, spirit. Therefore, the intellectuals found the bourgeois crass and pathetic. They castigated the bourgeois for being dull, joyless, unimaginative, conformist. Most damning of all, the bourgeois were unheroic. The old aristocrats had at least aspired to a certain grandeur. The peasants had a kiss of Christlike holiness. But these middle classes had no hint of the transcendent. They were prosaic and mediocre. There was nothing to spark the imagination, nothing loftier than their usefulness, their punctuality, their countinghouse concerns, their daily grind, their machines, their philistinism. Stendhal saw the bourgeois as "meticulous in advancing his own little schemes." They made him want "to weep and vomit at the same time." Flaubert saw the bourgeois as "plodding and avaricious." Zola later added, "The French bourgeoisie is too much the shopkeeper, too deeply sunk into its fat."

And most maddening of all, it was precisely the bourgeoisie's limitations that accounted for its tremendous worldly success. It was the merchants' petty-minded efficiency that allowed them to build successful companies and amass riches. It was their icy calculation that enabled them to devote themselves to the bottom line. It was their mechanical tinkering that enabled them to build the machines and factories and so displace the craftsmen and artisans. It was their concern for money that allowed them access to power and position. Nowadays we are used to the fact that sometimes the people who devote their lives to, say, marketing soap or shoes get to amass fortunes, live in big houses, and attract dinner party flattery, but in the 1830s all this was relatively new and shocking. It was the bourgeoisie's dullness that led to its power.

The intellectual set decided to hell with that, and they established their own alternative universe, which might forever be weak in economic terms but at least would be strong in the realm of spirit and the imagination. They considered it better, Graña notes, to be a regal outcast than an affluent worm. And so *la vie bohème* was born. Strictly speaking, bohemianism is only the social manifestation of the romantic spirit. But for clarity's sake, and because the word *romanticism* has been stretched in so many directions, in this book I mostly use the word *bohemian* to refer to both the spirit and the manners and mores it produces.

The French intellectuals set up ways of living that are by now familiar to us all. The sensitive souls flocked to run-down urban neighborhoods and created artistic communities and movements. In these places the poet and painter had higher status than the banker or president. And unable to ward off the growing strength of the bourgeoisie, the artists could at least shock them. After Flaubert finished *Salammbô*, his novel about Carthage, he predicted, "It will 1) annoy the bourgeois . . . ; 2) unnerve and shock sensitive people; 3) anger the archeologists; 4) be unintelligible to the ladies; 5) earn me a reputation as a pederast and a cannibal. Let us hope so." And so was born one of the war cries that was a hallmark of the bourgeois-bohemian feud: *Epater les bourgeois!*

The bohemian men grew their hair long and wore beards. They adopted flamboyant modes of dress by which they could easily be identified—red vests, Spanish cloaks. They celebrated youth culture and went in for provocations, whimsical humor, and practical jokes. The painter Emile Pelletier went on walks with his pet jackal. The poet Gérard de Nerval took a lobster on a leash on a walk through the Tuileries gardens. "It does not bark and it knows the secrets of the deep," he remarked. They developed a mordant fascination with the mystical and the macabre. They often wrote about suicide and sometimes performed it. They embraced novelty and sometimes applauded experimentation merely to demonstrate their contempt for the conservative middle classes.

The bohemians identified with others they saw as victims of the bourgeois order: the poor, the criminals, the ethnic and racial outcasts. They admired exotic cultures that were seemingly untouched by bourgeois mores. Many Parisians idealized Spain, which still seemed medieval. Flaubert marveled at the primitive way of life he found in Brittany. They idealized those they took to be noble savages, putting strange African artifacts in their bedrooms. They envied faraway societies, such as China, which seemed spiritually pure. They elevated sex to an art form (actually, they considered every aspect of life an art form) and scorned the prudery of the bourgeoisie. The more you read about the Parisian bohemians, the more you realize that they thought of everything. For the next 150 years rebels, intellectuals, and hippies could do little more than repeat their original rebellions.

Needless to say, in reality the conflict between the bourgeois and the bohemians was never as polarized as the polemics would indicate. The bourgeois were far more cultivated than Flaubert and his cronies gave them credit for. The Germans were sophisticated enough to distinguish between the property-owning bourgeoisie—*Besitzbuerger-tum*—and the cultivated bourgeoisie—*Bildungsbuerger-tum*. And the rebels were never as antimaterialistic as they pretended. Nonetheless, the mental categories entailed in this culture war did dominate people's thinking. The bourgeois prized materialism, order, regularity, custom, rational thinking, self-discipline, and productivity. The bohemians celebrated creativity, rebellion, novelty, self-expression, antimaterialism, and vivid experience. The bourgeois believed there was a natural order of things. They embraced rules and traditions. The bohemians believed there was no structured coherence to the universe. Reality could only be grasped in fragments, illusions, and intimations. So they adored rebellion and innovation.

The bourgeois realm was the realm of business and the market. The bohemian realm was art. The bourgeois preferred numerical and mechanistic modes of thought. The bohemians preferred intuitive and organic modes of thought. The bourgeois liked organizations. The bohemians valued autonomy and regarded the bourgeoisie as conformist herd animals. The bourgeois loved machines; the bohemians preferred the intimate humanism of the preindustrial craftsman. When it came to manners and consumption, the bourgeois admired poise and polish. The bohemians—with the exception of the Dandies, who came and went during the 19th century—admired authenticity and naturalness. The bourgeois worshiped success; the bohemians built a set of status symbols around antisuccess. The bourgeoisie sought tangible improvements. The great goal of the bohemian was the expansion of the self. Graña sums it up: "Romantic literature glorified strong passions, unique emotions, and special deeds. It despised normalcy, foresight, concern with customary affairs, and attention to feasible goals—everything of which the middle class was a daily example."

The Transcendentalists

The Parisian-style conflict between the Right and Left Banks would come to America soon enough. But the heyday of Greenwich Village bohemia—when it is possible to imagine flamboyant artists walking their lobsters through the park—was still at least 60 years away. In the mid-19th century the American artists and intellectuals who criticized bourgeois industrialism lacked the pranksterish humor and rebellious amoralism of their European counterparts. The American antimaterialists didn't seek to build a counterculture of urban rebels. They sought their alternative to the industrial economy amidst nature, in the simple life. Their aesthetic was more naturalist than artistic.

Richard Hofstadter called transcendentalism "the evangelicalism of the highbrows" because the transcendentalists always had enormous influence on the educated classes. They were mostly New England thinkers, writers, and reformers, such as Ralph Waldo Emerson, Henry David Thoreau, Bronson Alcott, and Margaret Fuller. They got their name because their goal was to transcend materialism and rationalism and so penetrate the inner spirituality that was at the core of each person. They began with the conviction, expressed by William Channing, that "there is something greater within [each individual] than in the whole material creation, than in all the worlds which press on the eye and ear; and that inward improvements have a worth and dignity in themselves."

The next step in this philosophy was to conclude that life is too precious to devote to money and things; material duties should be considered just a stepping stone to spiritual exploration. The transcendentalists did not totally reject the world. Emerson adopted a "gradational ethic" that held that people begin with their material needs and are meant to "ascend and ascend." In "The Young American" he wrote, "Trade is also but for a time, and must give way to somewhat broader and better, whose signs are already dawning in the sky." Thoreau bought and sold provisions but believed in living "simply and wisely" because "I wanted to live deep and suck out all the marrow of life, and to live so sturdily and Spartan-like as to put to rout all that was not life."

The transcendentalists lived in a bourgeois culture that was intoxicated by the possibilities of technology and by the "improvements," to use a popular word of the era, that would come with progress. The steam engine, the railway, the factory, scientific management—all of these things would eliminate distance, facilitate trade, and generate wealth. Man was on the verge of conquering nature, of redeeming the howling wilderness by making it productive. In his 1964 book, *The Machine in the Garden*, literary critic Leo Marx cites this quotation from an 1840s journalist named George Ripley as an example of what he calls the technological sublime:

> The age that is to witness a rail road between the Atlantic and the Pacific, as a grand material type of unity of nations, will also behold a social organization, productive of moral and spiritual results, whose sublime and beneficial character will eclipse even the glory of those colossal achievements which send messengers of fire over the mountain tops, and connect ocean with ocean by iron and granite bands.

Even Emerson was initially caught up in the excitement. But over time the transcendentalists concluded that while technology might bring material gain, it would also threaten nature and man's spiritual connection to nature.

"Things are in the saddle, / And ride mankind," Emerson famously complained. "We do not ride upon the railroad; it rides upon us," Thoreau echoed. Machines, wealth, and money, they believed, intercede between people and the experiences that really matter. The transcendentalists concluded that most of their fellow Americans worked too hard and too slavishly. They were able to calculate and measure but often did not take the time to sense and feel. Their middle-class neighbors were too concerned with their standard of living and not enough concerned with their reason for living.

The transcendentalists experienced their most vivid and profound experiences in the woods. Thoreau moved briefly to Walden Pond, where he lived "a border life" between the civilization of town life to his east and the primitivism of the frontier to the west. "The land," Emerson wrote, "is the appointed remedy for whatever is false and fantastic in our culture. The continent we inhabit is to be a physic and food for our mind, as well as our body. The land, with its tranquilizing, sanative influences, is to repair the errors of a scholastic and traditional education, and bring us into just relation with men and things." Striking a note that is the antithesis of the genteel culture of parlor society, Thoreau added, "Life consists with wildness. The most alive is the wildest." The civilization that erects barriers between man and nature can lead only to alienation and unhappiness.

It is a sign of the tremendous influence of the transcendentalists that the rhetorical flourishes of the 19th-century technologists now seem to us absurd, while the thoughts of the oddballs in the woods seem profound. They left a permanent imprint on American culture. Thanks in part to their influence, bohemia in America has usually been more naturalist, more devoted to the simple life, less nihilistic than its European counterpart.

The Culture War

The culture war between the bohemians and the bourgeoisie raged throughout the industrial age. It took different forms over time, and it was fought on different battlegrounds, but the main themes were pretty constant. There was always, in America, a bourgeois strain, materialist, rationalist, technological. It aspired to refined tastes and genteel manners. And there was always a bohemian strain, artistic, antirationalist, spiritual. It admired authentic furnishings, adventurous styles, naturalistic manners.

During the Gilded Age, for example, a bourgeois child would have read the *McGuffey Readers,* which contained moral tales for achievement-oriented kids, or Horatio Alger novels that had names like *Strive and Succeed, Luck and Pluck, Slow and Sure,* and *Fame and Fortune.* These books updated Benjamin Franklin's advice: work hard, be diligent, seize opportunities, be honest but not too intellectual, be pleasing to others, waste not want not. Such a child, if successful, would have grown up to live in a stately home, maybe on the hill above his town, or in one of the new commuter suburbs that were springing up. There, he might turn to Andrew Carnegie's essays, such as the hugely popular "Wealth," to take instruction in spending, giving, and getting.

But at the same time in another part of the country there would be writers like John Muir who rejected the "gobble gobble school" of bourgeois capitalism. There were furniture makers like Gustav Stickley who wanted to devise ways of living that would be comfortable and beautiful but that rejected the crass materialism of mainstream taste. Stickley was influenced by the Arts and Crafts movement that had been led in Britain by John Ruskin and

William Morris, who celebrated the simple virtues embodied in the preindustrial handicraft guild communities.

Stickley's magazine, the *Craftsman,* was the leading organ for their ideas. "We need to straighten out our standards," Stickley wrote, "and to get rid of a lot of rubbish that we have accumulated along with our wealth and commercial supremacy. It is not that we are too energetic, but that in many ways we have misused our energy precisely as we have wasted and misused so many of our wonderful natural resources." So the homes and furniture Stickley designed would not be mini-palaces for the aspiring bourgeoisie. They would encourage a simple and naturalist style of life. They would offer "an escape" from the "machine of commercial tyranny" where people could get their spiritual lives in balance. Stickley meant his Arts and Crafts and Mission styles to be a craftsmanlike alternative to the grandiose styles of the merchant princes, though, the bourgeoisie being the bourgeoisie, the merchants quickly co-opted his products. The Astors and the Rockefellers hired Stickley to furnish their country retreats. Henry Ford filled his Manhattan apartment with Mission furniture.

In the 1920s the bourgeois and the bohemian impulses took different forms. On the one hand, there were classic bourgeois presidents like Harding, Coolidge, and Hoover. There was a massive expansion of upscale suburbs; mansion after mansion sprung up in places like the Main Line outside Philadelphia and Westchester County near New York. There was an expanding class of petty bourgeoisie, who set up parlors in their small bungalows in Chicago, Los Angeles, and elsewhere. The members of the new parlor set might hardly ever use these rooms. Their homes were so small they really couldn't spare the space. Nonetheless, the parlors sat there, valued as symbols of newly earned, if slightly outdated, gentility. And there were millions of aspiring bourgeois buying books like Bruce Barton's *The Man Nobody Knows*. Barton argued that Jesus was actually best understood as a great business executive and a successful networker. "A kill-joy! He was the most popular dinner guest in Jerusalem!" Barton exclaimed. "A failure! He picked up twelve men from the bottom ranks of business and forced them into an organization that conquered the world." In 1926 bookstores sold more copies of *The Man Nobody Knows* than of any other nonfiction book.

On the other hand, there was a literary assault on bourgeois values and a flourishing bohemian alternative in Greenwich Village and elsewhere. During this period such writers as Sinclair Lewis, Thorstein Veblen, John O'Hara, John Dos Passos, Ernest Hemingway, and Gertrude Stein rejected bourgeois values, going off to Paris or Moscow, engaging in radical politics, or otherwise railing against the rise of provincial Babbittry. Malcolm Cowley, a Greenwich Village habitué who was also a writer and editor, summarized the priorities of early-20th-century American bohemians in his 1934 book, *Exile's Return*. The bohemians, he said, stood for the following ideas: "the salvation by the child"—each of us is born with special potentialities that are slowly crushed by society; "the idea of self-expression"—the purpose of life is to express the full individuality of one's inner being; "the idea of paganism"—the body is a temple, so there is nothing unclean about nudity and sex; "the idea of living for the moment"; "the idea of liberty"—every law and convention should be shattered; "the idea of female equality"; "the idea of psychological adjustment"—people are unhappy because they are repressed or maladjusted; "the idea of changing place"—truth could be found if one got on the road and moved to someplace new or vital.

Then came the 1950s, seemingly the high point of the bourgeois era but at the same time the moment when it was being undermined. It was the era of President Eisen-

hower, the Organization Man, Junior League clubs, and
Leave It to Beaver television culture. On the other hand,
there were squads of rebel bohemians hitting the road and
smoking pot. Like their bohemian predecessors, the Beats
celebrated spontaneity and sensation. They enjoyed
shocking the bourgeoisie. They rejected money and comfort for the sake of liberation and freedom. And they despised what Allen Ginsberg called the "Moloch whose
mind is pure machinery."

And there were writers and intellectuals who saw in
the Beat styles the first glimmerings of a social revolution.
In his 1960 book, *Growing Up Absurd,* Paul Goodman
rhapsodized about the Beats: "Their main topic is the 'system' with which they refuse to cooperate. They will explain that 'good' jobs are frauds and sells, that it is
intolerable to have one's style of life dictated by Personnel,
that a man is a fool to work to pay installments on a useless refrigerator for his wife," and so on. Goodman's main
assault was on "the organization," the great interlocking
system of bureaucracies and structures, which Goodman
and the Beats felt stifled autonomy and creativity. Society
needed to be disrupted and disorganized. But Goodman
was savvy enough to notice something else about the
Beats. Though they were dissidents and though they rejected affluence and all that, the Beats actually lived pretty
well. It was their spirit of pleasure that made them so at-
tractive. In a passage that brilliantly anticipates the Bobo
consumerism of today, Goodman observed, "The Beat
subculture is not merely a reaction to the middle class or
to the organized system. It is natural. Merging with the
underprivileged, the Beats do not make a poor go of it.
Their homes are often more livable than middle class
homes; they often eat better, have good records, etc. Some
of their habits, like being unscheduled, sloppy, communitarian, sexually easy-going and careless of reputation, go
against the grain of the middle class, but they are moti-

vated by good sense rather than resentment: They are probably natural ways that most people would choose if they got wise to themselves." This was a different notion: bohemia was a lifestyle most people would choose to live if they got wise to themselves. If you had taken that idea in 1960 and made it the cornerstone of your investment choices, you would be a billionaire today.

In the sixties, of course, the bohemian subculture turned into a mass movement, suitable for the covers of *Life* and *Look* magazines. The hippie assaults on the bourgeois lifestyle are so well known they don't really need to be summarized at great length here. But briefly, and leaving aside the civil rights movement and Vietnam and all the complex and substantive political turmoils of that decade, here are a few of the countercultural straws in the wind: In the realm of public theater, Abbie Hoffman threw dollar bills down on the traders of the New York Stock Exchange. The Diggers, a group of San Francisco performance artists, declared "The Death of Money and the Birth of the Free." In the literary realm, Norman Mailer explored what it meant to be a hipster. In his collection of essays, *Advertisements for Myself,* Mailer published, glossy-magazine style, a list of what was hip and what was square, and his list corresponds to the traditional split between the bohemian and the bourgeois. Night, he wrote, is hip, whereas day is square. Crooks are hip, whereas the police are square. The body is hip, whereas the mind is square. Questions are hip; answers are square. Induction, thinking intuitively, is hip; deduction, thinking more rationally, is square.

Theodore Roszak, the chronicler of the 1960s revolt, summarized the hippie critique of the middle classes in *The Making of a Counter Culture:* "The bourgeoisie is obsessed by greed; its sex life is insipid and prudish, its family patterns are debased; its slavish conformities of dress and grooming are degrading; its mercenary routinization of life is intolerable." The bourgeois floated on a swell of affluence, so the student leaders rejected materialism. The bourgeois admired politeness, elegance, and decorum, so the student leaders were raw. The bourgeois were neat, so the student leaders were haphazard. The bourgeois had short hair, so the student leaders had long hair. The bourgeois were technological, so the student leaders were natural. The bourgeois were career oriented, so the student leaders were experience oriented. The bourgeois pretended to be chaste, so the student leaders pretended to be promiscuous. The bourgeois practiced conspicuous consumption, so the students practiced conspicuous nonconsumption. The bourgeois celebrated work, so the students celebrated pleasure. The bourgeois ate meat and processed food, so the student leaders ate soybeans and other organic foods. In the 1960s millions of people figured out you could go up in your peers' estimation by going down in lifestyle and dress. And swelling with great numbers, the romantic counterculture actually overshadowed the bourgeois mainstream culture. More than a century after Flaubert and his Parisian cronies first raised the banner *"Epater les bourgeois,"* the bohemian movement had grown from a clique to a horde. For a time it seemed like the ideas of bohemia would actually rout what remained of Benjamin Franklin's bourgeois ethos.

The Bourgeois Counterattack

Then in the 1970s and 1980s, a funny thing happened. The bourgeois ethos began fighting back. For the previous century the argument between the bourgeois and the bohemians had been one-sided. The bohemians would launch their articulate attacks, but the bourgeoisie would just follow the advice of their throw pillows: Living well is the best revenge. They would just go on living their lives, semi-oblivious to the countercultural assault. They might sneer at the radicals or the eggheads, but they didn't produce a comprehensive critique of bohemianism. But after the sixties and seventies, the party of the bourgeoisie could not help but notice the party of bohemia. The counterculture was everywhere. The personal was political. The bourgeoisie had to respond.

Among those who formulated the response were the neoconservatives. These were writers and academics such as Irving Kristol, James Q. Wilson, Gertrude Himmelfarb, Norman Podhoretz, and Midge Decter, who, at least in the 1970s, still tended to accept the policies of the New Deal and the Great Society. Neoconservatism started as a movement dominated by social scientists. The journal *Public Interest* was founded in 1965 by Irving Kristol and Daniel Bell to publish cool-headed, technocratic analyses of public policies. The assumption was that the great ideological wars were over and that now policy disputes would be settled by hard-headed social science scrutiny. Daniel Patrick Moynihan wrote an essay in that first issue called "The Professionalization of Reform," which was a manifesto for rule by the intellectual class: "Men are learning to make an industrial economy work. . . . The ability to predict events, as against controlling them, has developed even more impressively." But like many successful magazines, *Public Interest* and its sister neocon publication, *Commentary*, found themselves engaged in a project totally antithetical to the one for which they had been created. The neoconservatives, mostly lower-middle-class kids, were appalled by the antibourgeois attitudes of the countercultural intellectuals and student radicals. And they produced something rare in the history of this dispute, an articulate defense of the bourgeoisie and a telling critique of bohemia.

The basic neoconservative argument started with a series of concessions. It acknowledged that the bourgeois lifestyle is not heroic or inspiring. "Bourgeois society is the most prosaic of all possible societies. . . . It is a society organized for the convenience and comfort of common men and common women," Irving Kristol wrote in an essay called "The Adversary Culture of the Intellectuals." Therefore bourgeois society aims to improve material conditions; it does not devote huge energies to transcendence, to classical virtue, to spiritual transfiguration. Bourgeois societies produce happy civilizations but not grand and immortal ones. What's more, Kristol wrote, an "amiable philistinism" is inherent in bourgeois society. The high arts are not accorded a lot of respect, but popular culture flourishes (and every movie has a happy ending). Bourgeois societies are usually free societies, but they are not always just societies. Often it is the narrow-minded brute who ends up with the most money and success while the truly wise person languishes unrewarded.

On the other hand, bourgeois culture does have one massive historical accomplishment to its credit, the neoconservatives argued. It provides an effective moral context for capitalism. With its emphasis on prudence, frugality, punctuality, thrift, piety, neighborliness, responsibility, and industry, it restrains some of the greedy passions that might otherwise make a market economy barbaric. Moreover, with its reverence for institutions such as family, organized religion, manners, ceremonies, and community groups like the Rotary Club or the PTA, bourgeois culture fosters institutions that keep a free society from descending into amoralism. Furthermore, the neocons added, let's not underestimate the importance of material progress. The bourgeoisie's talent for wealth creation has made life longer and more pleasant for billions of people around the world. Technology has brought untold improvements to everybody's lives. The tinkering of the entrepreneur may not be the stuff of grandeur, but commercial improvements produce real benefits. For instance, bourgeois capitalism leads to unprecedented social mobility.

The bohemians may aspire to grand spiritual transcendence, the neocons continued, but what they often end up with is self-indulgent nihilism. The neoconservatives disdained the perpetual rebelliousness of the counterculture. They were offended by what they took to be the New Left's snobbery, its contempt for middle America. The rejection of authority and custom doesn't lead to blissful liberation, they argued; it leads to self-destructive behavior. The romantic searchers throw off conventional morality, but their antinomianism is subversive of all morality, of all civil restraint. Egotism takes over. Pretty soon fathers are abandoning their families, and the sanctity of the two-parent family is delegitimized. Children raised without clear moral guideposts slip into criminality and drug abuse. Popular culture becomes more vulgar. People are recast as society's victims and so are not asked to accept responsibility for themselves.

Neoconservatives like Gertrude Himmelfarb pointed out that between 1860 and 1970—that is, through many of the horrors of the industrial age—the divorce rate remained essentially constant in America and Britain. But starting in 1970, when bohemianism became a mass movement and bourgeois culture found itself in retreat, divorce rates skyrocketed and illegitimacy rose dramatically, as did crime rates, drug use, and many other social pathologies. The assault on bourgeois values was a social disaster, the neoconservatives argued. The task ahead, many neocons believed, was to restore bourgeois values to their former influence.

The Dream of Reconciliation

Even while the bourgeois-bohemian clash was at its height, people dreamed of finding some balance between the two sides. In his 1915 book, *America's Coming-of-*

Age, Van Wyck Brooks complained of the social division between the "machinery of self-preservation and the mystery of life."

"We have in America," Brooks wrote, "two publics, the cultivated public and the business public, the public of theory and the public of activity, the public that reads Maeterlinck and the public that accumulates money: the one largely feminine, the other largely masculine." Brooks sought a "genial middle ground" between these two mentalities. He wanted to "bring the ideal into things," to make being good compatible with making good. Though some thinkers and writers might have longed for a reconciliation, the world was not, at least during the industrial age, ready for one. But in the information age, the world of ideas and the world of business have merged, and the much-longed-for reconciliation between the bourgeois and the bohemian has come to pass.

Look around America's upper-middle-class neighborhoods, like Wayne, Pennsylvania. A town like that certainly has its share of bourgeois elements. It's a suburb. It's affluent. There is obvious reverence for traditional bourgeois institutions like family and religion. But the new Wayne residents have adopted bohemian styles as well, the strong coffees, the grains, the casual manners. In his 1954 book, *The Tastemakers,* Russell Lynes could write of Gustav Stickley, "His name and his writings are now almost forgotten." But today you can't walk 15 feet in Wayne or in similar communities without stumbling across some bit of furniture inspired by the antimaterialist craftsman.

Indeed, one of the most interesting features of the town is the way the new educated-class consumers have taken the old styles of the genteel parlor society and stood them on their head. Everything the old gentry tried to make smooth, we in today's educated gentry try to make rough. They covered over ceiling beams. We expose them. They buried bulky stone chimneys in plaster and paint.

We unearth stone chimneys and admire massive rocky hearths. They prized delicate narrow floor planks. We like broad sturdy ones. They preferred marble. We prefer slate. They filled their homes with knock-off versions of high art. We like handicrafts. They covered their furniture in silk. We toss coarse Colombian throw rugs over our sofas, with maybe a few stray hairs from a long dead burro.

More broadly, they liked polish and high civilization. We like indigenous spirituality. They liked refined manners that demonstrated self-mastery. We like loose manners that demonstrate honesty. They made entertaining into a performance—the preparation was done by the servants somewhere in the dim recesses of the house. We invite our guests backstage into the kitchen and give them some veggies to chop. The old genteel style sprang from a belief that humankind is ascending from crude barbarism to a state of civilized grace. Members of today's affluent class are suspicious of refinement and genteel manners. So the new elite disdains all the words that were used as lavish compliments by the old gentry: delicate, dainty, respectable, decorous, opulent, luxurious, elegant, splendid, dignified, magnificent, and extravagant. Instead, the new elite prefers a different set of words, which exemplify a different temper and spirit: authentic, natural, warm, rustic, simple, honest, organic, comfortable, craftsmanlike, unique, sensible, sincere.

The Bobo class has moved into bourgeois haunts and infused them with bohemian sensibilities, at the same time watering down bohemian attitudes so they don't subvert bourgeois institutions. So today a "Days of Rage" T-shirt can be worn by health-conscious aerobicizers. The pseudo-transgressive photography of Robert Mapplethorpe can be hung in the guest bathroom of a weekend place, where people can gaze at it while soothing themselves in the oversized whirlpool. (And, as we'll see in the next chapter, the Bobos have moved into bohemian haunts and infused them with bourgeois sensibilities, similarly diluted.) Today it's almost impossible to divide towns along the old culture war lines. If you go to Berkeley or Greenwich Village, the old bohemian centers, you will find distressed-furniture boutiques that host workshops in cabinetry. There will be music stores with stacks of the local alternative weekly and yoga posters on the community bulletin board. But you will find these very same sorts of stores in Wayne, Pennsylvania, or Winnetka, Illinois, and the other epicenters of the old bourgeois elite. The educated class has conquered all and hegemonized its Bobo culture over affluent regions from coast to coast. Now the Babbitt lion can mingle with the beatnik lamb at a Pottery Barn, a Smith & Hawken, a Museum Shop, a Restoration Hardware, a Nature Company, a Starbucks, or any of the other zeitgeist-heavy institutions that cater to educated affluents. Today the culture war is over, at least in the realm of the affluent. The centuries-old conflict has been reconciled.

The Code of Financial Correctness

In its place we now have this third culture. And slowly, slowly a new set of rules and sumptuary codes is emerging to replace the competing codes of the bohemians and the bourgeoisie. This new set of codes organizes the consumption patterns of the educated class, encouraging some kinds of spending, which are deemed virtuous, and discouraging others that seem vulgar or elitist. They redefine what it means to be a cultured person.

Taken as a whole, this set of rules make it clear that the Thorstein Veblen era is over. Maybe off in Vegas there are still some rich peasants trying to conspicuously consume, buying big limousines, powerboats, and sports franchises and piling up possessions to demonstrate their net worth. But the Bobo renounces accumulation and embraces cultivation. He must show, in the way he spends his money, that he is conscientious and not crass. The emerging code of financial correctness allows Bobos to spend money without looking like one of the vulgar Yuppies they despise. It's a set of rules to help them convert their wealth into spiritually and intellectually uplifting experiences. A person who follows these precepts can dispose up to $4 or $5 million annually in a manner that demonstrates how little he or she cares about material things.

Rule 1. Only vulgarians spend lavish amounts of money on luxuries. Cultivated people restrict their lavish spending to necessities.

Aristotle made the ancient distinction between needs—objects we must have to survive, like shelter, food, clothing, and other essentials—and wants, which are those things we desire to make us feel superior to others. The Bobo elite has seized on this distinction to separate itself from past and rival elites. Specifically, the members of the educated-class elite feel free to invest huge amounts of capital in things that are categorized as needs, but it is not acceptable to spend on mere wants. For example, it's virtuous to spend $25,000 on your bathroom, but it's vulgar to spend $15,000 on a sound system and a wide-screen TV. It's decadent to spend $10,000 on an outdoor Jacuzzi, but if you're not spending twice that on an oversized slate shower stall, it's a sign that you probably haven't learned to appreciate the simple rhythms of life.

Similarly, it is acceptable to spend hundreds of dollars on top-of-the-line hiking boots, but it would be vulgar to buy top-of-the-line patent leather shoes to go with formal wear. It is acceptable to spend $4,400 on a Merlin XLM road bike because people must exercise, but it would be a sign of a superficial nature to buy a big, showy power-boat. Only a shallow person would spend hundreds of dollars on caviar, but a deep person would gladly shell out that much for top-of-the-line mulch.

You can spend as much as you want on anything that can be classified as a tool, such as a $65,000 Range Rover with plenty of storage space, but it would be vulgar to spend money on things that cannot be seen as tools, such as a $60,000 vintage Corvette. (I once thought of writing a screenplay called *Rebel Without a Camry,* about the so-cial traumas a history professor suffered when he bought a Porsche.) In fact, the very phrase "sport utility vehicle" is testimony to the new way Bobos think about tools. Not long ago *sport* was the opposite of *utility.* You either played or you worked. But the information age keyboard jockeys who traffic in concepts and images all day like to dabble in physical labor during their leisure time, so haul-ing stuff around in their big mega-cruisers with the four-foot wheels turns into a kind of sport.

And when it comes to a room as utilitarian as the kitchen, the sky's the limit. Up until the Bobos came along, the kitchen was a reviled part of the house. The 19th-century architect Calvert Vaux, for example, was dis-mayed at people who would eat in the kitchen. "This habit marks the low state of civilization," he remarked. In his 1972 book, *Instant Status; or How to Become a Pillar of the Upper Middle Class,* Charles Merrill Smith noted, "Upper class women never go into the kitchen. . . . Upper middle class women, of necessity, do go into the kitchen from time to time but wish to leave the impression they do not. A true upper middle class house, then, de-emphasizes domestic convenience." At the same time, but at the oppo-site end of the cultural continuum, Betty Friedan and her fellow feminists were also urging their sisters to get out of the kitchen. But today in the age of Bobo reconciliation, everybody is back in the kitchen, albeit on his or her own terms. Indeed, in today's educated-class homes, the kitchen has become the symbol of domestic bliss, the way the hearth used to be for the bourgeoisie.

That's why when you walk into a newly renovated upscale home owned by nice, caring people, you will likely find a kitchen so large it puts you in mind of an aircraft hangar with plumbing. The perimeter walls of the old kitchen will have been obliterated, and the new kitchen will have swallowed up several adjacent rooms, just as the old Soviet Union used to do with its neighbors. It's hard to tell where one of today's mega-kitchens ends. You think you see the far wall of some distant great room shimmering in the distance, but it could be a mirage reflected off the acres and acres of Corian countertop. And then when you turn into the pantry, you observe that it is larger than the entire apartment the owner lived in while in graduate school.

Kitchens this big require strategizing. The architects brag about how brilliantly they have designed their kitchens into "work triangles" to minimize the number of steps between, say, stove, dishwasher, and sink. In the old kitchens you didn't need work triangles because taking steps was not a kitchen activity. You just turned around, and whatever you needed, there it was. But today's infinite kitchens have lunch counters and stools and built-in televisions and bookshelves and computer areas and probably little "You Are Here" maps for guests who get lost on their way to the drink station.

As for kitchen equipment, today's Bobo kitchen is like a culinary playground providing its owners with a series of top-of-the-line peak experiences. The first thing you see, covering yards and yards of one wall, is an object that looks like a nickel-plated nuclear reactor but is really the stove. No more flimsy cooking cans with glorified Bunsen burners on top for today's domestic enthusiasts. Today's gourmet Bobos want a 48-inch-wide, six-burner, dual-fuel, 20,000 Btu range that sends up heat like a space shuttle rocket booster turned upside down. Furthermore, they want cool gizmos, like a lava-rock grill, a built-in 30,000 Btu wok burner, brass burner igniters (only philistines have aluminum ones), and a ½-inch-thick steel griddle. They want an oven capacity of 8 cubic feet minimum, just to show they are the sort of people who could roast a bison if necessary. And they want the whole awesome package covered in metal with such a high nickel-to-chromium content that magnets won't stick. That's how you know you have purchased the sort of utilitarian gear your family deserves. La Cornue makes an adequate stove with gas and electric simmer plates for about $23,500. The AGA 59-inch cooker, patented in 1922, has the unadorned sturdiness that suggests it was once used to recycle horses into glue, but it also features such conveniences as a warming plate, a simmering plate, a baking oven, a roasting oven, and an infinite supply of burners. It uses no direct heat, only radiant surfaces, and thus expresses a gentle philosophy of life. It costs only $10,000.

Presiding over the nearby quadrants of the kitchen will be the refrigeration complex. The central theme of this section is that freezing isn't cold enough; the machinery should be able to reach temperatures approaching absolute zero, at which all molecular motion stops. The refrigerator itself should be the size of a minivan stood on end. It should have at least two doors, one for the freezer section and one for the in-law suite, in case you want to rent out rooms inside. In addition, there should be through-the-door delivery systems for water (carbon filtered), ice (cubes, crushed, or alphabet style to help the toddlers with their letter recognition), and perhaps assorted microbrews. There should be gallon door bins, spillproof split shelves, sealed snack pans, full extension slides, and scratchproof bin windows, and the front doors should not be white, like those regular refrigerators they sell at Sears, but stainless steel—the texture of culinary machismo.

A capacious kitchen with durable appliances is a sign that you do your own chores, sharing the gritty reality of everyday life, just as Gandhi and Karl Marx would have wanted you to. It means you've got equipment with more power than all but six of the NATO nations. It means that when you throw those fish sticks into the oven, you know they will be browned evenly, and you could boil the water for the macaroni and cheese in eight seconds if you really turned the thing up full blast. It means that you have concentrated your spending power on where it matters, on the everyday places you and your family actually use. Spending on conspicuous display is evil, but it's egalitarian to spend money on parts of the house that would previously have been used by the servants.

Rule 2. It is perfectly acceptable to spend lots of money on anything that is of "professional quality," even if it has nothing to do with your profession.

Very few of us are actually professional sherpas, leading parties up Mount Everest, but that doesn't mean an expedition-weight three-layer Gore-Tex Alpenglow reinforced Marmot Thunderlight jacket is not a reasonable purchase. Just because you don't actually own a bagel shop doesn't mean you have to settle for a flimsy $29 toaster when you could select a $300 multipurpose industrial-strength toasting system that will be browning breakfast breads well into the 23rd century. Similarly, the fact that you are a only a part-time gardener doesn't mean you should settle for a $6 hoe when there are $55 ones at the gourmet gardening stores. Because while cultivated people would never judge each other on the costliness of their jewelry, they do judge each other on the costliness of their gear. When buying gear, you have to prove you are serious enough to appreciate durability and craftsmanship. You have to show you are smart enough to spend the very most.

To cater to this sentiment, upscale stores have adopted a set of clever disguises. They pretend to be selling hard gear-type stuff when they are actually selling soft boring stuff like clothing. The REI outdoor store will advertise its ice axes, knowing that they will make you feel virtuous as you walk by them up to the sweater section. Restoration Hardware trumpets its hardware, but it actually earns far more revenue from selling couches and chairs. The Lands' End company sells a lot of socks, but on their catalogue cover they will show a picture of hikers walking along the crest of Mount Everest.

One of the results of this trend is that there is an adventure gap opening up between members of the educated class and their belongings. The things they own were designed for more dangerous activities than any they actually perform. The hiking boots that were designed for the Andes spend most of their time in the farmer's market. The top-of-the-line fleece outergarments are used for nothing more strenuous than traversing the refrigerated aisle in the Safeway. The four-wheel-drive vehicles are never asked to perform any ordeal more treacherous than a bumpy road in the slush. But just as in the age of gentility hypocrisy was vice paying homage to virtue, so today among the Bobos rugged gear is comfort paying homage to adventure.

Rule 3. You must practice the perfectionism of small things.

It's kind of pretentious to build yourself a big estate with magnificently manicured grounds. But nobody can accuse you of getting too big for your britches if you devote fanatical attention to small household items, like selecting exactly the right pasta strainer, the distinctive doorknob, or one of those ingeniously designed corkscrews. Bobos practice what journalist Richard Starr calls the perfectionism of small things. They might line their bread drawer with terra-cotta; a small thing but it enhances breathability. They might spend hours contemplating backsplashes, devoting their massive powers of contemplation to finding one that is protective yet unobtrusive. They might dedicate their evenings so they can become insulation connoisseurs. They might scour the hardware catalogues until they find the Swiss-made KWC faucet, which many believe to be the world's finest pullout spray head. The idea behind all this effort is to show that you have so much brainpower to spare, you can even be thoughtful about your water flow.

The mental powers that were once devoted to organic chemistry finals and metaphysics term papers can now be lavished on appliance garages (it's important to get the ones with tambour doors). Bobos don't want gaudy possessions that make extravagant statements. That would make it look like they are trying to impress. They want rare gadgets that have not yet been discovered by the masses but are cleverly designed to make life more convenient or unusual. It's a sign you have mastered the art of living if you've built in a raised dishwasher so you don't have to stoop while unloading. It's a testimony to your commitment to your kids if your bathroom cabinet has view-at-a-glance, childproof plastic medicine containers. A person with an elevated sensibility gets a life-affirming rush while opening soup with a particularly brilliant can opener. If your Christmas tree lights are vintage 1933 with the slightly larger bulbs, your sophisticated guests will appreciate your nose for old-fashioned workmanship. Nobody wants to talk about a diamond necklace over dinner, but it's charming to start a conversation about the host's African-inspired salad serving forks. The smaller an item is, the more praiseworthy it is to have thought deeply about its purchase.

Rule 4. You can never have too much texture.

Smoothness may have been pleasing to Edmund Burke. And high-achieving but grasping yuppies of the 1980s may have surrounded themselves with smooth surfaces—matte black furniture, polished lacquer floors, and sleek faux-marbleized walls. But to demonstrate their superiority to such people, the educated elites prefer to build environments full of natural irregularities. For the Bobos, roughness connotes authenticity and virtue.

So the educated elites love texture. They prefer rough area rugs woven from obscure grasses over shiny wall-to-wall carpets, bumpy wooden toys over smooth plastic ones, thick and textured ceramics over smooth and dainty porcelain, crinkly and idiosyncratic wildflowers over smooth tulips. In accordance with our impasto longings, we in the educated class savor pummeled antique doorknobs, lichenous stone walls, scarred provincial cabinets, rough-hewn beams, weathered slates, raw Tibetan fabrics, and rammed-earth interiors. Really rich Bobos will hire squads of workmen with ball-peen hammers to pound some rustic wear into their broad floor planks. They'll import craftsmen from Umbria to create the look of crumbling frescoed plaster in their foyer. They'll want foundations built from craggy stones that look as if they could withstand a catapult assault, and interior beams built from logs that look as if they've been chipped by Paul Bunyan.

Any unreflective currency trader can choose clothing on the basis of pattern, but it takes an elevated sensibility to design a wardrobe by mixing textures. So Bobo shirts are flannel, not silk. Our collars are relaxed and folded, not starched and metallic. We will complement our linen slacks with a marled blouse, a Salvadoran folk-art fleece sweater, a hemp baseball cap, and, as it comes on the market, sisal underwear. When a group of Bobos stand together, observers will be awed by the subtle symphony of fabrics. Their mouths will hang open and they will think to themselves, "Wow, there goes a cloud of nubby people. I wonder if they know where I can get some fresh fava beans."

The texture principle applies to comestibles too. Everything the educated person drinks will leave sediment in the bottom of the glass: yeasty microbrews, unfiltered fruit juices, organic coffees. Bobo breads are thick and grainy, the way wholesome peasants like it, not thin and airy, as the old shallow suburbanites prefer. Even our condiments will be admirably coarse; rough, unrefined sugar is considered by many to be the height of refinement.

Rule 5. The educated elites are expected to practice one-downmanship.

Cultivated people are repelled by the idea of keeping up with the Joneses. Nothing is more disreputable than competing with your neighbors by trying to more effectively mimic the style of the social class just above you. Instead, as members of the educated class, you reject status symbols in order to raise your status with your equally cultivated peers. Everything about you must be slightly more casual than your neighbor. Your furnishings must be slightly more peasanty. Your lives should have a greater patina of simplicity. So your dinnerware will not have the sort of regal designs they use at Buckingham Palace. It will be basic white, like what they sell at Pottery Barn. Your shoes won't be snazzy pumps; they'll be simple but expensive penny loafers from Prada. Ostentation is a disgrace, but anything unadorned is a sign of refreshing honesty. You must learn to keep down with the Joneses.

The educated class pioneered this form of status inversion back in the 1960s when some anonymous genius discovered that you could sell faded blue jeans at a higher price than new blue jeans. Suddenly there was a class of consumers that wanted to reject the cult of newness that had hitherto been the guiding mode of consumerism. This taste for the faux archaic has now spread across the upscale marketplace. So now fancy furniture stores sell steamer trunks that are newly made but stained to look old, complete with torn destination stickers. Across the developing world there are factory workers busy beating up the goods they have just made in order to please American consumers, and one can only imagine what they think of us. But for us the payoff is clear. If your furniture is distressed, your conscience needn't be.

In the 1950s and 1960s the smart set wanted to appear relentlessly modern. A 1958 advertisement for the Invincible furniture company featured "Modernaire desks, modular Modernettes and Modernease chairs." Today these same styles are fashionable precisely because they are archaic. Being truly modern is out of date. Instead, restaurants splatter paint on their floors and dent their tables with hammers to exude a lived-in feel. The sales of self-consciously old-fashioned push lawn mowers skyrocket by 20 to 30 percent annually, catering to retro-chic professionals who could easily afford motor mowers. Meanwhile, roller-skate revivalists are powering a surge back to four-wheel skates and away from in-line models.

The course of status inversion is both back and down. It is not sufficient to buy stuff that is old. It is necessary in addition to go down the social scale and purchase objects that once belonged to persons much poorer than yourself. The aim is to surround yourself with products that purport to have no social status significance because they were once owned by people who were so simple and virtuous they didn't realize how fashionable they were. That is why the richer Bobos get, the more they live like Shakers. If you go into a Bobo home, you will possibly find Shaker-inspired stereo consoles and Shaker-inspired workstations. Bobo cabinets will have been converted from homely typesetting shops. Old closet doors will have been salvaged from an old sausage factory. The baby gates on the stairs will have been converted from 19th-century rabbit hutches. There will be ancient farm implements hanging from the wall as decorative devices. The tables will be arrayed with general store objets d'art, such as old cans of liniment salve, biscuit tins, kitchen utensils, and beat-up spice containers. Upending the hierarchies of the *ancien régime,* we want people to think we spent less on our stuff than we actually did.

We prize old things whose virtues have been rendered timeless by their obsolescence: turn-of-the-century carpentry tools, whaling equipment, butter churns, typesetting trays, gas lamps, and hand-operated coffee grinders. Lightship baskets made from rattan with oak bottoms now sell for between $1,000 and $118,000. We can appreciate the innate wisdom of the unlettered seaman and the objects he created. He saw his objects as tools, but we appreciate them as works of art.

Another essential element of one-downmanship is the co-optation of oppressed cultures. The old elite may have copied the styles of the European aristocrats or the colonial masters, but Bobos prefer the colonial victims. In fact, if you tour a super-sophisticated home, you will see an odd mélange of artifacts that have nothing in common except for the shared victimization of their creators. An African mask will sit next to an Incan statue atop a tablecloth fashioned from Samoan, Brazilian, Moroccan, or Tibetan cloth. Even some European cultures, such as the Celts, qualify for one-downmanship—they have been oppressed enough that an educated person can feel a sense of benevolence while appreciating the beauty of their iconography. Sometimes it will be the religious objects of an oppressed culture that will be displayed in an educated home: Amazonian figures, Native American totems, Egyptian deities, animistic shells, or Shinto statuettes. It is acceptable to display sacred items in an educated person's home so long as they are from a religion neither the host nor any of his or her guests is likely to profess.

We educated elites surround ourselves with the motifs of lives we have chosen not to live. We are busy meritocrats, but we choose goods that radiate pre-meritocratic calm. We march into the future with our Palm Pilots and cell phones, but we surround ourselves with rootsy stuff, the reactionary and the archaic. We guiltily acknowledge our privileges but surround ourselves with artifacts from the less privileged. It's not that we're hypocrites. It's just that we're seeking balance. Affluent, we're trying not to become materialists. Busy, we're trying not to lose sight of the timeless essentials. So we go around frantically shopping for the accoutrements of calm. We dream of building a home where we can finally sit still and relax, a place we can go where our ambition won't follow.

In this spirit we sometimes even reintroduce the old WASP styles into our eclecticism. The WASPs may have been racist and elitist. They may have been the establishment that we Bobos destroyed. But at least they weren't consumed by ambition. So when we look at those calm beautiful faces in the Ralph Lauren ads, we can't help feeling that they have something we long for. And so mixed in with our multicultural decor may be an item or two that could have come right out of the New York Yacht Club, maybe a faded leather chair or a dark wooden desk. The WASP Establishment is dead, and irony of ironies, the Protestant Establishment has been transmogrified into one of those extinct cultures destroyed by the march of technology and progress.

Rule 6. Educated elites are expected to spend huge amounts of money on things that used to be cheap.

As part of our effort to free ourselves from the corruptions of money, we in the educated elite spend a lot of time distancing ourselves from the moneyed elite, the people who are richer than us but less well educated. The members of the money class pour resources into big luxury items, like yachts and jewelry. They go in for products the lower classes could never purchase, such as foie gras, caviar, and truffles. But we in the educated elite go in for products the money classes would never purchase. We prefer to buy the same items as the proletariat—it's just that we buy rarefied versions of these items that the members of the working class would consider preposterous. So we will buy chicken legs, just like everybody else, but they'll likely be free-range chickens that in life were treated better than Elizabeth Taylor at a health spa. We'll buy potatoes, but we won't buy an Idaho spud. We'll select one of those miniature potatoes of distinction that grow only in certain soils of northern France. When we need lettuce, we will choose only from among those flimsy cognoscenti lettuces that taste so bad on sandwiches. The beauty of such a strategy is that it allows us to be egalitarian and pretentious at the same time.

Accordingly, we end up paying hugely inflated prices for all sorts of things that used to be cheap: coffee at $3.75 a cup, water at $5 a bottle, hemp clogs at $59 from Smith & Hawken, a bar of soap at $12, an Italian biscuit for $1.50, a box of gourmet noodles for $9.95, a bottle of juice for $1.75, and lemongrass at a few bucks a stalk.

Even our white T-shirts can run to $50 or more. We spend our money on peasant goods that are created in upscale versions of themselves. We are able to cultivate ever finer tastes about ever more simple things.

Rule 7. Members of the educated elite prefer stores that give them more product choices than they could ever want but which don't dwell on anything so vulgar as prices.

Members of the educated class are distinguished not only by what they buy but by how they buy. It's commonly observed, for example, that almost nobody in an upscale coffeehouse orders just a cup of coffee. Instead, one of us will order a double espresso, half decaf–half caffeinated, with mocha and room for milk. Another will order a vente almond Frappuccino made from the Angolan blend with raw sugar and a hint of cinnamon. We don't just ask for a beer. We order one of 16,000 microbrews, picking our way through winter ales, Belgian lagers, and blended wheats. Thanks to our influence on the market, all the things that used to come in just a few varieties now come in at least a dozen: rice, milk, tomatoes, mushrooms, hot sauces, breads, beans, and even iced tea (there are now at least 50 flavors of Snapple).

This is because educated people refuse to be merely pawns in a mass consumer society. Others may buy machine-made products or live in identical suburban tract homes or buy vulgar replicas of earlier vulgar mansions or eat conventional apples. But members of the educated elite do not want to be found to be derivative in their shopping oeuvre. We do not plagiarize our purchases. Shopping for us isn't just about picking up some stuff at the store. Rather, it is precisely by selecting just the right pasta bowls (hearty, not delicate; muted, not cute; Sienese, not Wedgwood) that an educated person can develop his or her own taste. In the realm of the Bobos, you become the curator of your possessions. You can, for example, be the Bernard Berenson of the mantelpiece, exercising your exquisite judgment in the realm of living room decor. You can choose candlesticks and picture frames that are eclectic and subversive—an array of statuettes and clocks that is at once daring and spontaneous yet also reflects an elegant unity of thought. You can push the boundaries of fireplace discourse, experimenting with new andirons and firewood formations. Each item you display will be understood to have been a rare "find." You will have picked it out from one of those new stores that organize themselves like flea markets. Thousands of less cultivated shoppers will have gone over it before but lacked the wit to stop and appreciate its ironic emanations. But there it sits on your mantel, a lasting tribute to your taste and slight eccentricity. If T. S. Eliot were alive today and of a mind, he'd open a chain of home furnishings stores called Objective Correlatives, and each object in them would be the physical expression of some metaphysical sentiment.

Nor is it ever enough just to buy something; one has to be able to discourse upon it. That is why, for example, the Lands' End catalogue doesn't just show off, say, a nice tweed jacket. It has little bits of text all around describing the Celtic roots of tweed, relating an interesting 14th-century legend about tweed, explaining why the best lambswool is sheared in the first six months of a lamb's life, and noting that the jacket is made by adorable old men with lined faces. The Lands' End people surround their advertisement with edifying articles by such writers as Garrison Keillor to let us know that the document we hold in our hands is not merely a catalogue but is actually more like one of those money-losing highbrow magazines.

In this and myriad other ways, the companies that sell to us have developed careful marketing strategies for people who disdain marketing. They help make shopping seem a bit like an honors project at Bennington College. We don't just look for a toothpaste. We assign ourselves a curriculum in toothpaste-ology. We learn about all the different options: whitening (we feel guilty that we are vain), gum protection (which is responsible), baking soda (organic and virtuous sounding, if perhaps a bit rough on the enamel). Then we study the brand names, musing over the big corporate brands, like Crest and Colgate, and the charming and socially conscious brands, like Tom's of Maine, which seems to be made by such nice, unpretentious people. And it's only when we are feeling tired and lazy at the airport store that we just go ahead and pick the toothpaste that has the nicest box.

The companies that appeal to educated consumers not only are informing us about things but are providing a philosophic context for their product. Coffee shops like Starbucks decorate their wall trim with texts—the apt Emersonian maxim or the ironic comment from Napoleon. Grocery stores provide brochures delineating the company's notions about community. Ice cream companies now possess their own foreign policy doctrines. These stores offend us if they dwell overmuch on utilitarian concerns—such as what a great bargain we are getting—but they win our loyalty if they appeal to our idealistic hopes. Volvo advertises a "car that can not only help save your life, but help save your soul as well." Toyota counters with a slogan for its line of trucks that reads, "Haul some concrete. Move some lumber. Save the world." Johnnie Walker Scotch announces, "In a Crass and Insincere World, Something That Isn't." The ABC Carpet & Home store on 19th Street and Broadway in New York endorses Keats's dictum "I am certain of nothing but of the holiness of the heart's affections and the truth of the imagination." I don't know what that means, but it sounds elevated.

The Rowenta company doesn't just try to persuade us that its irons really press out wrinkles. It sends out little catalogues called "The Feng Shui of Ironing." "In Feng Shui terms," the literature informs us, "a wrinkle is actually 'tension' in the fabric. Releasing the tension by removing the wrinkle improves the flow of ch'i." Similarly, the enlightened Williams-Sonoma catalogue doesn't try to flog us morally neutral sausages. The sausage links it advertises derive, the catalogue informs us, from the secrets of curing that Native Americans taught the first European settlers in Virginia (the mention of Native Americans gives the product six moral points right off the bat). The "sausages are made from pure pork and natural spices, using family recipes passed down through the generations." This is not some Upton Sinclair jungle but a noble lineage of craftsman sausage makers, and we members of the educated elite are willing to pay $29.50 for 24 little links in order to tap in to this heritage. Shopping, like everything else, has become a means of self-exploration and self-expression. "Happiness," as Wallace Stevens wrote, "is an acquisition."

Nor is it only our own selfish interests that we care about on our shopping forays. We want our material things to be bridges that will allow us to effect positive social change. We select our items from catalogues that have plain models in free-flowing dresses. It is by choosing just the right organic fiber shirt in the perfect tone of earth brown (the production of which involved no animal testing) that we use our consumption power to altruistically improve the world. We dine at restaurants that support endive cooperatives, and browse through department stores that have been endorsed by size-rights activists. We have put our Visa cards at the service of environmental concerns and so created a cleansing consumerism. And we put them away for the same reason. Some members of the educated elite can categorize their friends on the basis of which reason they give for boycotting tuna.

We members of the educated elite attach more spiritual weight to the purity of our food than to five of the Ten Commandments. And so we insist upon natural ingredients made by pesticide-averse farmers who think globally and act locally.

Midas in Reverse

Marx once wrote that the bourgeois takes all that is sacred and makes it profane. The Bobos take everything that is profane and make it sacred. We have taken something that might have been grubby and materialistic and turned it into something elevated. We take the quintessential bourgeois activity, shopping, and turn it into quintessential bohemian activities: art, philosophy, social action. Bobos possess the Midas touch in reverse. Everything we handle turns into soul.

3

Business Life

I'M HOLDING up traffic. I'm walking down the street in Burlington, Vermont, and I come to a corner and see a car approaching, so I stop. The car stops. Meanwhile, I've been distracted by some hippies playing Frisbee in the park, and I stand there daydreaming for what must be 15 or 20 seconds. The car waits.

In a normal city cars roll through these situations; if they see an opening, they take it. But this is Burlington, one of the most socially enlightened cities in America, and drivers here are aware that America has degenerated into a car-obsessed culture where driving threatens to crush the natural rhythms of foot traffic and local face-to-face community, where fossil-fuel-burning machines choke the air and displace the renewable energy sources of human locomotion. This driver knows that while sitting behind the wheel, he is ethically inferior to a pedestrian like me. And to demonstrate his civic ideals, he is going to make damn sure that I get the right of way. No matter how long it takes.

Finally he honks politely and I wake up from my reverie and belatedly cross the street. But by the time I reach the next corner, I'm lost in my thoughts again, and seeing a car coming, I stop. This car stops too. And waits. I have to go through this embarrassing ritual about a dozen times before I finally adapt to local mores and trudge straight into the intersections. In Burlington we pedestrians have inherited the earth. Social enlightenment rules.

Burlington is a Latte Town.

Latte Towns are upscale liberal communities, often in magnificent natural settings, often university based, that have become crucial gestation centers for America's new upscale culture. They tend to be the birthplaces of the upscale retailers, gourmet bread stores, handmade furniture outlets, organic grocery stores, and the rest of the uplifting enterprises that make up Bobo consumer culture. Boulder, Colorado, is a Latte Town, as are Madison, Wisconsin; Northampton, Massachusetts; Missoula, Montana; Wilmington, North Carolina; and half of the towns in northern California, Oregon, and Washington state. There are, all told, hundreds of Latte Towns in America, and even in non-Latte Towns there are often Latte Neighborhoods. You know you're in a Latte Town when you can hop right off a bike path, browse in a used bookstore with shelves and shelves of books on Marxism that the owner can no longer get rid of, and then drink coffee at a place with a punnish name before sauntering through an African drum store or a feminist lingerie shop.

The ideal Latte Town has a Swedish-style government, German-style pedestrian malls, Victorian houses, Native American crafts, Italian coffee, Berkeley human rights groups, and Beverly Hills income levels. There should be some abandoned industrial mills that can be converted into lofts, software workstations, and organic brownie factories. And in utopia a Latte Town would have Rocky Mountain views to the west, redwood forests downtown, a New England lake along the waterfront, and a major city with a really good alternative weekly within a few hours' drive.

For most of this century, literary types have portrayed small towns as stifling enclaves of Babbittry and reaction, but today these micro-cities are seen as refreshing oases from mass society and as potential centers of community and local activism. To take a stroll down the pedestrian mall in Burlington, for example, you start at Leunig's, the indoor/outdoor bistro where some of the local business-men gather for breakfast each morning, wearing Timber-lands, no socks, collarless shirts, and jeans. An executive with flowing gray hair will be chatting amiably with an-other who sports a Jerry Garcia beard, their cell phones tucked into their black canvas briefcases. The Birkenstock sandal store around the corner will have a sign in the win-dow pointing out that its wares make nice corporate gifts.

As you stroll up the street, you see young parents pushing those all-terrain baby carriages that are popular with the outdoors set. The high-end fashion chain Ann Taylor has its Burlington outlet cheek by jowl with the Peace and Justice Store, nicely showing how haute couture now cohabits effortlessly with hippie thrift-shop eclecti-cism. The pedestrian mall is lined with upscale candy, muf-fin, and ice cream stores. There are any number of stores with playful names like Madhatter and Muddy Waters. Ironic allusions and oppressive wordplay are key ingredi-ents to the Latte Town sensibility, where people are not shy about showing off the cultural literacy (the University of Vermont sits up on the hill in Burlington, looking down on the commercial center and Lake Champlain beyond.) There are several fine bookstores in Burlington, of course. You can't get the *New Republic* or any magazine to its right, but you can browse through *Curve*, the wonderfully titled lesbian magazine, or any number of French glamour journals while listening to World Music or New Age disks like *Wolf Solitudes* on the headphones. The bookstores do carry some books on politics, but the current affairs sections tend to be tucked away in the back. The sections that are featured right at the front of the store, and that presumably do the most business, are the sex section, the psychology section, the cooking section, the ethnic studies section (which is mostly books about women), and the alternative lifestyle section (which is 80 percent about gay issues). And this does seem to be a pretty accurate reflection of local priorities.

Burlington boasts a phenomenally busy public square. There are kite festivals and yoga festivals and eating festivals. There are arts councils, school-to-work collaboratives, environmental groups, preservation groups, community-supported agriculture, antidevelopment groups, and ad hoc activist groups. The result is an interesting mixture of liberal social concern and old-fashioned preservation efforts to ward off encroaching modernism and, most important, development. And this public square is one of the features that draws people to Latte Towns. People in these places apparently would rather spend less time in the private sphere of their home and their one-acre yard and more time in the common areas.

If old-line suburbs like Wayne used to be the quintessential bourgeois suburbs, Latte Towns like Burlington and Berkeley used to be the epicenters of bohemian culture. They were once cultural opposites. But in Burlington, just as much as in Wayne, all that is changed. For the most striking thing about Latte Towns is that, though they are havens for everything that now goes by the name "alternative"—alternative music, alternative media, alternative lifestyles—they are also fantastic business centers. Towns like Napa are wine centers; Santa Monica and Soho have the cultural-industrial complex. University towns have everything from biotech to carpentry, and Burlington, too, is a thriving commercial hub. Ben & Jerry's, the most famous company in town, is not even among the 20 largest employers. People with Burlington mores now apparently feel comfortable working at IBM, which has a facility here, as do General Dynamic, GE, Bank of Vermont, and Blodgett Holdings. And business is chic in Burlington. There are four local business publications that heavily cover the town, and sometimes you can read two or three sentences in a row in each of them before some executive says something about the need for businesses to practice socially responsible investing.

The Couple's Business Guide, a featured book at the Burlington bookstores, tells about 10 couples who gave up careers in places like New York and Boston, moved up to Vermont, and started making and selling things like Positively Peach Fruit Sauce, Summer Glory Vinegar, and Putney Pasta. The case studies tend to start out with a highly educated couple disenchanted with their fast-lane urban lifestyle. They have a dream—to make the best jasmine bread in the world—so they move up to the Green Mountains and work slavishly to perfect their recipe. Then they discover how hard it is to market their product. But after five years of toil and tribulation, they have revenues of $5 million a year, and now they can rest on the veranda of their refurbished Victorian cottage with their lovely children, Dylan and Joplin, and savor the turning of the seasons.

George McGovern bought a New England bed-and-breakfast after giving up on politics, so perhaps it's inevitable that up here the man in the gray flannel suit should be replaced by the man in the weather-beaten clogs. Ben and Jerry, the ice cream mavens, represent the quintessence of Latte Town capitalism, and you can't go anywhere in Burlington without seeing an image of their two faces staring down at you, like a couple of scruffy Big Brothers.

I was sitting at an outside table at Leunig's one day, eating lunch, counting the total number of earrings my waitress had on her ears, nose, lips, and bellybutton (19, I think), and trying to read Thoreau's *Walden* (when in Rome . . .). But I kept getting distracted by an aging hippie at the next table who would not shut up about zero-based budgeting and the differences between preferred and common stock. Gray ponytailed and casual about his grooming, he was lecturing like a professor at the Harvard Business School to a young Woodstock wannabe in granny glasses and a peasant dress. She was taking notes on a yellow legal pad, and intermittently they would digress and talk about some bookkeeping practice or management technique they could adopt at their own company. And it has to be said that the aging hippie knew what he was talking about; his description of the capital markets was precise, clear, and knowledgeable.

It occurred to me as I was bouncing back between Thoreau and this conversation that *Walden* is in its own way a business book. Thoreau is constantly tallying up his expenses, and when he can turn his frugality into a profit he's not shy about boasting of his accomplishment. So maybe it's not surprising that the 1960s-era rebels who once lived on communes named Walden would, in the fullness of time, discover that business can be converted into a spiritually satisfying lifestyle. But the philosopher of Walden Pond would no doubt be a bit taken aback by how avidly the tree-hugging set has gone for the business culture.

Today's Latte Town mogul remembers that business is not about making money; it's about doing something you love. Life should be an extended hobby. Moreover, business, which was once considered soul destroying, can actually be quite enriching if you turn your profession into a craft, using natural products, like apples, and transforming them via old-fashioned artisanship into wholesome products like cider. In your packaging you can exercise high aesthetic judgment, employing cutting-edge artistic design to give your product a cosmopolitan feel. If you own a restaurant or an inn or a cafe, you can transform your business into a node of civil society, a meeting place with books and magazines and toys, where people can come to form a community. In this way business nourishes the whole person.

And the whole world. For surely the most famous feature of this kind of enlightened capitalism, which requires little description because it is so ubiquitous, is the way it links profits to progressive causes. You can save the rainforest, ease global warming, nurture Native American values, support family farms, spread world peace, and reduce income inequality, all without leaving the refrigerated aisles of the supermarket. It used to be thought that the pursuit of profit inevitably crushes values. But now many companies have determined that good values lead to greater profits—as long as there is a large educated populace willing to pay a little extra for the sake of social progress. "You can't separate your social goals from your business," says Judy Wicks, the founder of Philadelphia's leftist White Dog Cafe. Everybody makes fun of the excesses of cause capitalism—all those wheat germ toothpastes that don't kill the bacteria in your mouth, they just ask it to leave—but most educated people still favor the companies that share their values. Liberation marketing may be silly at times—there are now gardening companies that have dedicated themselves to solving the compost crisis—but it doesn't do much harm and it may do some good. Anyway, it's just another sign of how the activist ethos has been absorbed into mainstream America since the 1960s. And been altered by it, because while once people thought a true painting or a poem or a protest march could revolutionize society, now you have people such as Nike's Phil Knight who talk as if a sneaker can.

"The sensual pleasure of eating beautiful food from the garden brings with it the moral satisfaction of doing the right thing for the planet and yourself," former student radical and current upscale restaurateur Alice Waters told the *New Yorker* recently. Her outlet in Paris, she continued, is not really a business. Rather, as she wrote in its mission statement, it is "a platform, an exhibit, a classroom, a conservatory, a laboratory and a garden. It must be, in a phrase, an art installation in the form of a restaurant, expressing the sensuousness of food. . . . The restaurant must feel human, reflecting the spirit of the farm, the *terroir,* and the market, and it must express the humanity of the artisans, cooks and servers who work there."

The Countercultural Capitalists

Indeed, one of the ironies of the age is that the one realm of American life where the language of 1960s radicalism remains strong is the business world. If anything, the hippie moguls of Burlington are the mellow ones. If you want to find a place where the Age of Aquarius radicalism is in full force, you have to go higher up the corporate ladder into the realm of companies listed on the New York Stock Exchange. Thirty years after Woodstock and all the peace rallies, the people who talk most relentlessly about smashing the status quo and crushing the establishment are management gurus and corporate executives. It's the big mainstream business leaders that now scream revolution at the top of their lungs, like billionaire Abbie Hoffmans. It's Burger King that tells America, "Sometimes You Gotta Break the Rules." It's Apple Computer that lionizes "The crazy ones. The misfits. The rebels. The troublemakers." It's Lucent Technologies that adopted the slogan "Born to be wild." It's Nike that uses Beat writer William S. Burroughs and the Beatles song "Revolution" as corporate symbols. It's *Wired* magazine and its Silicon Valley advertisers who use the color schemes of 1968 Jefferson Airplane street posters.

And this tone is heard not only in the advertisements of companies that want to show how hip they are. The language of radicalism and rebellion is no less common in the business magazines or on the management channels on airplane headsets, or wherever else the ethos of American business culture is set. Home Depot's senior vice president urges his colleagues, "Think revolution, not evolution." Management gurus like Tom Peters stand in front of thousands of America's business elite and rave, "Destruction is cool!" Software companies have opened up offices in the Netherlands to help them recruit workers who want to live there to take advantage of the lax marijuana laws. Bob Dylan and Crosby, Stills and Nash now play concerts at private conferences hosted by Nomura Securities. Practically every company now portrays itself as a social movement, complete with apostate goals (smash the big competitors), a high social mission (a computer in every home), a revolutionary counterculture (Southwest Airlines calls itself "A Symbol of Freedom"). The dirtiest word in the corporate lexicon is *mainstream;* every company in America seems to be an evangelical enterprise rocking the establishment.

What's happened is simple enough. The Bobos have invaded the business world, and they have brought their countercultural mental framework with them to the old conference rooms of the bourgeoisie. It's no accident that the Bay Area, the center of the Summer of Love, is now also the home base for a disproportionate number of educated-class retailers, like the Gap, Restoration Hardware, and Williams-Sonoma. And there are also straitlaced Republicans who were never hippies but who have adopted a descendant of 1960s radicalism as a corporate philosophy. There is the hybrid culture of Silicon Valley, which mixes antiestablishment rebelliousness with Republican laissez-faire.

Especially in the business sectors dominated by information age elites—high technology, the media, advertising, design, Hollywood—business leaders have embraced an official ideology that will look very familiar to radicals and bohemians: constant change, maximum freedom, youthful enthusiasm, radical experimentation, repudiation of convention, and hunger for the new. You've got to think outside the box, the current cliché goes. You've got to be on the edge. You've got to be outside a box that's on the edge. If you're not braving the cutting edge, today's corporate leaders tell us, it's off to the ash heap of history. "Experience is out. Inexperience is in," says the founding editor of the new wave business magazine *Fast Company.* "I'm not interested in anything else but the youngest, the brightest, and the very, very talented," says Bernard Arnault, chairman of LVMH Moët Hennessy Louis Vuitton.

Today's countercultural capitalists live, or at least think they live, for new ideas, new thinking, new ways of thinking. Even the rules of language have changed. They use short sentences. Nouns become verbs. They eliminate any hint of a prose style and instead tend to talk like 15-year-old joystick junkies. Next year's cost projections? They're insanely great. The product pipeline? Way cool. How'd the IPO go? It cratered. The San Jose conference? Flipped my nuts. Serious mind rub. Real-time life experience. In their conversation and especially in their e-mail, they adopt the linguistic style of Jack Kerouac. Be spontaneous above all, the Beat poet advised. Be fast and free. Remove literary, grammatical, and syntactical formalism. Be wild and fluid so you can be pure and honest. "Something you feel will find its own form," Kerouac insisted. If Kerouac were alive today, he'd be reading to squads of enthralled vice presidents at corporate seminars in Aspen. Even dead, he is now starring in ads for Gap khakis.

I Am Not a Businessperson; I'm a Creator Who Happens to Do Business

In 1949 Leo Lowenthal wrote a much discussed essay in which he traced the evolution of profile stories in popular magazines, such as the *Saturday Evening Post*. His point was that in the early part of the century the "heroes of production" were celebrated, people who made bridges and dams and built companies. But more and more the magazines were shifting their attention to "heroes of consumption," such as movie stars and sports celebrities, who were the superstars of the leisure world. Even when politicians were profiled, he observed, the attention was on the hobbies and private personality of the subject, not his or her on-the-job accomplishments or behavior.

Today we are witnessing another redefinition of media heroism. If you look at the flattering profiles in the business magazines, you don't see men and women celebrated for being great builders or efficiency maximizers or tough-minded managers. The key is to be youthful, daring, and avant-garde, to personify change. The center of gravity of the American business culture has moved westward and youthward. Impressive formality has been replaced by open-minded daring. Corporate America has gone more casual. Microsoft executives appear on the cover of *Fortune* with beanie propeller hats on their heads. Others are photographed looking like mellowing rock stars, wearing expensive collarless linen shirts or multicolored sweaters and rag-wool socks under funky but expensive sandals. Often they'll be shown in jeans, standing proudly in the main hallway of a Rocky Mountain log mansion. You'd never find a bunch of people in blue suits, white shirts, and red ties in a software firm. These wild things will be wearing clunky boots, ripped jeans, tattered university sweatshirts, and those tiny European glasses that give you as much peripheral vision as an astigmatic worm.

In 1950s *Business Week* profiles, an executive would be shown sitting in an impressive mahogany and brass office or perhaps with his sleeves rolled up at a work site. Now the predominant visual prop is the wacky accoutrement. DreamWorks' Jeffrey Katzenberg will be shown with his Supersoaker water cannon. Others prefer Nerf guns or yo-yos or laser pens. Some will be lounging around their desk gazing at their kitsch collections. Richard Saul Wurman, an entrepreneur who stages conferences where countercultural capitalists pay big bucks to mind-meld, collects ashtrays (which, of course, are obsolete in the modern office). Others display a snowboard that is hanging from the ceiling next to an ominously broken piece of bungee cord. In Silicon Valley offices the remnants of a comic book collection may be tacked to the wall near the torn cover from a Curious George book or a photo of Gandhi. An amazing number of executives are pictured with domesticated birds like cockatoos perched on shoulders and heads, or with ugly dogs of obscure breeding panting on their laps. Marilyn Carlson Nelson, the CEO of the travel conglomerate Carlson Cos., poses with her in-line skates. Scott Cook, co-founder of Intuit, is depicted in the *Wall Street Journal* at his favorite lunch place, Taco Bell. These images up-end the old business style. Today's business leaders want to show they are playful free spirits. Members of the older business elite wanted their photos to show how much they embodied Benjamin Franklin's virtues: industriousness, thrift, reliability.

In 1963 Richard Hofstadter's *Anti-Intellectualism in American Life* described the anti-egghead prejudices of the business community. Moguls in Hofstadter's day considered intellectualism vaguely feminine and airy-fairy. Today the business leader wants to show he or she is a hero of intellection. The quintessential hero of the *Forbes* magazine profile doesn't only run an efficient business; he or she plays the flute, paints, explores, performs in a rock band with an ironic middle-aged name like Prostate Pretenders. "Sandy Lerner cofounded Cisco with her husband Len Bosack," *Forbes* writes. "Now she jousts, rides Harleys and supports animal rights and the study of British women writers. He funds weird science."

Mutual fund managers are depicted as cerebral superstars, memorizing baseball statistics, perfecting their piano technique, jetting off to bridge tournaments and philosophy symposia. Today corporate reports are often introduced with quotations from Emile Zola and Toni Morrison. Executives are busy "applying" the insights of classic thinkers to next quarter's sales strategy so they can be seen walking around with books with titles such as *Aristotle on Management* or *Shakespeare on Strategy* or *The LBO Secrets of Pliny the Younger.* Advertising executive Rosemarie Roberts tells the readers of *Fast Company* that her most influential books are *No Exit* by Jean-Paul Sartre ("Contains my basic philosophy on living: ultimately what goes around comes around") and Machiavelli's *The Prince* ("Focus, focus, focus"). They pepper their conversations with phrases like "That's a pretty interesting heuristic you've got there." Or "I don't see that surviving in the post-Gutenbergian era." Or "He's the best phenomenologist of all the vice presidents." They may snort derisively at some notion they regard as an overhyped meme. On the other hand, this will not prevent them from issuing pronouncements on the quarter hour: "Distance is dead"; "Progress has hypertrophied"; "Time has warped."

Once businessmen spoke with gravitas to project an image of calm and caution. Now they speak like sociological visionaries. Today being a CEO means that you have such lofty and daring theories and ideas that you need a team of minions chasing you around with ropes just to tie you down. And if you want to serve as consultant or guru to the corporate types, you've got to expand your mind ever bigger, to cosmic proportions. Everybody is trying to envision the Next Big Thing, and they unleash their imaginations with almost gold rush intensity.

You need a complete breakfast to keep up with the visionary thinking of today's business leaders. "We are at the very point in time when a 400-year-old age is dying and another is struggling to be born," announced Dee Ward Hock, the man responsible for the Visa card, who is now a management guru. "We're at a point of absolute, positive, supreme discontinuity," declares the consultant Watts Wacker. "So I don't study just change. I study how change is changing—the delta of the delta."

In *Fortune,* management guru Gary Hamel counters, "We live in a discontinuous world—one where digitalization, deregulation, and globalization are profoundly reshaping the industrial landscape. What we see is a dramatic proliferation of new economic life forms: virtual organizations, global consortia, net based commerce, ad infinitum. . . . We have reached the end of incrementalism in the quest to create new wealth. . . . There is an inflection point where the quest for divergence is transformed into a quest for convergence, and a new collective viewpoint emerges."

In this new era you've got to use the phrase "We're moving from an age in which . . ." a lot. After all, we are moving from a power society to a knowledge society, from a linear society to a postlinear society, from a hierarchical society to a networked society, from a skim milk society to a 2-percent-fat milk society. So everybody has to make lots of predictions. Moguls like Time Warner's Gerald Levin or Viacom's Sumner Redstone or TCI's John Malone don't mind if their predictions are proven false. The shareholders don't seem to mind! The important thing is to make predictions that are big and daring. Titans of the information age walk around comparing the size of their predictions. As long as their world historical paradigm is massive, they can dominate any room they enter. Bill Gates called his first book *The Road Ahead*. America went through a time when futurology was restricted mostly to gloomy science fiction writers. But now the mood has shifted. The future looks bright once again, and the oracles of the age are businesspeople with extravagant intellectual aspirations.

Of course, the radicalism and occasional utopianism of today's moguls are not exactly the same as the radicalism and utopianism of the student leaders of the 1960s. In some ways the business elites are just in love with the idea of radicalism. They are not as interested in specific ideas that would actually up-end the social order. An entire magazine, the *Baffler*, exists to point out the follies of this hip capitalism. Its editor, Thomas Frank, makes fun of the pseudo-transgressions of the corporate class and all their socially approved deviances. Actually, all this is another form of conservative conformity, Frank argues. But the *Baffler* is wrong to suggest it is all hypocrisy or that the capitalist bosses are merely co-opting the lovely ideals of the counterculture. In fact, it's not so sinister or so one-sided. These renegade executives are both corporate and genuinely countercultural. The two cultural rivals have embraced and co-opted each other.

The Intellectual Origins of the Cosmic Capitalists

Look at how thoroughly the standard critique of American business has been accepted by the leaders of American business. For a century writers and bohemians have been lambasting the businessman in such works as *The Jungle, Babbitt, The Great Gatsby, The Gilded Age, Death of a Salesman, Something Happened* (Joseph

Heller's business novel), and a thousand other novels, plays, movies, and TV shows (remember J. R. Ewing in *Dallas?*). In each case the businessman is anti-intellectual, antispiritual, conformist, and philistine. He is a strangled individual who has killed whatever tender or creative capacities he may once have had in order to climb the greasy pole and accumulate money. His workplace is an arid bureaucracy filled with petty schemers. To this portrayal today's business trendsetters respond, All true! Guilty as charged! They've simply gone out and tried to create a different kind of businessperson, one more in keeping with bohemian values.

In 1956 William H. Whyte wrote *The Organization Man*. Sociologists differ over how much the Organization Man existed in real life, but there is no question that the concept remains powerful in the mental framework of the educated class. Even those who have not read Whyte's book—and that includes almost everybody these days— have a picture of what the Organization Man is, and they know they don't want to be one. This Organization Man is content to be a cog in a great social machine. He feels that, alone, he is too weak to control his destiny, so he integrates himself into some large institution and surrenders to its imperatives. He believes that the organization offers him security and opportunity without any trade-offs between the two. "The young men have no cynicism about the 'system,' and very little skepticism," Whyte wrote; "they don't see it as something to be bucked, but as something to be cooperated with." Moreover, Whyte argued, they adopt a "social ethic" in which creativity and imagination are valued less than having a smooth and pleasing personality. The Organization Man was "obtrusive in no particular, excessive in no zeal."

Whyte was anticipating the sorts of arguments that would be made with greater fervor in the 1960s, particularly in the way he described the psychological effects of large organizations. The old kind of boss, Whyte said, wanted just your labor, but the new kind wanted "your soul."

Whyte's book is a brilliant broadside at the prevailing management theories of the time. He criticized companies that used personality tests to weed out those workers who might not adapt themselves to the group. He described science labs that purged quirky or difficult talents for the sake of efficiency. The companies he described sought well-socialized team players, not idiosyncratic visionaries. For example, Monsanto recruited scientists with a film that declared, "No geniuses here; just a bunch of average Americans working together." The Socony-Vacuum Oil Company distributed a booklet that read:

No Room For Virtuosos

Except in certain research assignments, few specialists in a large company ever work alone. There is little room for virtuoso performances. Business is so complex, even in its non-technical aspects, that no one man can master all of it; to do his job, therefore, he must be able to work with other people.

Whyte rejected the Organization Man's social ethos. He argued that the relationship between the individual and the organization was out of balance in American corporations. The needs of the group were overvalued and the needs of the individual were given short shrift. Whyte wasn't calling on people to drop out of organizations, merely to adjust the way they related to them. He advised the Organization Man to fight the organization, but not self-destructively. "He may tell the boss to go to hell," Whyte wrote, "but he is going to have another boss, and unlike the heroes of popular fiction, he cannot find surcease by leaving the arena to be a husbandman." Whyte was looking for a world in which individuals would work within corporations, but as self-confident and assertive individuals who would value their own needs at least as highly as those of the organization. They would have multiple loyalties. He was looking for organizations that would value a person with quirky and creative genius, not exile him because he wouldn't fit into some bureaucratic flow chart.

Technocracy

A decade later elements of Whyte's argument were picked up by a more radical book that, in ways the author could never have envisioned, would also have a tremendous influence on how today's capitalist conceives of business life. Theodore Roszak's *The Making of a Counter Culture* was published in 1969, the smartest contemporary summary of the 1960s assault on the establishment. Like Whyte, Roszak described an America dominated by large organizations. Like Whyte, he analyzed the psychological wounds suffered by those who live and work within these bureaucracies, which he preferred to call technocracies. They exert a gentle tyranny on their victims, he wrote, making life comfortable and bland while smothering individuality, creativity, and imagination. Like Whyte, Roszak condemned the social ethic that emphasized congenial personalities and tepid social relations.

But there was a central difference between Whyte and Roszak. Whyte was a reporter at *Fortune* magazine. Roszak was a countercultural radical. While Whyte was ambivalent about bourgeois values, Roszak's criticism of the organization was much broader and deeper. He argued that the problem with society wasn't just this or that management theory or this or that way of recruiting employees into a company. Corporate structures were symptoms of a deeper cultural disease. For Roszak the real problem was the whole rationalistic mentality, which he called the objective consciousness.

"If we probe the technocracy in search of the particular power it holds over us," Roszak argued, "we arrive at the myth of objective consciousness. There is but one way of gaining access to reality—so the myth holds—and this is to cultivate a state of consciousness cleansed of all subjective distortion, all personal involvement. What flows from this state of consciousness qualifies as knowledge, and nothing else does. This is the bedrock on which the natural sciences have built; and under their spell all fields of knowledge strive to become scientific." Roszak is describing the counting-book mentality of the accountant, the cold scientist, the calculating businessman, the dry bureaucrat, the narrow engineer. The apotheosis of this consciousness, Roszak wrote, is the machine. The machine "is the standard by which all things are to be gauged." In the mind of the technocrat, companies, universities, and even nations are supposed to run as smoothly as a well-oiled machine.

So it's no wonder that people in organizations become cogs, machinelike. To hammer home this point, Roszak quoted the French writer Jacques Ellul:

> Technique requires predictability, and, no less, exactness of prediction. It is necessary, then, that technique prevail over the human being. For technique, this is a matter of life and death. Technique must reduce man to a technical animal, the king of the slaves of technique. Human caprice crumbles before this necessity; there can be no human autonomy in the face of technical autonomy. The individual must be fashioned by techniques . . . in order to wipe out the blots his personal determination introduces into the perfect design of the organization.

This is the constant bohemian critique. We could perceive truth and beauty if only we would stop to sense the world around us, but instead we enslave ourselves to artificial gods. We chain ourselves down with stifling social structures and inhuman ways of thinking. Bohemians had been bridling against these overrationalized ways of thinking since the days of Flaubert and his cronies in Paris. They had been seeking, as the transcendentalists did, more imaginative, mythopoetic, intuitional modes of perception. Like a century of bohemians before him, Roszak emphasized self-expression over self-control. He believed that self-expansion is the purpose of life. "What is of supreme importance," he wrote, "is that each of us should become a person, a whole integrated person in whom there is manifested a sense of the human variety genuinely experienced, a sense of having come to terms with a reality that is awesomely vast."

And Roszak's solution to the problem of technocracy was also bohemian. "The expansion of the personality is nothing that is achieved by special training, but by a naive openness to experience." He thought people living in industrial capitalist societies needed to rediscover more natural and more childlike modes of perception. "We must be prepared to trust that the expanded personality becomes more beautiful, more creative, more humane than the search for objective consciousness can make it." A more playful approach to life, he believed, could transform the reality around us: "This, so I have argued, is the primary project of our counter culture: to proclaim a new heaven and a new earth so vast, so marvelous that the inordinate claims of technical expertise must of necessity withdraw in the presence of such splendor to a subordinate and marginal status in the lives of men. To create and broadcast such a consciousness of life entails nothing less than the willingness to open ourselves to the visionary imagination in its own demanding terms."

Well, that was never going to work. If there was going to be a solution to the problems Whyte and Roszak identified with the organizational structure of American life, it wasn't going to be accomplished by the creation of a cosmic consciousness that would embarrass rationalistic thinking into submission. Roszak was being too grandiose. But that doesn't mean that he and Whyte were wrong when they criticized technocracies or the conformist and artificial social ethic they engendered. It simply means that it would take a more down-to-earth writer to provide a more practical way of rethinking organizations and social structures.

Jane Jacobs, Proto-Bobo

In fact, when Roszak was writing, the seeds of that rethinking had already been planted. In 1961 Jane Jacobs published *The Death and Life of Great American Cities,* which remains the most influential book on how Bobos view organizations and social structures.

Jane Jacobs was born in Scranton, Pennsylvania, in 1916, the daughter of a doctor and a teacher. After high school she went to work as a reporter for the *Scranton Tribune.* She lasted a year, then ventured to New York and worked in a series of jobs as a stenographer and freelance writer before landing a junior editorial position at *Architectural Forum.* In 1956 she gave a talk at Harvard expressing her skepticism about the High Modernist urban-planning philosophy that was sweeping away entire neighborhoods and replacing them with rows and rows of symmetrical apartment buildings, each surrounded by a windswept and usually deserted park. William H. Whyte invited her to turn her lecture into an article for *Fortune,* which, after some internal nervousness from the executives at Time Inc., was published as the essay "Downtown

Is for People." Jacobs then extended her argument in her book *The Death and Life of Great American Cities*. It's mostly about city planning, but Jacobs's vision transcends urban design. She creates in that book a description of the good life, a vision that has appealed to more and more people each year and that has attracted devoted followings on both the bohemian left and the bourgeois right.

At first glance, Jacobs seems pure bohemian. Here is a writer living in Greenwich Village, the bohemian Mecca. She is rising up to challenge the rationalists, the big developers who want to clear away neighborhoods and put up neat, orderly housing projects, parks, and high-tech expressways. She rails against monotony, sameness, and standardization. She is appalled by the rich and monumental tastes of the establishment. Meanwhile, she celebrates serendipity. Like any bohemian, she has a taste for exoticism, the African sculpture or the Romanian teahouse. She is a nonconformist, and she dresses in that downtown coffeehouse style that has since come back into fashion. In fact, her critics, the planners of the period, took her as an alienated bohemian and condemned her "bitter, coffee-house rambling."

But pause in the middle of *The Death and Life of Great American Cities* to see who the heroes of her ideal community are. Jacobs's most beautiful and influential passages describe life on her own little block of Hudson Street in Greenwich Village (pages 65–71 in the Modern Library edition). And the people who made life on that street so special were shopkeepers—Joe Cornacchia, the local deli owner, Mr. Koochagian, the tailor, Mr. Goldstein, the hardware store owner. Napoleon thought he had come up with the ultimate antibourgeois put-down when he called England a nation of shopkeepers. In bohemian literature up to that point, the small businessman had been taken as the epitome of petty-minded bourgeois values. But Jacobs does not disdain the merchants for being grubby and materialistic. It is precisely their ordinary activities she admires: their bustle, their cleanliness, their mundane neighborliness. One of them keeps the keys for people in the neighborhood. Another trades local gossip. They all keep an eye on the street. It is precisely their bourgeois virtues that Jacobs admires.

That lovely, lyrical set piece describes the grocer, the launderer, and the passersby as dancers in a ballet. She is likening their movements to high art. A fruit man appears and waves, the locksmith goes over to gossip with the cigar store owner, kids roller-skate by, people gather around the pizzeria. "The ballet is never at a halt," she writes, "but the general effect is peaceful and the general tenor even leisurely." It is hard to think of any passage of prose that so sweetly describes the everyday world of the ordinary street with the ordinary shops and their ordinary rituals.

Jacobs's tone, in fact, is part of the secret to her success. It is not overcharged or histrionic, the way the voices of contemporary writers like Jack Kerouac and later radicals like Theodore Roszak are. Neither is it pompous and directive, the way much intellectual writing of the 1950s is. Jacobs utterly rejects the utopianism and extremism that were an integral part of romanticism. She rejects the notion of the intellectual who is removed from the everyday world and lives instead in a world of ideas. As a result, she is relaxed and conversational. She is looking at things with an eye for down-to-earth details (it may be no accident that it was a woman who could exemplify this way of observing reality). The urban planning of the epoch may make Jacobs indignant, but she does not rain thunderbolts down upon her enemies. She suggests the answer is not to theorize or to rebel, but simply to sit quietly and be sensitive to our surroundings. The bourgeois epistemology often appealed to reason. The bohemian epistemology to imagination. Jacobs asks us to appreciate a mode of perception that requires both sense and sensibility. It requires the practical knowledge of the shopkeeper as well as the sensitive awareness to surroundings that we might expect from a painter or novelist.

Most important, Jacobs reconciles the bourgeois love of order with the bohemian love of emancipation. A city street, she argues, looks chaotic, but it really is quite orderly. "Under the seeming disorder of the old city," she writes, "wherever the old city is working successfully, is a marvelous order for maintaining the safety of the streets and the freedom of the city. It is a complex order. Its essence is intricacy of sidewalk use, bringing with it a constant succession of eyes. This order is all composed of movement and change, and although it is life, not art, we may fancifully call it the art form of the city and liken it to the dance." This passage encapsulates the key reconciliations, freedom and safety, order and change, life and art. The good life, she implies, is composed of flux, diversity, and complexity, but underneath it all is an inner harmony.

The planners who destroyed neighborhoods did not see this because their conception of order was mechanical. The developers and Modernists like Le Corbusier saw the city as a machine—"a factory for producing traffic" in one of Le Corbusier's phrases—and so, of course, they sought to reduce it to a mechanism that would be simple and repetitive. But if you read Jacobs's description of the street, it becomes clear that she is not talking about a machine or even a place with all the connotations of rush and tension that many associate with city life. She is almost describing a forest. The shopkeepers come out onto the sidewalk almost like leaves choosing their own angle to catch the sun. The passersby come and go like animals, each performing his or her little unconscious service to the ecosystem. Jacobs is seeing the city in organic terms, not in mechanical terms. She has taken the pastoralism of Emerson and Thoreau and reconciled it with modern urban life. The city was always thought of as the ultimate renunciation of nature, but here she treats the healthy city almost as a work of nature.

In order for the ecosystem to function, it must have many different players. It must have diversity. The word *diversity*, which has become one of the key words of our age, was central in *The Death and Life of Great American Cities*. The entire second section of the book is called "The Conditions for City Diversity." It is complexity she admires, the small unplanned niches where specialized activities can thrive. These are places whose use is not determined from above but grows up from small particularized needs.

In the years since *The Death and Life of Great American Cities* was published, Jacobs's way of seeing has been vindicated again and again. The urban plans she criticized are now universally reviled. The disastrous failure of social-engineering projects across the developing world have exposed the hubris of technocrats who thought they could reshape reality. The failure of the Communist planned economies has taught us that the world is too complicated to be organized and centrally directed. We are, with Jane Jacobs, more modest about what we can know, more skeptical of planners and bureaucrats. We're more likely to trust modest individuals like Jacobs, who take the time to sit quietly and observe closely.

The Pastoral Organization

Now we can return to the workplace of today. If you look at today's management theorists or the restructuring that has been instituted by cutting-edge companies, you are immediately struck by how deeply they have been influenced first by Whyte's and Roszak's objections to the old business structures and then by Jacobs's vision of what constitutes a healthy community. Today's executives will tell you, and they will tell you again and again until you want to plug up your ears with cotton, how fervently they have rejected the old Organization Man models. "Organizations are disappearing!" Tom Peters shouts at his audiences. "At HP, people don't become cogs in some giant corporate machine," the recruiting literature from Hewlett Packard opens. "From their first day of work here, people are given important responsibilities and are encouraged to grow." Indeed, the companies that are celebrated by the management gurus are those that have stood the Organization Man on his head. Companies like DreamWorks throw out job titles because they seem too hierarchical. Others boast of cutting their management layers from seven to three, from fourteen to four. Companies today, the mantra goes, have to think biologically. They have to create lean, decentralized, informal participatory systems. They have to tear down rigid structures and let a thousand flowers bloom. The machine is no longer held up as the standard that healthy organizations should emulate. Now it's the ecosystem. It's the ever-changing organic network that serves as the model to define a healthy organization, filled with spontaneous growth and infinitely complex and dynamic interconnections.

Big companies break themselves up into flexible small teams to create what some experts call "ensemble individualism." Pitney Bowes Credit Corporation has actually designed its offices in Connecticut to resemble a small village, with cobblestone-patterned carpets, faux gas lamps, a town square–style clock, and street signs at the intersections of the hallways—Main Street crosses Center Street and so on. At AOL's building, Creative Center One, desks are arranged into neighborhoods where workers brainstorm with their neighbors for the project amidst Silly Putty sculptures and piles of caffeinated beverages. At In-

hale Therapeutic Systems, chairman Robert Chess got rid
of executive offices; now everybody sits in large areas called
"bullpens," where they can bounce ideas off each other all
day. The hearing aid firm Oticon puts everybody's desks on
wheels so they can be wheeled around the vast workspace
and grouped according to the ensemble arrangement of the
moment. (Oticon is only one of many firms experimenting
with the schools-without-walls concept that was popular
with progressive educators in the 1960s.) At Procter &
Gamble, elevators, which are thought to destroy give-and-
take conversations, are out, while escalators, which are
thought to enhance them, are in. Nickelodeon installed
extra-wide stairs to encourage exchange and schmoozing.
IDEO, another design company, has long rolls of butcher
paper spread out over conference tables for brainstorming
and doodling. All these companies and hundreds of others
are trying to recreate little Jane Jacobs environments, complete with chance meetings, spontaneous exchanges, small
gathering places, and the sort of constant flexibility that is
really a dynamic order.

In the old organization it was the system that was
king. Now, so we are told, relationships matter most. In
1967 Kenneth Keniston completed *Young Radicals*, a
study of the 1960s counterculturalists in which he observed that "in manner and style, these young radicals are
extremely 'personalistic,' focused on face-to-face, direct
and open relationships with other people; hostile to for-
mally structured roles and traditional bureaucratic patterns of power and authority." That's an excellent
summary of the management philosophy that prevails
today in corporate America. Now companies go on expensive retreats at which employees play noncompetitive
games or wacky Olympics to build those relationships.

Information age companies are also trying to provoke
a certain type of thinking. Gone is the old emphasis on
scientific analysis and narrow specialization. Gone are

Robert McNamara–style rationalists with their sharp white shirts. Now messy desks are admired, along with the tousle-haired geniuses who sit behind them. Companies hire hyperkinetic motivators to serve as in-house Ken Keseys and inspirational Merry Pranksters. Gordon MacKenzie is an aging hippie who wears bright tie-dyed shirts and blue jeans and goes from corporation to corporation exhorting them to "orbit the giant hairball." The hairball in his lexicon is the bureaucracy, and to orbit it is to spin out into an individualized realm of creative vibrancy. MacKenzie worked for 30 years at Hallmark, ending up with the self-invented job title "creative paradox." Now he does consulting for IBM, Nabisco, and the FBI— not exactly the outfits that one associates with Byronic romanticism. Creativity is seen as the new key to productivity, having replaced the Organization Man's virtue, efficiency.

ZEFER, a Boston-based Internet consulting firm, asks job applicants to take a "Lego/Play-Doh Test" so their creative faculties can be evaluated. Kodak has "humor rooms" with games, toys, and Monty Python videos. Ben & Jerry's has a Joy Committee to liven things up. Rosenbluth International has a "thought theater" where employees can watch videos selected by the manager for culture development. Paul Birch worked as a "corporate jester" at British Airways. Meanwhile, the "learning person" at Xerox Business Services threw a "learning Woodstock" session, held in a dark room with moons and stars and planets hanging from the ceiling.

A lot of this, especially at the extremes, is silly. But at their best, today's management techniques do follow in Jane Jacobs's epistemological footsteps. They are based on the idea that the best way to learn and think is not by breaking problems down to their narrowest specializations, as a technocrat does, but on the contrary, by being sensitive to the flow and rhythms of the situation. These techniques encourage employees to see old problems in new ways, to be imaginative, to feel their way intuitively to deeper understandings of the reality that confronts them. The marketplace is not to be conceived of as a machine but as an organism filled with feedback mechanisms, interconnections, and flux.

Metis

In other words, the companies are trying to cultivate in their employees a faculty that in classical times was known as *metis*. This is an ancient Greek term that has been revived by Yale anthropologist James C. Scott. The French might call metis *savoir faire*. We might call it practical knowledge, cunning, or having a knack for something. Odysseus was the model of a person with metis because of his ability to improvise his way through unexpected situations. Scott himself defines metis as "a wide array of practical skills and acquired intelligence in responding to a constantly changing natural and human environment."

This trait cannot be taught or memorized. It can only be imparted and acquired. The philosopher Michael Oakeshott would say that you can study grammar in a classroom, but the ability to speak can only be acquired slowly through experience. Similarly, metis is acquired as a series of random acquisitions that only gradually form a whole picture. People sharing metis do not lecture; they converse. They work side by side. To acquire metis, a person must not only see but see with comprehension. He or she must observe minutely to absorb the practical consequences of things. He or she must develop a feel for the process, for the interrelationships of things. The person who acquires metis must learn by doing, not by reasoning or dreaming.

For example, an apprentice may learn the rules of cooking, but only a master chef will have the awareness to know when the rules should be applied and when they should be bent or broken. A graduate student may read a book on pedagogy, but only a metis-rich teacher will be able to guide and lead a class. Metis exists only when it is in use; often the person who has it will not be able to put his or her gifts or methods into words. It is an awareness of the flow of things, knowing which things can go together and which can never go together, which way to react when the unexpected happens. It means being able to tell what is really important and what is mere distraction. Isaiah Berlin was getting at metis when he wrote in his classic essay "The Hedgehog and the Fox": "It is not scientific knowledge, but a special sensitiveness to the contours of the circumstances in which we happen to be placed; it is a capacity for living without falling foul of some permanent condition or factor which cannot be altered, or even fully described or calculated." This sort of knowledge consists in perpetual improvisation, a sort of wise muddling through. Rejecting universal solutions, the person who prizes metis welcomes a diversity of approaches, to use that word which was so important to Jane Jacobs and all subsequent Bobos.

In this atmosphere leadership is also perceived differently. The CEO is no longer a chess grand master, an imposing, aloof figure moving pieces around the board. Now he or she is likely to be portrayed, and to portray himself or herself, as an inspirer, a motivator, or an orchestra leader. Today's CEOs boast about trying to inspire the creativity in others. With their hair-trigger sensitivity to authoritarianism or repressive authority structures, they talk about fostering collaborative relationships. The good ones do not so much dominate as lead by example, as head artist in the workshop. For example, hanging around the corporate headquarters of Restoration Hardware in Marin County for a few days, I was struck by the number of times employees praised CEO Stephen Gordon for being "loose" and "real." His associates happily recount the time Gordon led a water balloon fight and a game of Red Rover during their company retreat. Gordon's clothing is just as casual as everybody else's at the place. His office is not especially bigger or nicer than the offices of the people who work for him. The company has a liberal dog policy, so when people bring their pooches to work, they can wander into his space as freely as anybody else's. Twice a week the buyers at Restoration hold meetings to determine which new items they should carry in their stores, and in keeping with the quasi-egalitarian ethos of Bobo enterprises, everybody at the meeting gets a vote, but somehow Gordon's is decisive. The buyers happily admit that for all the creativity each of them brings to their jobs they are really just executing Gordon's vision. And so we arrive at one of the paradoxes of information age enterprises: though they flatten hierarchies and promote equality, today's CEOs tend to dominate their companies even more than those at the old corporations. In the companies Whyte described, the ethos of the organization set the tone; now it is the vision of the charismatic leader. As Xerox's John Seely Brown told *Fortune,* "The job of leadership today is not just to make money. It's to make meaning."

The Higher Selfishness

As in so many spheres of Bobo life, all that was profane has been made holy. Businesspeople talk like artists. Corporations enthuse about their social missions. Managers emphasize creativity and liberation. Phenomenally successful corporate consultants like Stephen Covey seem more like spiritual advisers than efficiency experts. Meanwhile in this through-the-looking-glass world of capitalism, the people in the marketing department talk about how much they detest marketing. The CEO says he is ambivalent about expansion. The zillionaires say they are in it for the self-expression, not the money. "The money hasn't changed a thing," Rob Glaser of RealNetworks told the *Wall Street Journal* in one interview. "The money has not changed a thing in my life," Steve Case of America Online told the *Journal* in another. "The money has not changed a thing in my life," said Jeff Bezos of Amazon.com in a third.

Workers in this spiritualized world of Bobo capitalism are not the heroes of toil. They are creators. They noodle around and experiment and dream. They seek to explore and then surpass the full limits of their capacities. And if a company begins to bore or stifle them, they're gone. It is the ultimate sign of privilege—to be able to hit the road in search of new meaning whenever that little moth of tedium flies in the door. Self-cultivation is the imperative. With the emphasis on self.

So this isn't a crass and vulgar selfishness, about narrow self-interest or mindless accumulation. This is a higher selfishness. It's about making sure you get the most out of yourself, which means putting yourself in a job that is spiritually fulfilling, socially constructive, experientially diverse, emotionally enriching, self-esteem boosting, perpetually challenging, and eternally edifying. It's about learning. It's about working for a company as cool as you are. It's about finding an organization that can meet your creative and spiritual needs. When Anne Sweeney contemplated taking over the presidency of the Disney Channel, she didn't think in résumé or financial terms. She asked herself, "Would this job make my heart sing?" and she decided yes. The PR firm Porter Novelli doesn't recruit employees with appeals to crass self-interest. Instead, it runs ads in various magazines showing a young woman in jeans sitting on a rocky beach. The copy asks, "What do *you* want?" The answer, expressed in the woman's voice, is this:

> I want to write my own ticket. High tech is a wide-open field. I'm helping to create public relations programs for companies that are on the leading edge of software development. What I'm learning is making one fabulous career. I want to hit the beach. I grew up on the West Coast. The ocean has always been my second home. Whenever I need to think things through, this is where I come. I want to keep climbing. Each year, my role gets bigger. My managers support my growth with professional development and mentoring programs. It's like being back in college. I want to go to Africa. Next year, I hope. (Incidentally, our health insurance plan is great.) I want to be my best. If there's a limit to what I'm capable of achieving, I'm not sure where it is or when I'll reach it. Never, I hope.

This is Bobo capitalism in a nutshell. College, learning, growth, travel, climbing, self-discovery. It's all there. And it's all punctuated with that little word "I," which appears in that short paragraph 15 times. The Organization Man is turned upside down. Whyte described a social ethos that put the group first. The current ethos puts "me" first.

Work thus becomes a vocation, a calling, a metier. And the weird thing is that when employees start thinking like artists and activists, they actually work harder for the company. In the 1960s most social theorists assumed that as we got richer, we would work less and less. But if work is a form of self-expression or a social mission, then you never want to stop. You are driven by a relentless urge to grow, to learn, to feel more alive. Executives who dreamed of turning themselves into refined gentlemen may have valued leisure, but executives who aspire to be artists value work. Companies learn that Bobos will knock themselves out if they think they are doing it for their spiritual selves, for their intellectual development. Lee Clow is chairman of the advertising firm TBWA Worldwide. He has established a set of work expectations that would have led to strikes decades ago. Now they are considered enlightened. "It's a rare weekend in this agency when you won't find people at work," he told the *Wall Street Journal* a few years ago. "Sometimes I'm asked what I say to people to get them to work on Saturday and Sunday. We don't say anything. But our creative people know what we expect from them. They know they'll have a chance in this big sandbox. It's designed to be a stimulating place, a fun place, an interactive place, a social place." Don't dare call it a sweatshop. It's a sandbox! This isn't business. This is play!

The Cultural Contradictions of Capitalism—Resolved!

In 1976 Daniel Bell wrote an influential book, *The Cultural Contradictions of Capitalism*. He argued that capitalism is built upon two contradictory impulses. People in a capitalist society have to be self-disciplined and a bit ascetic so they will show up to the factory on time and work hard. But they also have to be acquisitive and a little hedonistic so they will constantly want to consume more and more of the things they make. Following Max Weber, Bell thought that for a long time the Protestant Ethic had reconciled these two impulses into a single belief system. But, Bell argued, the Protestant Ethic was fading. He foresaw a world in which self-restraint had become extinct. He located two primary culprits: first, the culture of romanticism, which sought to destroy order, convention, and tradition for the sake of sensation, liberation, and self-exploration, and second, capitalism's need to continually stoke ever greater levels of consumption. Once you had massive consumer credit without shame, Bell argued, people would discover that consuming was more fun than self-restraint and begin to live more and more for the pleasures of the moment. Hedonism would increasingly trump frugality, and display would increasingly replace modesty. In Bell's future world, "the culture was no longer concerned with how to work and achieve, but with how to spend and enjoy," he wrote.

In the 1970s Bell saw antinomianism, the feeling that people should be freed from laws and restraints by virtue of personal grace, all around him. Indeed, it seemed to many that the work ethic was eroding, that the ladder of ambition was being delegitimized. Bell's thesis struck a chord. It seemed plausible to think that capitalism would unleash cultural forces that would end up destroying it.

But it hasn't happened. On the contrary, the people most influenced by the romantic cultural forces Bell described, the Berkeley-style baby boomers, have become hard-working capitalists, oriented toward the long term. The hedonism of Woodstock mythology has been domesticated and now serves as a management tool for the Fortune 500. Americans haven't even adopted European-style vacation schedules. Instead, they pull all-nighters at Microsoft and come in weekends at Ben & Jerry's. And the people who speak most devoutly about smashing order and instituting a perpetual revolution—the capitalists of the corporate world—are the ones who strive most earnestly for success. This is Modernism for the shareholders. Bell looked at America and observed a culture that emphasized antirational hedonism, and he saw an economic structure that depended on technocratic reason.

He concluded that the two forces must clash. Instead, they've blurred to create something new.

Countercultural capitalists are not restrained by the old puritanical or Protestant code. Instead, they have constructed their own ethos that creates a similar and perhaps more rigorous system of restraint. They have transformed work into a spiritual and intellectual vocation, so they approach their labor with the fervor of artists and missionaries. Their collars may not be buttoned up and their desks may not be neat, but they are, after a fashion, quite self-disciplined. Members of the educated class often regard work as an expression of their entire being, so of course they devote themselves to it with phenomenal energy. For many there is no time when they are not at work; they are always thinking.

Nor do the denizens of the Latte Town microindustries or the surfers in the countercultural workstation go in for the lavish display and hedonistic lifestyle that Bell predicted. They have created an ethos of environmentalism, healthism, and egalitarianism that makes it bad form to live in the ostentatious style that characterized the old moneyed elite. This, too, serves as a substitute for the restraint system of the much-debated Protestant Ethic. If these people believe in nothing else, they believe that you shouldn't damage your own body, which means that drinking, drugs, and carousing are out. Coffee shops replace bars as the central gathering places. As we'll explore in greater detail in later chapters, self-disciplined activities like jogging and cycling are in; by working out, these people have reduced even leisure time to a form of self-discipline.

The 1960s unleashed wild liberationist forces into American society, but that antinomianism has merged with the enterprising ethos we associate with the 1980s. This fusion has legitimized capitalism among the very people who were its most ardent critics, and it has legitimized countercultural poses amongst the business elites. Whatever its flaws, the Bobo ethos has been fantastically good for the bottom line. American businesses have thrived over the past decade and established American dominance in sector after sector. American companies are creative and efficient at the same time. Bell thought he was witnessing the end of the bourgeoisie, but at the moment it looks as if the bourgeoisie has, in fact, revived itself by absorbing (and being absorbed by) the energy of bohemianism.

4

Intellectual Life

IN 1954, Irving Howe wrote an essay for *Partisan Review* called "This Age of Conformity." His subject was the degradation of American intellectual life. "The most exciting periods of American intellectual life tend to coincide with the rise of bohemia," Howe argued. Ideas and innovations pour forth at these moments, when thinkers and artists detach themselves from bourgeois life, with its well-worn customs and conventions, and live apart in the realms of art, ideas, and spirit. But Howe sensed that the idea of bohemia was beginning to lose its force. And the culprit was money. "Some intellectuals, to be sure, have 'sold out' and we can all point to examples, probably the same examples," Howe noted. "But far more prevalent and far more insidious is that slow attrition which destroys one's ability to stand firm and alone: the temptations of an improved standard of living." Intellectuals, to use Howe's words, were no longer standing "firm and alone." They were going to work for government agencies. They were sitting on public committees, going on lecture tours, writing for mass publications, and teaching adult education classes. In sum, they were putting a foot in the worlds of commerce and politics.

What was lost in this process, Howe continued, was "the whole intellectual vocation—the idea of a life dedicated to values that cannot possibly be realized by a commercial civilization." In joining with mainstream bourgeois culture, intellectuals, Howe felt, were surrendering their total freedom. They were debasing themselves. Indeed, Howe wrote, in lamentation mode, "Writers today have no choice, often enough, but to write for magazines like the *New Yorker*—and worse, far worse." Some who did so survived with their independence intact, he concluded, but "for every short-story writer who has survived the *New Yorker* one could point to a dozen whose work became trivial and frozen after they had begun to write for it."

Well, if the Irving Howe of 1954 was upset by what was going on then, it's a good thing he's no longer around to see what is going on now. These days it doesn't even occur to us to fear for a writer's literary soul if we find her writing in the *New Yorker.* We don't feel a novelist has sold out if he gets a book on the bestseller list. We don't object much if tenured professors go off on lucrative lecture tours. Better them than yet another squad of motivational speakers. Today we have almost entirely lost the belief, which was still common in Howe's day, that intellectuals should cut themselves off from commerce and from pop-culture temptations. Just as the cultural forces of the information age have created businesspeople who identify themselves as semi-artists and semi-intellectuals, so nowadays intellectuals have come to seem more like businesspeople. We now use phrases like "the marketplace of ideas," "intellectual property," and "the attention economy" to meld the realm of the mind with the realm of the market. Intellectuals have seen their job descriptions transformed. Once so aloof, they now mingle with the rest of the educated elite, producing a new sort of intellectual for the new Bobo age.

From today's vantage point, the intellectual landscape of the 1950s really is a strange and unfamiliar place. When you go back to the writings of Lionel Trilling, Reinhold Niebuhr, Sidney Hook, William Barrett, Hannah Arendt, and the crowd that contributed to *Partisan Review,* you are struck immediately by the tone of high seriousness that prevailed. Those intellectuals went in for big "The World in All Its Aspects" essay topics that would be regarded as pompous by most writers today. Niebuhr wrote a book called *The Nature and Destiny of Man,* which certainly covers a lot of ground. They adopted prose styles that, while clear and elegant, were also portentous and loaded with authority and learning.

They were not shy on the subject of their own importance. They spent lots of time signing petitions, making statements, convening congresses, and otherwise taking "stands." Their memoirs are filled with intellectual melodrama: When Edmund Wilson published his review of so-and-so, they recount, we knew life would never be the same again, as if a book review could alter reality, as maybe in those days it could. They considered themselves, and perhaps were, shapers of history. "A single stroke of paint, backed by work and a mind that understood its potency and implications, could restore to man the freedom lost in twenty centuries of apology and devices for subjugation," wrote the painter Clyfford Still, apparently without being ridiculed. They went in big for capital letters. "These three great forces of mind and will—Art, Science and Philanthropy—have, it is clear, become enemies of Intellect," Jacques Barzun declared in 1959, launching off into characteristically grand territory. And they issued the sort of grand and often vaporous judgments that today strike us as ridiculous. Here's a statement by Bertrand Russell featured on the cover of *Dissent* in the fall of 1963, which embodies the tone of heroic denunciation that you can muster only if you have drunk deeply from the cup of your own oracular majesty:

> Kennedy and Khrushchev, Adenauer and de Gaulle, Macmillan and Gaitskell are all pursuing a common aim: the ending of human rights. You, your families, your friends and your countries are to be exterminated by the common decision of a few brutal but powerful men. To please these men, all private affections, all the public hopes, all that has been achieved in art and knowledge and thought, and all that might be achieved thereafter is to be wiped out forever.

At the heart of this style was an exalted view of the social role of the intellectual. In this view the intellectual is a person who stands apart from society, renouncing certain material advantages and instead serving as conscience for the nation. Intellectuals are descendants of Socrates, who was murdered by the polis because of his relentless search for truth. They are inspired by Emile Zola's *J'Accuse*, which confronted orthodoxy and challenged authority in the name of higher justice. They are influenced by the Russian notion of the *intelligentsia*, a secular priesthood of writers and thinkers who participated in national life by living above it in a kind of universal space of truth and disinterestedness, rendering moral judgments on the activities below. One of the most influential descriptions of the intellectual's Olympian role—as the intellectuals themselves conceived it—was written by Edward Shils in a

1958 essay, "The Intellectuals and the Powers: Some Perspectives for Comparative Analysis":

> In every society . . . there are some persons
> with an unusual sensitivity to the sacred, an un-
> common reflectiveness about the nature of the uni-
> verse, and the rules which govern their society.
> There is in every society a minority of persons who,
> more than the ordinary run of their fellow men, are
> inquiring, and desirous of being in frequent com-
> munion with symbols which are more general than
> the immediate concrete situations of everyday life,
> and remote in their reference from both time and
> space. In this minority, there is a need to external-
> ize the quest in oral and written discourse, in poetic
> and plastic expression, in historical reminiscence or
> writing, in ritual performance and acts of worship.
> This interior need to penetrate beyond the screen of
> immediate concrete experience marks the existence
> of intellectuals in every society.

That's a stark social divide. On the one side is the vast
majority who live in a world of "concrete situations." On
the other are the few whose lives are defined by their "sensitivity to the sacred" and their "reflectiveness about the
nature of the universe." But this gap was absolutely essential to the intellectuals of the day, in Europe and to a lesser
extent in the United States, because it was only by staying
aloof from society that they could see it clearly and hon-
estly, or so they believed. In a later book called *The Life of
the Mind*, Hannah Arendt made this point by quoting a
parable ascribed to Pythagoras: "Life is like a festival; just
as some come to the festival to compete, some to ply their
trade, but the best people come as spectators, so in life the
slavish men go hunting for fame or gain, the philosophers
for truth." Only the thinker who frees himself from large

organizations and worldly alliances can hope to perceive that truth, argued C. Wright Mills in *Power, Politics and People:* "The independent artist and intellectual are among the few remaining personalities equipped to resist and to fight the stereotyping and consequent death of genuinely living things."

Intellectuals in the 1950s sometimes seemed to nurture this sense of embattlement, of continually being under assault from the coarse world of commerce. They armed themselves against invasions by journalism, advertising, and the celebrity culture, fighting off the Babbitts and the philistines. "The hostility of the common man toward the intellectual is of all times and places," wrote Jacques Barzun in *The House of Intellect.* Richard Hofstadter's *Anti-Intellectualism in American Life* was a salvo in the war between mind and matter.

The biggest threat to the independent intellectual was money and its temptations. Commerce was the enemy of art. Norman Mailer got into a lot of trouble with his intellectual friends when his novel *The Naked and the Dead* became a bestseller. Its commercial success was taken as prima facie evidence that there was something wrong with it. And commercial culture didn't just attack intellect head-on with crass financial offers. It came up disguised in Trojan Horse form as middlebrow culture.

It's hard now to understand the ferocity highbrow intellectuals of the 1950s brought to bear in their assault on the middlebrow. Middlebrow culture was the sort of popular but moderately high-toned writing, art, and music that could be found in magazines like *Saturday Review* (which ran such turgid headlines as "The Future Belongs to the Educated Man" and "Art: Giver of Life and Peace") or in books recommended by the Book-of-the-Month Club or in the plays of Thornton Wilder. Middlebrows consumed high culture with an air of worthy self-congratulation, because it is good for you. Looking back on the middlebrow culture of the 1950s, it seems a little dull and pretentious but well intentioned, and certainly better than some of the proudly illiterate culture that has taken its place.

But that is not how highbrows of the 1950s saw it. They attacked it with a viciousness that takes your breath away. Virginia Woolf had decades earlier fought the same war, calling the middlebrow "sticky slime" and "a pernicious pest." Clement Greenberg called it an "insidious" force that was "devaluating the precious, infecting the healthy, corrupting the honest and stultifying the wise." Dwight Macdonald wrote the most famous attack in an essay called "Masscult and Midcult," in which he blasted the "tepid ooze" of the Museum of Modern Art and the American Civil Liberties Union and summarized middlebrow culture as "the danger . . . the enemy outside the walls . . . the swamp."

Middlebrows were not interested in joining a secular priesthood devoted to ideas. Rather, they wanted to take the realm of ideas and drag it back to earth, into the clutches of middle-class America and commercial mediocrity. They wanted to co-opt intellect and make it serve the utilitarian interests and amusements of the bourgeoisie. They wanted to read the Great Books to impress friends, to add sparkle to their conversation. The intellectuals had to crush the tentacles of commercial culture, even if it snuck up bearing reproductions of Michelangelo.

Intellectual Entrepreneurs

There is something admirable and at the same time delusionally self-confident about the intellectual self-image of this era. Who wouldn't want to live with such passionate commitment to ideas? And in truth, in those days books and ideas did seem to matter more. At the same time, the self-importance of those thinkers was often hard to take. In cutting themselves off from political insiders, intellectuals cut themselves off from the reality of what was going on. They invented conspiracies; they made bold pronouncements about the state of things that look absurdly gloomy in retrospect. In any case, today all that is as dead as the dinosaurs. Now intellectuals tend to minimize or deny the gap between themselves and everyone else, not defend it. The central feature of the information age is that it reconciles the tangible with the intangible. It has taken products of the mind and turned them into products of the marketplace. So, of course, the bifurcations that were so important to the intellectuals of the 1950s would seem archaic in this new age. Today a young college student who wants to become an intellectual looks out into the world and does not see awesome literary critics with the authority of an Edmund Wilson or a Lionel Trilling. But he or she will see dozens of academic stars, people who cross lines by succeeding in intellectual realms and also on TV, in private consulting firms or on op-ed pages, themselves a hybrid institution that didn't exist in the 1950s. The young intellectual will see such six-figure celebrities as Henry Louis Gates, the entrepreneurial Harvard professor who also hosts documentaries for PBS, writes for the *New Yorker* and *Talk,* and seems to spawn an infinite variety of conferences, encyclopedias, and other projects; Henry Kissinger, who emigrated from studies of Metternich to politics to economic consulting; Duke's Stanley Fish, who is often off on a lecture circuit road show with a conservative counterpart; E. J. Dionne, who serves as a public intellectual from the ever expanding world of think tanks; and Esther Dyson, who spins out her theories at expensive technology conferences.

In the 1970s a group of conservative intellectuals developed the theory of the New Class, which posited that a small and politically liberal intellectual class had gained disproportionate influence over American culture by controlling the commanding heights of academia, media, and culture. But with the rise of a mass educated class, it has become ever more difficult to draw the line between the world of the intelligentsia and the rest of America. The gap between intellectuals and everyone else is now a continuum. The landscape is filled with people who are quasi-scholarly, quasi-political, quasi-rich. Harvard academic Daniel Yergin wrote some books on the history of oil, then seized the opportunity to open a consultant's shop for energy companies (the Cambridge Energy Research Associates, with revenues over $75 million a year). Strobe Talbott turned his interest in Russian studies into a career at *Time*. He writes books on diplomatic affairs, publishes poetry, and became the deputy secretary of state. The information age economy has meant that people who have a talent for research, for analysis, for mathematics, for writing or any other realm of intellection have enormous nonacademic opportunities—in finance, in Silicon Valley, or in the multiplying realms of the commentariat: journalism, think tanks, foundations, government, and so on. The jobs off campus and beyond the little magazines often pay better. The opportunities for advancement come quicker. And the intellectual stimulation can be just as intense, the experiences more exciting. In sum, the relationship between thinking and doing has become closer.

The very meaning of the word *intellectual* has changed over the last 50 years in the way the word *gentleman* changed in the 50 before. Once *intellectual* referred to a small and select group. Then its meaning broadened and broadened to include more people. Now it has almost lost its meaning as so many different types lay claim to it.

There is no longer a small, rarefied intelligentsia living with their hangers-on in bohemian neighborhoods in New York, San Francisco, and Boston. Now there is a massive class of educated analysts and "opinion leaders" who have made the old bohemian neighborhoods unaffordable for anybody without stock options or large royalty checks. Now universities blast-fax press releases to let reporters know that their faculty members are available to comment on the controversies of the day on cable talk shows. Now writers and cultural studies professors embrace mass culture and devote conferences to Madonna or Marilyn or Manson or Marilyn Manson. In the 1950s the scene of maximum glory was to be found in the sphere of the literary critic. Today it is in the first-class section of transatlantic flights, where airborne academics hop from conference to conference, racking up frequent flyer miles and comparing notes on duty-free opportunities around the globe. Fifties intellectuals discussed *No Exit*. Contemporary intellectuals discuss no-load mutual funds.

But the crucial change is not merely that more money and greater opportunities are available for those who are good with ideas. It's the way intellectuals conceive of themselves. Columbia professor Edward Said, who is unhappy with the trend, describes the change in *Representations of the Intellectual:* "The particular threat to the intellectual today is not the academy, nor the suburbs, nor the appalling commercialism of journalism and publishing houses, but rather an attitude that I will call professionalism. By professionalism I mean thinking of your work as an intellectual as something you do for a living, between the hours of nine and five with one eye on the clock, and another cocked at what is considered to be proper, professional behavior—not rocking the boat, not straying outside accepted paradigms or limits, making yourself marketable and above all presentable."

Intellectuals have come to see their careers in capitalist terms. They seek out market niches. They compete for attention. They used to regard ideas as weapons but are now more inclined to regard their ideas as property. They strategize about marketing, about increasing book sales.

Norman Podhoretz was practically burned alive for admitting in his 1967 memoir, *Making It,* that he, like other writers, was driven by ambition. That book caused outrage in literary circles and embarrassment among Podhoretz's friends. Now ambition is no more remarkable in the idea business than it is in any other. Now Henry Louis Gates, who is chairman of Harvard's African American Studies Department, casually remarks to a reporter from *Slate* magazine, "By impulse, I'm an entrepreneur. If I weren't in the academy, I could be a CEO. Quincy Jones is my hero. I have a picture of Vernon Jordan on my wall, right over one of John Hope Franklin."

The Economy of Symbolic Exchange

The only amazing thing these days is that universities haven't opened business schools for aspiring intellectuals. The schools send marketing and finance people off into the world with full training in how to manage and rise in the business world. But intellectuals have to make their way in the job market with no official training on how to amass foundation grants, no courses on how to blurb their colleagues' books, no case studies on how to market a bestseller, no quantitative models on how to determine when a certain subject niche will become hot and how long its vogue will last. Today's intellectuals learn career strategies the way fourth graders used to learn about sex—from the bad kids in the bathrooms.

If a university were to offer a course of study on the marketplace of ideas, the writer who would be at the heart of the curriculum would be Pierre Bourdieu. Bourdieu is a French sociologist who is influential among his colleagues but almost entirely unread outside academia because of his atrocious prose style. Bourdieu's aim is to develop an economy of symbolic exchanges, to delineate the rules and patterns of the cultural and intellectual marketplace. His basic thesis is that all intellectual and cultural players enter the marketplace with certain forms of capital. They may have academic capital (the right degrees), cultural capital (knowledge of a field or art form, a feel for the proper etiquette), linguistic capital (the ability to use language), political capital (the approved positions or affiliations), or symbolic capital (a famous fellowship or award). Intellectuals spend their careers trying to augment their capital and convert one form of capital into another. One intellectual might try to convert knowledge into a lucrative job; another might convert symbolic capital into invitations to exclusive conferences at tony locales; a third might seek to use linguistic ability to destroy the reputations of colleagues so as to become famous or at least controversial.

Ultimately, Bourdieu writes, intellectuals compete to gain a monopoly over the power to consecrate. Certain people and institutions at the top of each specialty have the power to confer prestige and honor on favored individuals, subjects, and styles of discourse. Those who hold this consecration of power influence taste, favor certain methodologies, and define the boundary of their discipline. To be chief consecrator is the intellectual's dream.

Bourdieu doesn't just look at the position an intellectual may hold at a given moment; he looks at the trajectory of a career, the successive attitudes, positions, and strategies a thinker adopts while rising or competing in the marketplace. A young intellectual may enter the world armed only with personal convictions. He or she will be confronted, Bourdieu says, with a diverse "field." There will be daring radical magazines over on one side, staid establishment journals on another, dull but worthy publishing houses here, vanguard but underfunded houses over there. The intellectual will be confronted with rivalries between schools and between established figures. The complex relationships between these and other players in the field will be the tricky and shifting environment in which the intellectual will try to make his or her name. Bourdieu is quite rigorous about the interplay of these forces, drawing elaborate charts of the various fields of French intellectual life, indicating the power and prestige levels of each institution. He identifies which institutions have consecration power over which sections of the field.

Young intellectuals will have to know how to invest their capital to derive maximum "profit," and they will have to devise strategies for ascent—whom to kiss up to and whom to criticize and climb over. Bourdieu's books detail a dazzling array of strategies intellectuals use to get ahead. Bourdieu is not saying that the symbolic field can be understood strictly by economic principles. Often, he says, the "loser wins" rule applies. Those who most vociferously and publicly renounce material success win prestige and honor that can be converted into lucre. Nor does Bourdieu even claim that all of the strategies are self-conscious. He says that each intellectual possesses a "habitus," or personality and disposition, that leads him or her in certain directions and toward certain fields. Moreover, the intellectual will be influenced, often unwillingly or unknowingly, by the gravitational pull of the rivalries and controversies of the field. Jobs will open up, grants will appear, furies will rage. In some ways the field dominates and the intellectuals are blown about within it.

Bourdieu hasn't quite established himself as the Adam Smith of the symbolic economy. And it probably wouldn't be very useful for a young intellectual to read him in hopes of picking up career tips, as a sort of Machiavellian Guide for Nobel Prize Wannabes. Rather, Bourdieu is most useful because he puts into prose some of the concepts that most other intellectuals have observed but have not systematized. Intellectual life is a mixture of careerism and altruism (like most other professions). Today the Bobo intellectual reconciles the quest for knowledge with the quest for the summer house.

How to Be an Intellectual Giant

So let's take a look at how the world looks to, say, a young woman newly graduated from a fancy university who dreams of establishing herself as the Henry Kissinger of her generation. She'll emerge from college saddled with debt, but she will nonetheless find herself landing a barely paying internship at a politically safe outfit like, say, the Brookings Institution. She'll start off doing Nexis searches for some former secretary of commerce who spends his three-hour workday preparing for panel discussions on the topic "Whither NATO?" Her mood will swing from euphoria to despair. Stendhal wrote, "The first love affair of a young man entering society is generally one of ambition," and that is true for a person entering the intellectual marketplace. Her famous boss can send her on the path to fame and fortune (if he places the right call on her behalf to the editor of the *New York Times* op-ed page), or if he doesn't like her, he can block her entry into the commentariat and so compel her to begin applying to law schools. The intern will come to long for his approval, glowing when he gives it and sinking into the depths when he does not.

For the sake of her own self-respect, she will indulge in tiny afterwork rebellions. Sitting around with her friends, she will bitingly ridicule the boss she wants so badly to impress. In the warrens of every foundation, think tank, publishing house, newspaper, and magazine are young interns who can do scathing imitations of their superiors. Making fun of the boss is the careerist's form of blasphemy. The young serfs in intellectual organizations will gather around the buffet tables at book parties and conference receptions, chomping free shrimp while gossiping meanly about their secure superiors. If a bomb were to go off in one of these settings, think tank reports across America would go out filled with typos for months.

Fortunately, this initial period of torment and anxiety does not last long. If the young intellectual does make it one rung up the ladder, she will begin to experience the sense of exaggerated self-importance that will be her prime satisfaction for the rest of her life. Her first full-time job will be as a minion. This sounds lowly, but in reality it is not.

In most intellectual organizations, the hard work of researching, thinking, and writing is done by the people who are too young to get out of it. A two-tier system develops. There are paper people—the young intellectual climbers who read and write things—and there are front people—the already renowned intellectuals, government officials, magazine editors, university presidents, foundation heads, and politicians whose primary job is to appear in places, delivering the research findings, speeches, and talking points the paper people have gathered for them. The front people go to meetings, do *Nightline*, speak at fundraisers, host panel discussions, and give interviews on NPR. They get to take credit for everything. When they are not showing their faces to photographers from *U.S. News and World Report,* they are talking on the phone. Indeed, some days their job consists of coming into work, talking on the phone for three hours, going to lunch, talking on the phone for four more hours. And while they are on the phone they tell each other how much they are looking forward to the weekend, when they can get some reading done. Somehow, almost against their will, their lives have been turned inside out.

The front people get the glory and the contacts, and the paper people control the substance of what gets said.

The young intellectual at this stage of her career gets to write the scathing memos and op-eds castigating people four decades her senior for their ignorance and cowardice ("Campaign Finance Retreat: A Shameless Failure of Nerve"). She is the one who evaluates the policy ideas, companies, scripts, or tenure-track candidates that come across a front person's desk. In some ways she is at the peak of her actual power. For example, a few years ago a friend of mine ghostwrote an op-ed piece for a business executive on a bill before Congress, which was published in a national magazine. Then my friend went to work for a presidential candidate. The business executive sent the op-ed to my friend's candidate. So my friend got to write a letter in the politician's name lavishly praising the op-ed piece he had written under the business executive's name.

As penance for such gratifications, the junior paper person is forced to undergo superficial humiliations. She must hover in a cloud of consultation behind her front person as he walks down the hall (like four-year-olds, famous people seem to have a horror of going anywhere alone). In addition, front people, who don't have to carry anything, walk very fast to demonstrate their vitality. Paper people, who have to carry their own documents as well as the documents of their front, have to scurry behind in an undignified manner just to keep up. Sometimes the front will leave a room or climb into a car and pull the door shut behind him. The poor paper person will have to juggle her files and reopen the door and remind the front she exists.

Still, this buttboy stage in the career is very important because it is during this period that the young intellectual learns about the various players in the field, who is important and who is not. Thanks to the position of her famous boss, the young intellectual has access to places and people that would be closed to her if she were unaffiliated. She will be making contacts with all of the editors and other gatekeepers she will need to know if she is to forge her own career as a publicity intellectual. The difficult moment comes a few years hence, when she is, say, 28 and must break away from her front person and start to make herself a front person. If she does not perform this difficult self-weaning, she will find herself reduced to perpetual valet status. Her ability to think independently will deteriorate. She will begin to use the word *we* when asked her opinion, as in "We wrote an essay on that a few weeks ago." She will begin to confuse her own status and the status of her boss (self-aggrandizement is the opiate of the anonymous).

Subject Niche

Once she breaks free, she will have to determine her field of specialty. The purpose of a field of specialty is to give her a market niche so that when talk-show bookers, editors, or search committees are looking for someone who knows about, say, Chinese missile programs, her name will come immediately to mind. This is a difficult selection. The young intellectual must estimate future market demand—thousands of intellectuals mastered the arcane field of arms control, only to find the market reduced after the end of the Cold War. The young intellectual must also gauge market supply. If there are ten thousand young intellectuals setting out to write books about communitarianism and the theory of civil society, does she want to be another? Here she must be subtle, because in the intellectual arena sometimes it's best to follow the crowd. The more people are specializing in civil society, the more civil society conferences will be organized. More civil society arguments will be put forward and therefore there will be more demand for people to comment on or rebut them. Because each person in the field will read (slightly) more than he writes, each new entrant in this specialty increases the demand for critics and panelists. That's Say's Law. The more people are saying, the more there is to be said.

The young intellectual must also evaluate the prestige and visibility of her market niche. During the Cold War it was easy to find the prestigious intellectual specialties. You could draw a chart, and at the top corner there would be foreign policy issues that involved banks. If your specialty was East-West capital flows, you could be assured that you'd be spending a lot of time going to conferences in $300-a-night Kempinski Hotels in Budapest and Jakarta. Then, the further you got away from foreign policy and banks, the less prestigious a specialty would be. At the bottom there were fields, such as welfare and abortion, that had no banking implications whatsoever. If you went to a conference in one of these fields, you would be surrounded by people with ill-fitting sports jackets, stubby fingers, and facial hair. But the end of the Cold War has scrambled all that. Foreign policy has sunk in prestige, while domestic issues like education have risen. An expert on Latin America can now go years at a time without getting a call from a producer from *The NewsHour with Jim Lehrer.* Specialists on racial issues, on the other hand, can scarcely go a month without getting a genius grant from the MacArthur Foundation.

The young intellectual has to pick a specialty that will be in the news. She can pick the federal budget, because there has to be a budget process every year. But that is so worthy, her chances of breaking out of the PBS/NPR orbit and into the ABC/CBS/NBC orbit are slim. She could become an expert on Middle Eastern affairs, but suppose there were to be peace in the Middle East; that would be calamitous. Some young intellectuals develop a plan— how to redesign the U.N. or how to restructure the college loan system—but this is always a mistake because nobody cares about some academic's policy idea and constant rejection tends to make intellectuals who promote programs pushy and annoying. The opposite temptation is to become an expert in a field that is too much in the news. Some intellectuals go out and become specialists in subjects people in the media are actually interested in, such as teenage sexuality. But the intellectuals who do this are too obviously publicity hungry. They tend to be the kind of people who use the letters Ph.D. after their names on the title pages of their books. It's better to have a specialty in a prestigious field so you can pretend to bring respectability to the discussion of teenage sexuality that the prime-time newsmagazine is broadcasting.

The budding intellectual must at the same time recognize that having a specialty is just a novice's tool—like punditry training wheels—to get her rolling. Once she becomes famous, she will no longer need a specialty to have bookers or editors calling. They will want her for her name. At that point she can leave her field of expertise long behind. She can comment on anything at all. In fact, she will be compelled to do so by the marketplace. There is no subject she will not be asked about. And if she refuses to give an answer, on the grounds that she is not knowledgeable enough to say, she will find that people feel insulted. They will regard her as a pompous prude.

Demeanor

After finding a specialty, the young intellectual must find a demeanor. It's possible to succeed in the marketplace of ideas with any set of ideas; there are fabulously successful moderates and fabulously successful radicals. And it's possible to succeed with any demeanor. There are happy people who make it, as well as angry people. But you cannot succeed if your ideas clash with your personal-

ity. You cannot be a mellow radical or an angry moderate.
There is little audience for such creatures.

The main job of radicals in the Noam Chomsky or
G. Gordon Liddy mode is to go around from one scruffy
lecture hall to another reminding audiences that while
they may be disdained or ignored by the mainstream culture, they are actually right about everything. The radical
bases his career on the assumption that the world is deeply
out of sorts and is in fact run by a deceitful establishment
that tricks the masses into holding opinions that are incor-
rect. In order to prosper, the radical must be out of sorts.
His audience will demand vehemence, a tinge of paranoia,
omniscience (the intellectual must be able to see the truth
through the establishment's web of deception), and a willingness to broadcast his brave contrarianism.

To qualify as heroic, the radical must establish his un-
fashionableness. He can do this by wearing brown shirts
or excessively heavy boots, outfits that are unfashionable
at Brooks Brothers and therefore de rigueur among radical
book buyers and thought consumers. In addition, radicals
have to go around finding revered figures to attack in
order to demonstrate that they intend to remain deeply
unfashionable despite their contracts with such magazines
as *Vanity Fair*. For the same reason, comfortable academics are compelled to find ever more transgressive subjects—sadomasochism, queer studies—to research. Artists
have to find ever more offensive themes. Radicals who get
suddenly fashionable are immediately regarded as craven
social climbers. They lose their standing with their audience, as well as most of their foundation grants and career
prospects.

Moreover, the radical intellectual cannot build his career just by saying things his supporters like; he must say
or do things his opponents hate. If he does no more than
flatter his audience, he will achieve only modest success.
If, on the other hand, he is vilified by his opponents, then

his audience, his patrons and various foundation officers will rally to his side. He will become a cause, a person his audience takes into their hearts. His audience will be willing to shell out large amounts of money to buy his books or attend his lectures. They will give him standing ovations when he is introduced because the very idea of him has become sacred in their minds. (Often he will get only tepid applause after he has finished his remarks because in intellectual combat it's the combat the audience craves, not the intellectual part.)

In order to be reliably vilified, radical intellectuals and public figures must get themselves paired off with counterparts on the other extreme—Jerry Falwell and Norman Lear, gay activists and Operation Rescue. By joining these symbiotic bogeymen relationships, both sides can raise money and support off the villainy of the other. They can go out of their way to outrage their opponents—by sticking a crucifix in a jar of urine or engaging in some other prefab gesture. This earns them two weeks on the talk shows trading charges, and it stokes up the troops. Each side will claim to be more unfashionable than the other, and this war to be seen as more persecuted than your rival becomes the central preoccupation of the dispute.

While a radical intellectual must be vehement, contentious, and unhappy, moderate intellectuals must be civil, slow-talking, and placid. Moderates appeal to consumers who are basically happy with the world and therefore disturbed by commentators who generate too much heat and disharmony. Moderate audiences want to see a civil exchange of views and are impressed more by subtleties than by bold, slashing rhetorical strokes. They are attracted by genial intellectuals who say things like "I would like to associate myself with the remarks that Mr. Moyers made during his intervention." The moderate intellectual, in turn, will feel that he is so important he does not need to be interesting. So he will speak slowly and carefully, as if from a great height. Afterward he will be regarded as a thoughtful person, but nobody may remember any single thought he has uttered.

Marketing

The intellectual today does not come up with an expertise and a demeanor and then market it to the great thinking public. The production and marketing evolve simultaneously, with each process looping back and influencing the other. In her early thirties our young intellectual will still spend most of her time writing. Before she can get on TV or the lecture circuit, she must have been published enough so that her name rings a bell. As her publishing career is getting started, she will imagine that if she could write just one really notable essay in one really prestigious publication, then her career would be made. She will learn that this is untrue. On the day her first big essay is published—perhaps it is called "The Decline of Discourse" in *Harper's*—she will imagine her world has changed. But she will walk around all day, and other people will be leading their lives just as before, treating her no differently than they did yesterday. Many will have not noticed her piece—which has been the object of her fevered attention for weeks—while others who have will treat it as just another scrap in the media confetti.

Nonetheless, she must continue to get published. The *New York Times,* the *Wall Street Journal,* the *L.A. Times,* and the other newspapers and magazines receive hundreds of thousands of submissions every year, and regular appearances in such places is the way intellectuals now remind others and themselves of their existence. So within the first few hours after a news event, such as a court decision on gay marriage, our intellectual will phone the right subeditor at the right op-ed page to say that the line being taken by the shallow TV pundits is 180 degrees off the mark. Print editors like to be told this so they can be assured they have not been rendered obsolete by Geraldo Rivera. She will mention her friendship with the publisher of the newspaper (the editor will doubt the truthfulness of this tie but won't be totally sure). In making her pitch, she will assure the editor that "this piece will really move the debate." She will also describe how she can work a pop culture reference into her essay, comparing the Supreme Court to the creature in the number-one box office movie of the moment. Editors like this sort of mass-media integration, first because it gives them a way to illustrate the piece, and second because they are under the delusion that pop-culture references will propel a piece's readership into the five-digit area. Besides, this is the sort of desperate mixing of high and low that Bobo intellectuals strain to achieve in their effort to persuade people that they are not elitist or boring.

Once the editor gives a provisional go-ahead for the piece, the young intellectual will have up to four hours to write it, which doesn't exactly leave a lot of time for Edmund Wilson–like throat clearing. Nonetheless, she must conceive the piece along the lines of Chartres Cathedral. The prose style should be permanent and solid but appear light. The first two paragraphs should be like a facade—dazzling and all-encompassing. The next several paragraphs should be like a walk down the apse, always heading in a straight line toward the predictable climax but also offering glancing views of interesting side chapels. Finally, the ultimate paragraph should be like arriving at the transept, with light flooding in from all sides. Also, as journalist Michael Kinsley advises, it is best not to use semicolons, as they can be thought pretentious.

The article should also contain healthy dollops of autobiography, forcing the reader to glance down at the biographical tagline that accompanies the piece. If the article

mentions some celebrity—perhaps a recently dead politician—the author will want to mention some pointless detail from her last meeting with that person or the emotions
she experienced when learning of the subject's death.

To get the most attention, the essay should be wrong.
Logical essays are read and understood. But an illogical or
wrong essay will prompt dozens of other writers to rise
and respond, thus giving the author mounds of publicity.
Yale professor Paul Kennedy had a distinguished but
unglamorous career under his belt when he wrote *The
Rise and Fall of the Great Powers,* predicting American
decline. He was wrong, and hundreds of other commentators rose to say so, thus making him famous and turning
his book into a bestseller. Francis Fukuyama wrote an
essay called "The End of History," which seemed wrong
to people who read only the title. Thousands of essayists
wrote pieces pointing out that history had not ended, and
Fukuyama became a global sensation.

After the article has appeared, the young intellectual
will want to let the editor of the piece know what a massive impact the article is having at the White House/the
Federal Reserve/the film industry or wherever its intended
target is. If she is well connected with other intellectuals,
bits of praise will come in. Praise is the currency of the
realm among the thinking classes. In the fifties intellectuals seemed to be forever screaming condemnations at each
other, but now they endlessly praise each other. And since
giving out praise doesn't cost a person anything but actually wins affection, praise is ladled out freely and praise
inflation occurs. The value of each unit of flattery declines,
and pretty soon intellectuals have to pass over a wheelbar-
row full of praise just to pay one compliment. To accurately measure how much people actually like her work,
our young intellectual will be wise to develop a praise de-
flation formula. If someone says he liked a piece, that
means he saw it but didn't read it. If he says he loved the

piece, that means he started it and made it at least halfway through but can't remember what it was about. If he calls it brilliant, that means he finished it. It is only when a reader offers the following highest form of praise that the writer knows for sure the person is being sincere: "That was an absolutely outstanding piece; I've been saying the same thing myself for years."

If our intellectual is successful, she will be offered a column. This seems like the pinnacle, but while a dozen people get riches and fame from column writing, thousands do it in wretched slavery—compelled like circus animals to be entertaining once or twice a week. The ones who succeed in that line of work have a superb knowledge of one thing: their own minds. They know what they think and they have immense confidence in their judgments. This is not as simple as it sounds, for most people don't become aware of their own opinions until someone else has put them into words. But a columnist can read an article on brain surgery for 20 minutes and then go off and give a lecture to a conference of brain surgeons on what is wrong with their profession.

For intellectuals who do not possess this gift, the next step up the ladder involves writing a book. Aside from the obvious paramount thing about a book—who the author can get to blurb it—there are three important factors the author needs to concern herself with: the publishing house, the title, and the one phrase people will remember from it. A writer's career should be traceable through her publishing houses. Her first rigorous book will be with the University of Chicago Press or some such. Her next serious book should go to W.W. Norton. Her big-think prestigious book should go to Simon & Schuster or Knopf, and at the end of her career, her blockbuster memoir—when she will finally persuade an editor to put her photo on the cover—will go to Random House. The title of her first book will begin with the phrase *"The End of . . ."* The benefit of endism is its dramatic finality; few people will remember a book called *Ideology Is Ailing*. But decades after its publication, the title *The End of Ideology* will still be referred to (even as its contents are utterly forgotten). The difficulty in writing an endist book is in finding things that haven't already ended. History, equality, racism, tragedy, and politics have all been taken, and *The Death of . . .* takes in just about everything else. *The End of Gardening* just doesn't have the ring of a bestseller.

If the endist strategy doesn't work out, the writer might go for the approach pioneered by Leon Uris in a series of bestselling novels and then taken up by Thomas Cahill in the sphere of nonfiction: ethnic brown-nosing. The way to do that is to give the book a title like *Irish People Are Wonderful: But English People Suck* and then follow it up with another book called *Jews Are Great*. An author can go decades without running out of high book-purchasing demographic groups to flatter *(Book Buyers Are Really Smart)*, and where is the *New York Times Book Review* going to find a critic willing to say otherwise? A wise soul once declared that the ultimate power of the writer is that he has the choice of whom he wants to be co-opted by. In making his first book topic selections, a writer can select which audience he will spend the rest of his career flattering. However, considering the fan mail he will receive from pet lovers, a writer has to have a strong stomach before he launches off on a career with a book called *The Secret Sorrows of Cats*.

Intellectuals on book tour will need a catchphrase that talk-show interviewers can scan seconds before a segment and then use to start a conversation. For educated audiences the catchphrase might be a paradox that seems sophisticated and appeals to the Bobo's desire for the reconciliation of opposites. So a writer might say her book is an argument for sustainable development, cooperative individualism, the social market, liberation management, compassionate conservatism, practical idealism, or flexible commitment. The most successful oxymoron, *Simple Abundance,* has already been taken by Sarah Ban Breathnach in her mega-selling book of that title, and *Complicated Poverty* probably won't work.

If the author can't come up with a phrase, she will probably have to go nude unless she is already a famous TV celebrity. Going nude doesn't mean the author has to literally strip off her clothes (although it has been done by Elizabeth Wurtzel and others). Rather, just as movie stars in a career lull will sometimes pose shamelessly for *Vanity Fair* in order to get back in the buzz, authors will sometimes accept exhibitionist embarrassment for attention. They will divulge their orgasm patterns or, better yet, those of their predatory stepfathers. If they have been lucky enough to land a job in a glamorous industry such as Hollywood or Wall Street, they will divulge the embarrassing secrets of the mentors who gave them their first big break or the companies that paid them or, in a pinch, the spouses who loved them.

Conferences

Magazine writers sometimes argue that there's no sense writing a book because a magazine article can reach millions more people and costs a fraction of the effort. But book writing—aside from whatever pleasures can be derived from actually knowing something about your subject rather than just boning up on it for a few days—turns the author into panel fodder. An intellectual entering mid-career should be sitting on at least three panel discussions a month, because at the end of life the intellectual who sits on the most panels wins.

This quota is easy to fill because conferences have become ubiquitous in the information age. It is hard to imagine Andrew Carnegie and John D. Rockefeller sitting between evenly spaced bottles of mineral water and discussing "The Future of Corporate Responsibility" with Mark Twain as the celebrity moderator, but these days we are all intellectuals, and intellectuals have to panel. So even sales shows for the floor coverings industry have taken on the academic trappings of, say, the Modern Language Association (while scholarly conferences like the MLA are like sales shows). Big hotels are divided into microscopic seminar rooms. Coffee urns are arrayed on tables in the hallways, supplemented by fruit bowls and small danishes for panelists to gather around during break time. And everywhere there is the buzz of presentations on everything from the musculature of the ankle to the dinner menus in the novels of Henry James.

Whatever other purposes conferences serve—and they do build solidarity among people who think about the same things, they do offer organizations a forum in which they can flatter their donors, they do give disheveled intellectuals a chance to go to places like Orlando and San Francisco without their families—the main purpose of the conference is to serve as a status stock exchange. From the amount of attention and sycophancy a conference goer attracts, she can judge where her stock price stands in relation to the rest of the market. With a brilliant presentation and some acute hobnobbing, she can send her valuation skyrocketing, thus laying the groundwork for future job offers and other opportunities.

The first task at a conference is to be a panelist. If the midcareer intellectual isn't on a panel, she probably shouldn't be at the conference, since nonpanelists are conference lambs, and lambs soon learn that the conference lions hang out only with each other. Second, she should be the least famous person on her panel, just as in real estate it's better to buy the least expensive house in an expensive neighborhood. In the first place, it will be easier to shine

among more senior intellectual celebrities. They are probably living off past cultural capital and so are likely to
have done no preparation for the event. As her session
gets underway, the first few minutes will be spent counting
the number of people in the audience and comparing it to
attendance at other panels. Then the symposiasts will listen intently to their introductions. The organizer—who
usually assigns himself the moderator role in order to get
some publicity compensation for his work—will inflate
the brilliance of each panelist so as to reflect glory on his
ability to draw big names. Listening to her puffed-up introduction will probably be the most enjoyable moment of
the entire conference. This joy is marred only when the
moderator goes on for too long. I was once at a conference with a long-winded moderator, and a member of the
audience sketched a running bar chart comparing the
length of the introductions to the length of *Berlin Alexan-
derplatz*.

The successful symposiast begins her remarks with
preapproved jokes. At a conference of economists one
should begin by telling the one about a few billion here
and a few billion there and pretty soon you're talking real
money, or the one about how if you laid a thousand economists end to end they still wouldn't reach a conclusion,
or the one about how economists look for keys under the
street lamp because that is where the light is. At least one
speaker per panel should refer to Yogi Berra, and everybody in the audience must chuckle to prove how unpretentious they are. Then the speaker will have to judge how
dull she can afford to be. Very eminent panelists are expected to be dull, since their words carry great weight.
High government officials, university presidents, and corporate leaders are expected to speak in the Upper Institutional mode—a vocabulary so dense and vague of content
as to cause people's mouths to hang open and their eyes to
water. But climbing intellectuals cannot plod along like

aging silverbacks. There is nothing more off-putting than a young intellectual who presumes he has won the right to be tedious without having actually achieved the requisite eminence or responsibility. Those who have not won major awards or who do not occupy powerful posts should not be using such phrases as "I would like to suggest . . ." or "My contention therefore . . ."

The average audience can remember only one point from each presentation, so the acute panelist will want hers to be large enough to generate a little butt bouncing among members of the audience. The surest way to generate such excitement is to make startling predictions about the future. But this must be done in a socially acceptable manner. Crude futurologists are considered charlatans. There are two ways to get away with it. The first is no-escape historical determinism, which means arguing that the tides of history make certain dramatic changes inevitable: the PC era is over, an age of socialist renaissance is just around the corner, the growth of evangelical Christianity will have wonderful implications for the financial services sector. The second technique is promiscuous historical parallelism. This is achieved by observing that the current moment resembles another significant date: the political climate of 1929. At that point another panelist will counter that in fact the correct comparison is to 1848, and another will impressively state that the true parallel is to the state of the Holy Roman Empire in 898.

The purpose of these chronological acrobatics is to generate questions during the discussion period. There is nothing worse for a climbing intellectual than to have to sit silently for the last half of the session as all the Q&A interventions go to other panelists. That is a sign of stock market decline. But if the panelist can put forward one theory that is sweeping and inexact, that should stir a few rebuttals. To cover her backside from people who think her notion absurd, she can emphasize that her idea is

something she is merely testing, though these equivoca-
tions rarely help. The cleverer protective device is to pad
out the remainder of her time by lavishly citing her fellow
panelists. Three quotations from a colleague's work is
what students of peacock behavior call a love display.

As the session winds down, each person in the room
will crouch in a sprinter's position in order to make a
quick exit to the coffee urn, where the schmoozing and the
real point of the conference will take place. If you look
at the newsletter from any academic or professional organization, you will observe a series of awkward black-
and-white photographs that show three or four people
standing in a happy semicircle clutching wine glasses or
coffee cups to their bellies. These are intellectuals caught
in midschmooze. They are enjoying an activity that deli-
ciously combines work and play, which is a characteristic
reconciliation of the Bobo class. The people in the picture
look jovial, in part because they know their picture is
being taken ("Everyone a Celebrity" is the slogan for this
day and age) and in part because they are pleased to be in
the presence of people as important as themselves. During
the first rush of a schmooze session, if four or more conference lions gather in one place, they radiate a happy
glow—so thrilled are they to be in each other's company—
that they will laugh for 10 or 15 seconds at a joke nobody
bothered to tell.

An intellectual who can first-name his way across a
cocktail room, planting a 4.7-second seed of goodwill
with each familiar friend without ever being tempted to
stop and pay more sustained attention, is either an intellectual superstar or a top official at the Ford Foundation.
On the other hand, an obscure person who does not
bother to introduce himself when meeting someone, on
the presumption that the other person must already know
who he is, suffers a decline. A person who interrupts
someone else's story to go off in search of more prestigious

company is a jerk, but a person who interrupts his own story to talk to bigger stars is a charming force of nature. One who hands out his own essays during schmooze sessions is in danger of falling off the exchange, while another who acts as if the first amendment was invented so he could mention his old friendship with Bobby Kennedy is also in trouble.

A person who is trapped outside a conversational klatsch and cannot induce anyone in the ring to step back and let him in is in desperate straits. The people on the other side of the klatsch see his social exclusion and observe that he lacks the celebrity kilowattage to subconsciously induce his peers to step back and grant him entrance. An aspiring intellectual will find it pretty easy to gauge her stock value by who stops to pay attention to her, how long they spend, whether or not they look at her as they speak, and how many of her field's top-dog consecrators idle by to acknowledge her existence. One must read the signs while pretending not to, acting instead as if the most important thing on one's mind is the need to spear a chicken shard from the traveling waiter's tray, dip it into mustard sauce, and bring the shard to one's mouth without spilling one's drink or getting sauce on one's chin.

Television

Books and panels are fine, but in the end, those who are not on television find their lives are without meaning. The days when all you had to do to become an intellectual giant was to write a literary masterpiece, such as *War and Peace* or *Being and Nothingness,* are gone. Now it is necessary to be able to pitch your ideas to Barbara Walters and Katie Couric. As today's intellectual gets more eminent, the places where she appears should grow less and less rarefied. So a career that starts out at tiny colloquia with bearded philosophers will end up, if all goes well, on the *Tonight Show*.

To achieve this level, the intellectual will first have to attract the attention of TV producers. These bookers are caught between the demands of their vain and temperamental hosts and the crotchety male retirees who are the bulk of their viewers, so they are always looking for someone who can make their life easier. An intellectual on the rise will wake up early in the morning, formulate her sound bites, and then call up bookers on MSNBC to let them know she's available (especially in August when they are hungry for guests). If the producers are interested, they will give her a preinterview, which is a telephone audition, during which she can deliver her idea nuggets in as throaty a voice as possible. Some of the time the bookers will call back later in the day to say, "We've decided to take the show in a different direction, so we won't be needing you." That means they have found a more famous commentator to say the same thing.

Or they will book her, which means she will get to drive to Fort Lee, New Jersey, or some such place so she can appear on a cable talk show that she wouldn't watch if forced under threat of death. She will be met at the entrance and deposited in the green room, which is a tiny chamber with a TV fixed to the station and its endless denture cream commercials. The producer will linger long enough to give her two contradictory instructions: "Don't be afraid to interrupt—we like it when people mix it up." And "This is a sophisticated program. We're not the McLaughlin Group here." Then a young woman will come in and bring her to the makeup room, where the intellectual will chatter incessantly so as to demonstrate that being on TV doesn't make her nervous. When she gets back to the green room, there will be an author touring his book on Stalin's death camps, the messiah of a religious cult, and an astronomer who thinks he is going on the air to downplay the risks of an asteroid hitting the earth but who at the last minute will bow to the pressure and end up sounding alarmist. Cable networks bring in pundits in waves, like line changes during a hockey game, because the idea minstrels are the cheapest way to fill air time. The intellectual has to hope that all the guests use Q-Tips, because often the TV channels don't change earpieces between pundits.

She'll be brought into a small studio and put in a chair in front of a dented photo of the New York skyline. A cameraman who has working-class contempt for anybody who would pontificate on TV will roll his camera in front of her, and all she'll have to do over the next four minutes is pretend to have sex with the black glass square that hides its lens. After she has done this enough times, she will successfully become a caricature of herself, which is the key to television success. If she is blonde, she will become a bleached blonde. If she is a partisan, she will become ferocious. If she is thoughtful, she will develop all the verbal accoutrements of the stock professors you used to see in Marx Brothers movies. And since TV is a visual medium, she will develop an audiovisual signature: something like Tom Wolfe's white suit, Robert Novak's vest, or Anne Coulter's legs.

Irony and sarcasm do not work on television, so the intellectual's best tactic is to pretend she is having the greatest time she's ever had in her life. As the host asks the question, she will beam a brilliant smile. She will answer the question while smiling and top off her answer with another three-second smile. She'll leave everybody with a warm glow. TV is an attention medium, not a persuasion medium. On many programs people will remember that she was on but will have no recollection of what she said. So content is not always vital, but it is important that she wave her hands a lot—for visual interest—and speak in the tones of one who has just finished her third cup of coffee.

The host will have been briefed on the guests' sound bites and often will steal them. If her plan has been to say that America is suffering a loss of community unparalleled since the early industrial age, the first question from the host will be "You know, America is suffering a loss of community unparalleled since the early industrial age. Do you disagree with that?" The guest's attempt to come up with a secondary thing to say will be hampered by the out-of-body experience that many people feel during the first few seconds of a TV appearance. The brain rises out toward the ceiling and looks down on the body, which is frantically trying to think of something to say. The brain will mischievously tell the body that one "fuck" or "shit" here will lead to a career meltdown, auto-pundicide.

Nonetheless, TV does introduce the intellectual to the magic of show business. At its best it offers all the attention and buzz of intellectual activity—adrenaline, fame, influence—with none of the actual work. After a few dozen appearances on *Nightline* or *Charlie Rose,* she will be stopped at airports and recognized in restaurants, a pleasure that Lionel Trilling or Irving Howe probably never experienced.

The Convergence of the Successful

In the premeritocratic age, a person's social life was based largely on proximity. People socialized with friends from the neighborhood or church or work or the local country club. But for many members of the educated class, social life is based on achievement. Social invitations come to the job as much as the person, so the higher a person climbs up the professional ladder, the more invitations there will be to dinner parties, receptions, and other gatherings. And this despite the fact that in all of American history, there has never been a recorded case of a person who has actually become *more* charming as he became more successful.

At the top of intellectual life are semiprofessional, semisocial institutions like Renaissance weekends, Jackson Hole conferences, the TED technology confabs, and the Colorado Conference on World Affairs. They bring together people who are often total strangers. The only thing the attendees have in common is that they are all successful. These meetings serve as meritocratic Versailles, exclusive communities for the educated aristocracy, to gather and chat about their various lecture fees. Except instead of Lord So-and-So conversing with Duke Such-and-Such, at these meetings Mikhail Gorbachev will be in the corner conferring with Ted Turner, Elie Wiesel will be lecturing Richard Dreyfuss, and George Steiner will be lost in conversation with Nancy Kassebaum Baker. These institutions are run by the new consecrators of social prestige, foundation officials. Program officers are like the hostesses of the French salons, great themselves for their ability to recognize success.

If our intellectual has succeeded with essays, books, panels, conferences, and TV appearances, she will find herself invited to retreats at an Arizona rock resort. She will be asked to attend boards of directors meetings hosted by associations, universities, and corporations (which in this day and age like to have a few deep thinkers hanging about, if only for their conversation). If she is deemed clubable, there will be invitation-only conferences to discuss the next millennium. There will be Alpha clubs to join, such as the Council on Foreign Relations, the Bilderberg meetings, and the Ditchley Park conferences in Oxfordshire. There will be working groups, presidential commissions, and special research groups. Her first trip to one of these get-togethers will be like Natasha's first ball in *War and Peace*. She'll stare proudly at her name on the roster, mingling so intimately with big names of past and present.

The successful intellectual will thus be able to rise above intellectual endeavors into that social canopy where everybody gets to bathe in the golden light of each other's accomplishments. The intellectual will find herself invited to dinners that mix the financial elite, the fashion elite, the Hollywood elite, and the political elite. After a lifetime spent amidst the theory types, she will find groups who are not ashamed to be interested in pleasure, who wear clothes that actually emphasize their waists or shoulders.

The intellectual will wonder why she has neglected pleasure all her life. She will discover new joys being amidst people who are careful about their toilet, whose cheeks have that buttery complexion that is the mark of a diet of fat-free sauces. And everybody will be so charming! By now familiarity will have led her to have a jaded view of her intellectual peers. But, being fresh, the top dogs in other fields will seem dazzling and impressive. The business tycoons will seem sharp and together. The movie directors will be surprisingly engaging. The politicians will have wonderful stories.

And she will find they are pretty much like her. Intellectuals once assumed that businessmen were unlettered boobs or that movie stars were glorified cheerleaders, but with the triumph of the educated class, the young intellectual finds that she has ties to most everyone. She went to the same college as a movie star, grew up on the same Upper West Side block as a research scientist, married the cousin of a financier. She's already met many of her new companions in the green rooms of various TV networks. Moreover, she discovers that whatever different realms they have traveled, they have actually all been engaged in the same profession. They have all spent their lives building a reputation. So they have mastered much of the same cultural literacy ("Toni Morrison made an important point on *Charlie Rose* the other night . . ."). They all know how to convey the impression that they have heard of you as they shake your hand ("Oh, of course! . . . How are *you?*"). They have all mastered the fine art of false modesty ("I made a proposal about that several years ago, but no one heeded me then"). And they all can tell you the trading range of the U.S. dollar.

The intellectual will find that she can even be dazzling in such company. She'll find people who do not regard it as a joke if she quotes Tocqueville, and pretty soon she starts rotating her conversational sawhorses: one Tocqueville, one Clausewitz, one Publius, and one Santayana per dinner party. She will learn the pleasures of tasteful thinking. Pretty soon she will announce that it is time to reject the false choices of both left and right. We must all move beyond tired old categories like liberal and conservative. "Labels don't really matter anymore," she will hear herself saying. Her conversation will assume that tone of exhortatory banality that is familiar from the addresses of those who are Gravely Concerned—about public apathy, the decline of civility, the collapse of literacy.

Slowly but surely, in manners and in mind, she will be absorbed into the ethos of the Alpha class. She will find that at the top levels the educated class really has reconciled old divisions. Businessmen can mingle with intellectuals and find that their politics are not too far apart, their tastes are not too far apart, their worldviews are not too far apart.

But this merger has, paradoxically, created one new tension. This is not a great cultural gulf, such as used to exist between intellectuals and corporate types. It's more like a social annoyance. It has to do with that inescapable subject, money.

Status-Income Disequilibrium

In the 1950s, when intellectuals socialized mostly with each other, they did not feel the pain of their own middle-class income. The rich were remote. In those days an investment banker went to Andover and Princeton, while a newspaper person went to Central High and Rutgers. But now the financiers and the writers both are likely to have gone to Andover and Princeton. The student who graduated from Harvard cum laude makes $85,000 a year as a think tank fellow, while the schlump she wouldn't even talk to in gym class makes $34 million as a bond trader or TV producer. The loser who flunked out of Harvard and never showered is worth $2.4 billion in Silicon Valley. Pretty soon the successful intellectuals start to notice that while they have achieved social equality with these money types, financially they are inferior.

Imagine, for example, our worldly intellectual, now middle-aged and well established, at a dinner for the Society for the Preservation of Historic Chicago at the Drake Hotel. All night long she has been telling stories about Ted Koppel (emphasizing her recent *Nightline* appearance) and Bill Bradley (recounting their joint Aspen Institute conference in August). She's kept the bankers and lawyers and doctors at her table enthralled. They retire afterward to the hotel bar for seven-dollar martinis and are joined by a consultant from Deloitte & Touche and his wife, a partner at Winston & Strawn—a two-ampersand couple. She is just as amusing at the bar, filling the air with inside dope about the publishing industry and magazine gossip. Feeling expansive, she decides to pick up the tab for drinks, putting it on her own credit card, even though any of the others could expense it, and when the whole group stumbles outside she is so overcome by the triumph of the evening that she blurts out, "Can I give anyone a lift? Anyone going south?"

There is an awkward silence. The ampersand couple says, "Actually, we're going north, up to Winnetka." One of the doctors says he is going north too, up toward Lake Forest. Suddenly it is all ash in her mouth. She knows what the neighborhoods are like on Chicago's North Shore. The million-dollar homes stretch on for mile after mile. Some are Tudor Revival and others are Prairie School and Queen Anne, but they all are massive and immaculate. There are no weeds on the North Shore. Each house is surrounded by a huge spread of flawless lawn and masterfully landscaped grounds, with hedges so neatly sculpted they look like they're made out of green marble. Even the garages are spotless, with baby joggers hanging neatly from pegs, and the Little Tikes kiddy cars arrayed in perfect rows, the floors swept and mopped. The renovators in those neighborhoods appear inside the house every seven years like cicadas, changing the paneling in the rotunda from cherry to walnut or back again. From the time those people wake up in the morning and set foot on their preheated bathroom floor to the waning moments of the evening, when they hit the remote to turn off the gas fireplace, they are reminded that life is good, America is just, and their lives are in control.

But the intellectual has to drive down to her university neighborhood in Hyde Park. She has to zip past the menacing housing projects, and when she returns to her neighborhood at 47th Street, she finds herself waiting at a stoplight looking over at a yellow check-cashing place and a storefront operation that offers low phone rates to El Salvador. Her building, which seemed such a step up from her earlier graduate school existence, is made of old and dark brick and is low and squat. The patch of ground out front, a scraggly excuse for a lawn, is practically bare, iron bars protect the windows, and the gate is rusted and ramshackle. She walks through the chipped marble vestibule —with its faint odors—and one flight up to her apartment. In Winnetka the doctors and lawyers are greeted by a grand entrance hall, but the intellectual has only a small excuse for a foyer, which has shoes and boots lining the wall. She steps over the threshold of her apartment and finds herself confronted by a cluttered dining room table and looking into the kitchen. Suddenly she is feeling miserable. She is suffering from Status-Income Disequilibrium, a malady that afflicts people with jobs that give them high status but only moderately high income.

The tragedy of the SID sufferers' lives is that they spend their days in glory and their nights in mediocrity. At work they go off and give lectures—all eyes upon them—appear on TV and on NPR, chair meetings. If they work in the media or in publishing, they can enjoy fancy expense-account lunches. All day long phone messages pile up on their desks—calls from rich and famous people seeking favors or attention—but at night they realize the bathroom needs cleaning so they have to pull out the Ajax. At work they are aristocrats, kings of the meritocracy, schmoozing with George Plimpton. At home they wonder if they can really afford a new car.

Consider the situation of our imagined intellectual. She's earning $105,000 a year as a full professor at the University of Chicago. Her husband, whom she met while they were studying at Yale, is a program officer at a boutique foundation that takes Robert McCormick's money and uses it to promote ideas McCormick despised. He makes $75,000. In their wildest imaginings they never dreamed they'd someday pull in $180,000 a year.

Or that they'd be so poor. Their daughter turned 18 last year, and her room and board at Stanford tops $30,000 annually. Their 16-year-old son, who has such a flair for music, consumes at least that much in tuition fees, when you throw in the prep school costs, the summer music camp, and the private lessons. The nanny who is home when their 9-year-old returns from the University of Chicago Lab School each afternoon eats up another $32,000 (they pay her legally because our intellectual still dreams of an administration post). Then there are the charity costs, which are high so they don't have to feel too ashamed when they face their accountant each April (Nature Conservancy, Amnesty International, etc.). All of which leaves them about $2,500 a month for rent, food, books, laundry, and living expenses. It feels like they are utterly poor, and of course they are suffering from bracket amnesia; as soon as they reach one income bracket, they forget what life was like in the lower brackets and so can't imagine how it would be possible ever to return there.

Modern intellectuals are good at worrying about their reputations. But the person who suffers from Status-Income Disequilibrium spends a lot of time worrying about money. And it is not as if the intellectual these days fills her days with thoughts about truth and beauty or poetic evocations of spring. It is not as if she is compensated for her meager $105,000 salary with the knowledge that she can rise above the mundane pressures of the world. She has to spend her working hours marketing herself, appraising the needs of her audience, selling herself to producers, journalists, and her academic colleagues. The SID sufferer who is in publishing spends his days thinking about market niches, the same as the estate-owning executive at AT&T. He has to do just as much artificial schmoozing as the partners at Skadden, Arps or the sellers at Goldman Sachs. It's just that they are working in big money industries and the SID sufferer is working in a small money industry.

Today's intellectual is at the butt end of the upper class. She is rich enough to send her kids to the private schools and to Stanford, but many of the other parents at these places make as much in a month as her family does in a year. Eventually the kids of the SID sufferer begin to notice the income difference between their family and their classmates' families. It happens around birthday time. The other kids have birthdays at Wrigley Field (they've bought out a section) or at FAO Schwarz (they've rented out the whole store for a Sunday morning). The SID kid has his party in his living room.

When the intellectual's oldest daughter comes home for Christmas break, she'll be invited to go hang out with her Stanford classmate who lives up in Winnetka. She'll notice that when she visits the home of her friend, everything is uncluttered. The house is filled with vast expanses of table space and counter space and floor space, all of it luxuriously spare. Spareness is also the rule at work. People in that branch of the educated class have big offices with wood surfaces. And they have secretaries to route the paper flow, and their secretaries have secretaries to file things away, so there is nothing left stacked up to cover the wide-open expanse of the predator's desk. The brief-cases of the financial services Bobos are wafer thin, with barely enough space to squeeze in a legal pad, because their lives are so totally in control they don't have to schlepp things from place to place. They travel luggage-free to London because, after all, they've got another wardrobe at their flat there.

The life of the SID sufferer, by contrast, is cluttered. She's got a small desk tucked upstairs in the social science building. And there are papers everywhere: manuscripts, memos, journals, magazine clippings. And at home the SID sufferer has jars and coffeemakers jamming the available counterspace, and pots hanging loosely from a rack on the wall. The SID sufferer has books all around the living room, most dating back to graduate school days (*The Marx-Engels Reader,* for example), and there are frayed copies of the *New York Review of Books* lying on the nightstand.

When an intellectual with a household income of $180,000 a year enters a room filled with moneyed types making $1.75 million a year, a few social rules will be observed. First, everyone will act as if money does not exist. Everyone, including the intellectual who can't pay her Visa bill in full, will pretend it is possible to jet off to Paris for a weekend and the only barrier is finding the time. Everyone will praise the Marais district, and it will not be mentioned that the financial analyst has an apartment in the Marais and the intellectual spends her rare vacations at one-star hotels. The intellectual will notice that the financial analysts spend a lot of time talking about their vacations, whereas all the intellectual wants to talk about is work.

When an intellectual enters a room filled with financial predators, there will be a nagging doubt in the back of her mind: do they really like me, or am I just another form of servant, one who provides amusement or publicity instead of making the beds? The sad fact is that the moneyed analysts tend not to think this way. The millionaires are plagued by the fear that while they have achieved success, they have not achieved significance. They suffer from a reverse SID—their income is higher than their status. They have Income-Status Disequilibrium (ISD). After all, they have not done much with their lives that would allow them to explore their artistic side or to achieve intellectual immortality or even to be dazzling in conversation. The millionaires notice that they have to pay for all the foundation dinners they attend while the intellectuals are thought to be important enough to get in for free. The rich are the johns of the think tank circuit.

Furthermore, the intellectuals are, in effect, paid to be interesting. They are paid to sit around all day reading things that they can then redirect into provocative prose and conversation (it's astonishing that so many do this job so badly). And the rich, meanwhile, are practically paid to be dull; they are given huge salaries to work on arcane deals that would make their dinner companions' minds go numb if they had to hear about them. Finally, the rich feel vulnerable because, despite their vast resources, they still rely on the publicity machine for their good reputations, which these professional dinner party ironists control.

Therefore, many millionaires think it would be neat to be a writer whose opinions are queried on *The News-Hour with Jim Lehrer*. Look at Mortimer Zuckerman, who owns the *New York Daily News, U.S. News and World Report,* and goodly chunks of Manhattan and Washington. He'll drive out to New Jersey to do a taping for the cable channel CNBC. It's not enough to have more money than some countries. Zuckerman wants to be a public intellectual.

The intellectuals react in diverse ways to Status-Income Disequilibrium. Some try to pass for members of the money wing of the educated class. They buy those blue shirts with white collars. They polish their shoes daily. The women in this category save up enough money to buy a Ralph Lauren or Donna Karan suit. And if they are in, say, media, publishing, or the foundation world, they use their expense account to the max. Like an asthma sufferer taking the cure at an Arizona resort, a SID sufferer can find temporary relief when traveling on business. She can stay at the Ritz-Carlton for $370 a night, with phones and televisions in every room. Hotel dry cleaning will be as nothing.

But then the business trip ends and it is back to earth. Which explains why other members of the intelligentsia go the other way and aggressively demonstrate that they still proudly adhere to their bohemian roots. You'll see them wearing Timberland boots with their suits, a signal that they are still rebelling against the money culture.

Their taste in ties and socks will tend toward the ironic; you might see one wearing a tie adorned with the logo of a local sanitation department, a garbage truck driving over a rainbow.

At home this sort of SID sufferer will luxuriate in his poverty. He will congratulate himself for the fact that he lives in an integrated neighborhood, though he couldn't afford the pearly white neighborhoods in such places as Winnetka or Grosse Pointe or Park Avenue. Most of all, he will congratulate himself on choosing a profession that doesn't offer the big financial rewards, for not devoting his life to money grubbing. He does not mention to himself that, in fact, he lacks the quantitative skills it takes to be, say, an investment banker and that he is unable to focus on things that bore him, the way lawyers can. There never was any great opportunity to go into a more lucrative field, so there was never any real moment of deliberate sacrifice.

The Death and Rise of the Intellectual

SID is painful for those who suffer from it, but in reality SID is like the coccyx. Just as the coccyx is thought to be an evolutionary remnant from when our primate ancestors had tails, SID is a remnant of the class war between the bourgeoisie and the bohemian. For centuries the bourgeois businessman and the bohemian intellectual glowered at each other from a distance and across barricades. But now their great class war has been reduced to dinner party friction. Now they mingle; they do not assassinate. Their great cultural conflict has been reduced to slight status jockeying as each tries to justify his own form of career success.

So the social role of the intellectual really has been transformed. Once the aloof member of a secular priesthood, she is now an anxious but basically comfortable member of a large class of people who are interested in ideas. Once the radical who sought to challenge the rule of mammon, she is now the worldly player, building a reputation and climbing the ladder of success. Say farewell to the self-absorbed intellectual quarrels and to all those alienated garret lifestyles; today intellectuals know their Château Margaux from their Merlot.

So what have we gained and lost? On one level it is hard not to admire the intellectual life of the fifties—Hannah Arendt and Reinhold Niebuhr, the *Partisan Review* crowd, poets and literary critics like Robert Penn Warren, sociologists like David Riesman. These were people who lived for ideas, words, and argument. They possessed minds that could soar up to rarefied heights, tossing off quotations from Hegel and Aristotle, Schiller and Goethe. This was the age before television punditry, before op-ed pieces, before jet-setting conference tours. The intellectual world seemed smaller but more intense and more vital.

And yet. And yet. There is something to be said for today's intellectual world as well, and I at least would not want to go back. Start with this question: how do we learn? Is wisdom best attained by sitting in a book-stuffed studio on Riverside Drive, reading Freud and the existentialists, engaging in intense debates with an insular crowd, most of whom live within a few square miles? Or is it gained through broader experience with the world, by putting one foot in the river of mainstream life and then by reflecting on what you found there? Is it gained by detaching oneself and judging the world from some rarefied height, or is it gained by involving oneself in the scramble and feeling the contours of reality immediately, then trying to describe what one has sensed? It's not only that modern writers have fatter wallets than the old kind. We have different epistemologies.

We are more skeptical of pure reason, of high-flown

abstractions and towering generalizations. We are more likely to follow in the footsteps of Jane Jacobs, who may not have been familiar with Heidegger, who may not have been able to match the intellectual acrobatics of the *Partisan Review* crowd, but was intimately familiar with the daily life around her. In the last chapter I described metis, the practical sort of wisdom that can be gained by doing and sensing more than by theorizing. We Bobo types prize metis more than abstract reasoning, and we are right to do so. We are right to be involved in the world, to climb and strive and experience the dumb superficialities of everyday life, just like everybody else. Our intellectuals understand the world better if they experience the same sorts of pressures that confront most people, the tensions between ambition and virtue, the distinctions between pleasant but shallow status and real accomplishment. Detaching oneself from commercial culture means cutting oneself off from the main activity of American life. That makes it much harder to grasp what is really going on. But today's intellectual, if she is honest about her own motives and compromises, can reach a more accurate sense of the state of the country and the world. Her declarations may not be as sweeping or as grand as the declarations that are made by a self-exiled intellectual who hurls thunderbolts down from the clifftops, but she will know the valley paths better, and her descriptions will be more true and her ideas more useful.

Look back again at the books of the 1950s. The years between 1955 and 1965 constitute a golden age of nonfiction. I've cited many books from that period already in this one, and I've left off some of the most influential, like Betty Friedan's *The Feminine Mystique* and Rachel Carson's *Silent Spring*. And with all due respect to people like Niebuhr and Arendt, many of the best and most influential books were written by people who would not have been considered intellectuals in that day: Jane Jacobs,

William Whyte, Betty Friedan, Rachel Carson, even Digby Baltzell. In some ways these writers and journalists had more in common with today's pundits and worldly commentators than with the intellectual mode Edward Shils defined. These people serve as better models for us today than the highbrows who self-consciously detached themselves into the realm of high culture, capital-letter Ideas, and bohemian alienation.

And they achieved one final thing. They gained an audience. The *Partisan Review* crowd was brilliant, but the journal's circulation was minuscule. Today there are more and more outlets to bring ideas to the millions, through public broadcasting, through the profusion of magazines, through the Internet. Surely writers and thinkers are right to take advantage of the new media to get ideas around, even if it means that one does have to pay more attention to the demands of different formats and learn how to smile when the TV camera flits on.

5

Pleasure

IF YOU'D like to be tortured and whipped with dignity and humiliated with respect, you really ought to check out the Internet newsletter of the Arizona Power Exchange, an S&M group headquartered in Phoenix. The organization offers a full array of services to what is now genteelly known as the leather community. For example, on a recent August 3, according to the summer newsletter, there was a discussion and humiliation session. On August 6 at 7 P.M., there was a workshop on caning. The next night the Bondage Sadomasochism Personal Growth and Support Group met with Master Lawrence, while on August 10, Carla helped lead a discussion on high heel and foot worship. A week later a visiting lecturer came to discuss "blood sports." All of these meetings were to be conducted with the sort of mature high-mindedness embodied in the organization's mission statement: "Treating the S&M, B&D and D&S experience with acceptance, car-

ing, dignity and respect." Dignity and respect are important when you're tied up on the ground worshiping
someone's boot.

The organization, which goes by the acronym APEX,
has a seven-member board of directors and a long list of
officers and administrators. There's a recording secretary,
a treasurer, an archivist, an orientation officer, a logistics
officer, and a Web page staff to design its Internet site,
which is more demure than the one that might be operated
by your average Rotary Club. APEX sponsors charity
drives. There's a special support group for submissives
who are too shy to vocalize the sort of submission they
like. There's a seminar on S&M and the law. There are 12-
step meetings for sadists and masochists recovering from
substance abuse. Finally, there are outreach efforts to
build coalitions with other bondage and domination
groups nationwide.

When you read through the descriptions of the APEX
workshops, you are struck by how much attention is devoted to catering these affairs. Topics like nipple piercing
and nude gagging are supposed to evoke images of de-
bauched de Sades, but in this crowd paddling and punish-
ing are made to sound more akin to bird watching or wine
tasting. You imagine a group of off-duty high school guidance counselors and other responsible flossers standing
around in nothing but a leather girdle and their orthotics,
discussing the merits and demerits of foreign versus domestic penile clamps. It's all so temperate and responsible.
It's so bourgeois.

Sex, especially adventurous sex, used to be the great
transgressive act. Dissolute aristocrats would gather their
whips and manacles and repair to the palace attic. Peasants would slobber their way through lewd drunken
orgies. Bohemians would throw off the fetters of respectability and explore the joys of Free Love.

But today that is obsolete. And it's not only organizations like APEX that try to gentrify norm-challenging Eros to make it responsible and edifying. There is now a thriving industry that caters to people who want to practice moral sex. There are shelves and shelves of Barnes & Noble erotica that owe more to the Iowa Writers' Workshop than to *Hustler* magazine. There are high-minded sex journals and catalogues, such as Good Vibrations, *Sex Life,* and the Xandria Collection, that advertise in the back of upscale magazines like *Harper's* and the *Atlantic Monthly.* (These high-minded sex journals are easy to distinguish because, to avoid committing the sin of lookism, they prominently feature ugly people having sex; to emphasize that sex is a life-long endeavor, they spend so much time on elderly sex you can practically hear the banging of the medical ID bracelets.) There are so many academic theoreticians writing about sexual transgressions that orgies must come to resemble an Apache dance at tourist season, done less for the joy of it than to please the squads of sociology professors who have flown in to quote Derrida.

In short, over the past few years the educated class has domesticated lust by enshrouding it in high-mindedness. The Bobos have taken sex, which for centuries has been thought to be arousing or sinful or possibly dangerous, and they have made it socially constructive.

Bobos turn out to be the parsons of the pubic region. Nearly gone are 1960s traces of Dionysian wantonness. Instead, "Play Safe" and "Play Responsibly" are the slogans that are repeated again and again in sophisticated sex literature. The practitioners talk so much about how healthy it all is that you'd think they were doing jumping jacks. To keep everything responsible and under control, weird activities are codified in rules and etiquette. Judging by the sexual encounter groups that describe their activities in newsletters, the rules at a group sex community meeting—when it is necessary to sign a legal waiver, when to wear latex gloves, when it is OK to smoke—are strictly adhered to. Theirs may not be the same as the etiquette that governed behavior in a 19th-century parlor, but in their relentless demands on self-control, they weirdly mimic those sorts of social codes.

Today's Marquis de Sades don't seem to want to create an immoral underground society. They're not trying to subvert normalcy. They're trying to join it. They want to win mainstream acceptance and so gain a respectable place in the middle-class world. "We affirm that loving more than one can be a natural expression of health, express joy and intimacy. This is a lovestyle we call responsible non-monogamy," reads the mission statement of *Loving More* magazine, the journal of polyamory. Every "affirmation group" (as they are now called) seeks a place in the land of the up-and-up: the bestiality community, the necrophiliacs, the cigar fetishists, the lovers of orthodontia, the piercists, the crush lovers (people who enjoy watching women smash things), and the macrophiliacs (people who fantasize about women who destroy buildings with their breasts).

In odd ways, these are moralistic people. Sex is now frequently seen as a way to achieve deeper moral understandings. The former monk Thomas Moore, who wrote *Care of the Soul,* followed it up with *The Soul of Sex,* just one of hundreds of the moral sex books that have been published over the past few years. Others can go to the Church of Tantra, which offers such courses as "Tantric Sex: The Spiritual Path to Ecstasy." Others use their sexual lives to advance social change. To avoid ethnocentrism, the orgies in the highbrow sex journals tend to be as diverse as the casts of kids on PBS children's shows: one Asian, one Hispanic, one African American, one Caucasian, and one Native American. I imagine that if there were a room full of people rubbing each other's ex-

crement over each other and somebody confessed he
didn't recycle, he'd be immediately expelled from the
group and told never to come back. It's a weird version of
propriety, but it's propriety nonetheless.

But Bobos do more than merely moralize what
was once subversive. They are meritocrats through and
through. So they don't just enjoy orgasms; they *achieve*
orgasm. Sex in this literature is like college; it's described
as a continual regimen of self-improvement and self-
expansion. It's amazing how many sex workshops, seminars, institutes, and academies there are out there to cater
to people who want to learn more about their bodies.
What's available at the Human Awareness Institute? The
Web site tells you: "Examine and shed limiting notions
about love, intimacy and sexuality. Relate and communicate more effectively with others. Significantly improve
your relationship with yourself. Be more loving, intimate
and fully self-expressive with others. Make exciting and
empowering choices in your life and relationships." Lady
Chatterley's lover becomes Lady Chatterley's empower-
ment counselor.

These practitioners work extraordinarily hard to improve their skills and master new techniques. It's not for
the Bobos to be content with the sort of normal practices
of the bedroom onanist. They have to turn it into graduate
school. JoAnn Loulan, the author of *Lesbian Passion:
Loving Ourselves and Each Other,* offers the following
exercises: "Look at your genitals every day in the mirror.
. . . Draw a picture of your genitals. . . . Write a letter to
your genitals. . . . Spend an hour of uninterrupted sensual
time with yourself. . . . Look at yourself in the mirror for
an hour. Talk with all parts of your body. . . . Spend an
hour touching your genitals without the purpose of having
an orgasm. . . . Masturbate for an hour." Even just reading about this curriculum is enough to give you an acute
case of carpal tunnel syndrome.

Everything in the Bobo life is purposeful. The most animalistic activities are now enshrouded with guidebooks, how-to videos, and magazine articles written by people with advanced degrees. Everything gets talked about and shared. Even masturbation can be measured and evaluated by the standards of connoisseurship. And it's not only the techniques of sex that can be continually worked on and improved; it is the perceptions and knowledge that come from sex that can be deepened and refined. Sex can't be just a fun thing between the sheets. It's also got to be a profound thing between your ears. It's got to be safe, responsible, and socially constructive. Hedonism sure has changed.

The Pleasure Wars

This isn't how the sexual revolution was supposed to end up. After all, it had its roots in the romantic movement which was supposed to be a rebellion against the repressed attitudes of the bourgeoisie. Historian Peter Gay has called them the "pleasure wars," the long-running disputes that had the bohemian sensualists flouting middle-class conventions. The bohemians were the ones jeering at plodding and unerotic Charles Bovary. They were the ones championing Anaïs Nin's diaries and the shocking novels of Henry Miller. They were crusading against the censorship of sexually explicit art and literature.

The counterculture was the place where life was free, where pleasure was available. In his evocative memoir of underground life, *Down and In*, Ronald Sukenick quotes *Village Voice* columnist Howard Smith: "I came to the Village because sex was very uptight in the fifties. I wanted to fuck. I wanted women who would talk to me. I wanted women who didn't wear padded wired bras with a slip over it and a sweater. . . . At Pandora's Box I used to go to that coffee shop all the time and this waitress would lean over and say, 'Anything else I can get you?' and she wore a low-cut peasant blouse and no bra and I would almost fall out of my chair."

In the sixties the hippies ridiculed the "blue meanies," the pleasure-robbing villains in *Yellow Submarine*. Students celebrated polymorphous perversity and condemned repressive desublimation, one of Marcuse's terms that seemed to have something to do with being uptight. "The more I make revolution, the more I make love," the radicals exclaimed. In the 1960s and '70s, nudity was deemed revolutionary and rock stars really seemed radical when they sang anthems to sex, drugs, and rock and roll. They made it seem as if raucous hedonism and revolution were the same thing, as perhaps they were. And there was a romantic rationale behind all this fast living: *Le dérèglement de tous les sens*. Deregulate the senses. Great truths come from great sensations. The best live passionately and for the moment. The brave ones live free and fast and penetrate into the profound realms.

By the 1970s it seemed obvious who was going to win the pleasure wars. Swinging, or at least talk about swinging, was hip. Gay Talese's *Thy Neighbor's Wife* was written during those years, chronicling the swingers who seemed to spend large amounts of time sitting naked in groups discovering new erogenous zones. Revered novelists like John Updike and Philip Roth described acts underground pornographers wouldn't have touched two decades before. *The Joy of Sex* was a massive bestseller. New York featured at least five nudie musicals; at the beginning of their runs they were actually considered kind of cool. Erica Jong made herself famous by describing the zipless fuck. Movies in that era celebrated drug use. "A Motion Picture for the Stoned Age" is how a film called *Black and White* promoted itself. The *New York Times* ran pages of advertisements for porn movies and strip bars, so that there would be ads for *Deep Throat* right next to those for *The Sound of Music,* a sign that people no longer knew where to draw the line between decency and indecency or whether there should be a line at all.

The forces of emancipation recorded triumph after triumph. In some places children were encouraged to explore their sexuality as a means of self-discovery. A New Jersey school curriculum advised, "Grown-ups sometimes forget to tell children that touching can give people pleasure, especially when someone you love touches you. And you can give yourself pleasure, and that's okay." Old taboos were falling. Old family structures began to seem passé. Old systems of etiquette seemed positively Neanderthal. Reticence seemed like hypocrisy. Sexual freedom, at least in the realm of public discourse, was on the march.

Indeed, some social critics believe the sexual revolution continues unabated to this day. In 1995 George Gilder wrote, "Bohemian values have come to prevail over bourgeois virtue in sexual morals and family roles, arts and letters, bureaucracies and universities, popular culture and public life. As a result, culture and family life are widely in chaos, cities seethe with venereal plagues, schools and colleges fall to obscurantism and propaganda, the courts are a carnival of pettifoggery." In 1996 Robert Bork's bestseller, *Slouching Towards Gomorrah,* argued that the forces of the sixties have spread cultural rot across mainstream America. In 1999 William Bennett argued, "Our culture celebrates self-gratification, the crossing of all moral barriers, and now the breaking of all social taboos."

But if you look around upscale America, it's not all chaos and amoralism, even among the sexual avant-gardists at the Arizona Power Exchange. What they are doing is weird and may be disgusting, but it has its own set of disciplines. And when you get to the educated-class mainstream, it's hard to find signs of rampant hedonism or outright decadence. Smoking is down. Drinking is down. Divorce rates are down. Rock stars now pose more as moralistic storytellers—in the tradition of fifties folk singers—than as hedonistic rebels.

Reregulating the Senses

It's no longer accurate to say that the forces of Anything Goes are sweeping through American culture (if indeed they ever were). Instead, the picture is far more complex and confusing. In humor, for example, we have become tolerant of sexual jokes over the past 30 years but extremely intolerant of ethnic jokes. We have become far more relaxed about things like posture and proper attire but far more restrictive about anger, spitting, and smoking. We have become more tolerant about frank sexual talk in public but more censorious about lewd banter or any talk that could be interpreted as harassment. We have these high-toned sex journals in the finest bookstores, but old-fashioned Harold Robbins–style bonkbusters are déclassé. Universities tolerate tattoos and piercing that would have seemed outrageous in the early 1950s, but they crack down on fraternity drinking rituals that would have seemed unexceptional. We feel we are less strict with our children, but in fact we intervene in their lives far more than did parents in the 1950s. In *Tom Sawyer,* for example, Aunt Polly may have tried to civilize Tom with beatings and strict table etiquette, but she also allowed him hours of unsupervised time to wander and adventure. Today we don't adhere to that etiquette, but we don't allow much wandering, either. Instead, we shepherd kids from one adult-organized activity to another.

In short, moral standards don't necessarily rise and fall at once, in great onslaughts of virtue or vice. The reality is more like mixed trading in the stock market, with standards rising in one area and falling in the next, making it very hard to determine whether in the aggregate we are tightening or loosening. In 1999 Carnegie-Mellon historian Peter N. Stearns published a book called *Battleground of Desire: The Struggle for Self-Control in Modern America,* in which he traced different self-control regimes that prevailed in America during the 20th century. Stearns concluded that while we certainly practice a different control regime than, say, Victorian-era Americans, it is not immediately clear that on balance we are more permissive or licentious. Rather, our taboos and restrictions "are different, involving a distinctive set of tolerances and restrictions and in some ways, demanding greater vigilance."

The truth is that Bobos have constructed new social codes that characteristically synthesize bourgeois self-control and bohemian emancipation. Now we have a new set of standards to distinguish permissible pleasures from impermissible ones. We have new social codes to regulate the senses.

Useful Pleasures

To get a firsthand glimpse of these new codes, go down to your local park in the summertime. You'll see women jogging or running in sports bras and skin-tight spandex pants. Imagine if the Puritans could get a load of this! Women running around in their underwear in public. They'd pull out the tracts on Sodom and Gomorrah. Even a cosmopolitan historian such as Edward Gibbon would take a first glance at these women and begin speculating about the decline of empires. But look at the bra joggers more closely. It's not wanton hedonism you see on their faces. They're not exposing themselves for the sake of exhibitionism. Any erotic effect of their near nudity is counteracted by their expressions of grim determination. They are working out. They are working. They're building their muscles. They're setting goals and striving to achieve them. You never see them smile. On the contrary, some of them seem to be suffering. These near-naked young women are self-discipline personified—no pain, no gain—and the reason they are practically naked, they will tell you, is that this sort of clothing is most practical, most useful for strenuous exercise. What we see at the park is near nudity, but somehow it's nudity in the service of achievement. Dionysius, the god of abandon, has been reconciled with Prometheus, the god of work.

The Bobos take a utilitarian view of pleasure. Any sensual pleasure that can be edifying or life-enhancing is celebrated. On the other hand, any pleasure that is counterproductive or dangerous is judged harshly. So exercise is celebrated, but smoking is now considered a worse sin than at least 5 of the 10 commandments. Coffee becomes the beverage of the age because it stimulates mental acuity, while booze is out of favor because it dulls the judgment. You can go to the beach near naked in a skimpy bathing suit and that is normal, but if you neglect to put on sun block to protect against skin cancer, people are astonished. It is admirable to eat healthy, but we use the word *guilt* more often in connection with unhealthy foods—high fat, high sodium, or high calorie—than in any other context. Contemplative pleasures like taking a long bath are admired, but dangerous pleasures like speeding on a motorcycle are disdained, and driving without a seatbelt is positively immoral. Sports that are aerobic, like cross-country skiing and Rollerblading, thrive, while sports that do little to improve cardiovascular health, like pool, bowling, and Ping-Pong, are low class. Even an afternoon spent playing with the kids is thought to be "a good thing" because we are invariably helping the little ones improve some set of skills (watch the Bobo parents taking part in their kids' "play") or at least we are building better relationships or self-esteem ("Good job! Good for you!").

We Bobos have taken the bourgeois imperative to strive and succeed, and we have married it to the bohemian impulse to experience new sensations. The result is a set of social regulations constructed to encourage pleasures that are physically, spiritually, and intellectually useful while stigmatizing ones that are useless or harmful. In this way the Protestant Work Ethic has been replaced by the Bobo Play Ethic, which is equally demanding. Everything we do must serve the Life Mission, which is cultivation, progress, and self-improvement.

It's perfectly fitting that the two leisure-time institutions that have thrived during the Bobo age are health clubs and museums. Both places offer sensual satisfactions in uplifting settings. At health clubs you can enjoy the pleasure of an ennobling muscle burn—you get off the Stairmaster, exhausted and sweaty after 35 minutes of pure exertion, and admire your virtuous self in the floor-to-ceiling mirrors. Meanwhile, at museums you can luxuriate in a sensual cornucopia, enjoying the colors and forms of the paint and materials, while being edified by informative Acoustiguides, scholarly texts on the walls, and the wonderful bookshop downstairs. Health clubs and museums have become the chapels and cathedrals of our age, the former serving to improve the body, the latter the mind.

It's also fitting that we Bobos have taken the ultimate symbol of Dionysian release, the party, and merged it with work. A couple of years ago in the *New Yorker,* James Atlas published an essay called "The Fall of Fun," which pretty accurately captured the transformation of the literary party scene and shed light on educated-class parties as a whole.

Next to the writers, poets and essayists of earlier

decades, Atlas argued, today's creative types are a pretty tame bunch. He recalled that the literary giants he admired during his student days at Harvard drank and caroused with abandon. "My gurus were the famously hard-drinking literati of an earlier epoch: a shaky hung-over Robert Lowell chain-smoking mentholated Trues at a seminar table in the Quincy House basement; a drunken Norman Mailer brandishing a bottle of whiskey and baiting the crows in Sanders Theatre; Allen Ginsberg toking up at a Signet Society dinner and chanting his poems to the hypnotic accompaniment of a harmonium. Postwar poetry was a hymn of excess."

These were artists living the bohemian way. Atlas described the booze-filled gatherings of the old literati, the smoky parties, the embarrassing scenes, the bitter feuds, and the ensuing divorces. Even the diaries of austere Edmund Wilson are filled with adultery and lewd drunkenness; Edmund found himself one day doing a threesome on a couch. Many of these people, in fact, caroused themselves to an early grave. Delmore Schwartz died at fifty-two; John Berryman killed himself at fifty-seven; Shirley Jackson died at forty-five; Robert Lowell died at sixty, relatively old for his group.

But nowadays people who drink and carouse that way are likely to be greeted with medical diagnoses—alcoholism, drug addiction, depression. Even in what used to be the bohemian quarters, as James Atlas eloquently testifies, the days of booze and brawling are over. Now parties tend to be work parties; a glass or two of white wine, a little networking with editors and agents, and then it's home to the kids. Almost nobody drinks at lunch anymore. People don't gather around kitchen tables staying up nights imbibing and talking. Everybody is healthier, more orderly, and more success oriented.

The same pattern has been acted out in other circles. Journalists used to be smoking, drinking vulgarians. Now, as the older reporters never stop reminding us, the campaign buses are filled with mild college grads sipping bottled water. Nobody gets drunk at journalist parties, and anybody who did would be regarded as a loser. Academic social life, the articles in the *Chronicle of Higher Education* tell us, is drier and tamer than it was two decades ago. Even Hollywood, which should be the epicenter of hedonism, is overrun by health consciousness, career consciousness, and (relative) moderation. More Bobos pass out business cards at parties than pass out under the table.

When it comes to alcohol consumption more generally, we are probably living through the most abstemious era since Prohibition, maybe in American history. In our age all the old terms are fading away—sours, slings, highballs, fizzes, nightcaps—despite a little self-conscious nostalgia at the cigar and martini bars. On cable I recently stumbled across an old episode of *Match Game* '73. Six celebrities were asked to complete the phrase "half-_____," and the contestant had to guess how they had filled in the blank. He guessed "half-drunk." That was a good answer because four of the six celebrities chose either "half-drunk" or "half-crocked." Today if the same *Match Game* question were asked, the most common answer might be "half-and-half."

One of the reasons the old bohemians were so wild and free was that they were rebelling against square bourgeois mores. But once the bourgeoisie assimilated the liberated culture of the 1960s, there was not much left to rebel against. Once bohemian symbols were absorbed into the mainstream, they lost some of their countercultural panache. The novels of Henry Miller seemed cool when they offended middle-class librarians, but they don't seem so daring now. Nude performance art may have been a thrilling statement once, but it lost its cachet when it became titillation for the tourist trade. When drugs were discovered by disco kids from Queens and yuppies from Wall

Street in the seventies and eighties, naturally they seemed less like mind-expanding tools and more like grubby playthings. Living for pleasure no longer makes the same rebellious cultural statement it once did.

Moreover, playtime in the earlier decades seemed more like release. People were stuck in boring jobs, so wanted a little revelry at night. Creative types felt themselves stuck in a boring society, so wanted to up-end the rules. But for Bobos work is not boring. It's challenging and interesting. So maybe it's not surprising they should make play more like work. Bobos are reconcilers, after all, so maybe it is inevitable they would strive to blur their duties with their pleasures, making the former more enjoyable and the latter more tame.

Useful Vacations

You're sitting in an outdoor cafe in the Piazza della Serenissima in one of those stone Tuscan hill towns, and you've just finished 20 minutes of rapture while touring a gemlike little basilica far off the normal tourist paths. You've pulled a few iron tables together to accommodate the urbane couples you met inside, and as you sip drinks that back home would qualify as cough syrup, you begin trading vacation stories. Somebody mentions a recent journey to the Göreme Valley of central Turkey and the glories of the caves the Hittites carved into the volcanic mud-ash, when suddenly a gentleman wearing a shirt with an enormous number of pockets leans back and interjects, "Ah, yes. But the whole Cappadocia region has just been ruined by all the tourists."

After a few minutes someone else at the table relates some fascinating bits she learned from the tour guides while on an eco tour of southern Belize. "It really hasn't been the same since electrification," the man with all the pockets laments. You have come face to face with a travel snob. There are a certain number of sophisticated travelers who wear their past destinations like little merit badges. Their main joy in life comes from dropping whopping hints that everywhere you are just going they went to long ago when it still meant something. It's hard to know where such people get the time to go all these places, unless some evil philanthropist pays them to go around the world making other travelers feel inferior about their cultural repertoire. They are masters of the insufferable question. "Didn't the atabeg of Damascus stop there in 1139?" one of them will ask at the mention of a certain faraway oasis before peering around the table with a hopeful expression, as if everybody else were going to jump in to confirm that little bit of data. They seem to spend their evenings boning up on obscure ethnic groups: "The Mobabi tribe once fished there, I believe, until the Contutis pushed them further upriver." And needless to say, they merge with that other atrocious population segment, language snobs: "I suppose you can get by with a little Chinook?" They don't say, "I know" such-and-such a language. They'll say, "I *have* a little Portuguese" or "I have a few of the romance languages, of course," in that faux offhand manner that makes you want to stick the person's head in a vise and squeeze it until the eyes pop out.

Unfortunately, few people act on this noble impulse, even though they know that when such a person appears, the Vietnam syndrome is not far behind. This is the psychosis that causes people to steer all their conversations to a single destination: their life-altering trip to Vietnam.

The travel braggart begins slowly. Just a few sly hints about his vast cultural capital. Then as the conversation goes along, he gets a little more voluble. He is biding his time, sucking you in. There will be a ray of hope when someone else in the group starts talking about Mount Everest. Ah, he's been Tibetted, you'll think. Surely he can't be so smug around someone who's been to Tibet. But, of course, he was doing Tibet before *Into Thin Air*.

And then it begins. He's describing his journey up the Ho Chi Minh Trail or the rail trip from Hue on the crowded non-air-conditioned train. He starts describing all the odd glories of North Vietnam, the aroma of camphor, the flurry of bicycles. Suddenly you realize you are in a quagmire. There will be much suffering. There is no way now to withdraw from the conversation with honor.

"I never knew that feeding geese could be such a spiritual experience," he will be saying while passing around photos of himself standing with a group of locals amidst the rice paddies near My Lai (he's the one in the sunglasses). He'll be describing a former VC whose oxcart he rode on up the Red River Valley. In his stories he always depicts himself as a masterful Dr. Livingstone, but you know that when he walked into a village, the locals saw him as this big flapping wallet with dollar bills flying out. If this person were suddenly found dead with a dozen butter knives up his nose, it would be like an Agatha Christie novel; everyone would have a motive.

I suspect that what keeps us from finishing off the travel braggart is that none of us is pure. All of us in the educated class are travel snobs to some degree. It's just that while we are snobs toward the hordes of fat tourists who pile out of vast buses and into Notre Dame, he is snobbish toward us. He's just a bit higher on the ladder of sophisticated travel.

The code of utilitarian pleasure means we have to evaluate our vacation time by what we accomplished— what did we learn, what spiritual or emotional breakthroughs were achieved, what new sensations were experienced? And the only way we can award ourselves points is by seeking out the unfamiliar sights, cultivating above-average pleasures. Therefore, Bobos go to incredible lengths to distinguish themselves from passive, nonindustrious tourists who pile in and out of tour buses at the old warhorse sights. Since the tourists carry cameras, Bobo travelers are embarrassed to. Since tourists sit around the most famous squares, Bobo travelers spend enormous amounts of time at obscure ones watching non-tourist-oriented pastimes, which usually involve a bunch of old men rolling metal balls.

Since tourists try to move quickly from sight to sight, the hard-working traveler selects the slowest possible means of transportation. Bobo travelers tour the Loire Valley by barge, looking down on the packs who zip through in cars. They cruise through New Zealand by bike, dismissive of those who take the train. They paddle through Costa Rica on a raft, feeling superior to those who jet past on airplanes. If tourists seem to be flocking to one sight, Bobos will make sure they are at another. "While most tourists in Tanzania go to Serengeti National Park to see the wildlife, the Selous Game Reserve is bigger and less disturbed," writes *Natural History* magazine editor Bruce Stuts in fine cultivated-traveler mode. It doesn't even matter if the Selous Game Reserve has less to see than the Serengeti. The pleasure the Bobo traveler derives from doing the more industrious thing more than compensates.

Lewis and Clark didn't return from their trip and say, "Well, we didn't find the Northwest Passage, but we did find ourselves." But that is the spirit of Bobo travel. Our travel dollars are investments in our own human capital. We don't just want to see famous sights; we want to pierce into other cultures. We want to try on other lives.

But not just any other lives. If you observe Bobo travel patterns and travel literature, you will detect a distinct set of preferences. The Bobo, as always, is looking for stillness, for a place where people set down roots and repeat the simple rituals. In other words, Bobo travelers are generally looking to get away from their affluent, ascending selves into a spiritually superior world, a world that hasn't been influenced much by the global meritocracy. Bobos tend to relish People Who Really Know How to Live—people who make folk crafts, tell folk tales, do folk dances, listen to folk music—the whole indigenous people/noble savage/tranquil craftsman repertoire.

Therefore, Bobos are suckers for darkly garbed peasants, aged farmers, hardy fishermen, remote craftsmen, weather-beaten pensioners, heavyset regional cooks—anybody who is likely to have never possessed or heard of frequent flier miles. So the Bobos flock to or read about the various folk locales where such "simple" people live in abundance—the hills of Provence, Tuscany, Greece, or the hamlets of the Andes or Nepal. These are places where the natives don't have credit card debts and relatively few people wear Michael Jordan T-shirts. Lives therefore seem connected to ancient patterns and age-old wisdom. Next to us, these natives seem serene. They are poorer people whose lives seem richer than our own.

The small things—an olive grove or a small chapel—take on greater meaning to a Bobo on vacation. Ideally, Bobo travelers want to spend a part of each day just savoring. They'll idle away at a trattoria so far removed from the crush of events that the natives don't even feel compelled to have an opinion about Bill Gates. They will swoon over some creamy polenta or a tangy turtle soup and even educate their palate with some dish that prominently features bone marrow. They will top off their coffee cup with cream squeezed straight from the cow and enjoy the sturdy obesity of the peasant woman in the kitchen, the picturesque paint peeling off the walls, the smiles of the other diners who seem to be welcoming them into their culture.

The pace of life is so delicious in such places. But the lease on the vacation rental only goes for two weeks, so Bobo travelers had better do their spiritual development

quickly. Most Bobos come up with a few serendipity techniques that will allow them access to a few moments of
authentic peasant living. Hovering on the edges of local
weddings often works. Exaggerating their genealogical
connection to the place while conversing with the locals is
another winning tactic: "Actually my grandmother's second husband came from Portugal." If done correctly, these
techniques can allow the Bobo pilgrim to have 6 unforget-
table moments a morning, 2 rapturous experiences over
lunch, 1.5 profound insights in the afternoon (on average), and .667 life-altering epiphanies after each sunset.

Enriching Misery

At the tippy top of the leisure status system are those
vacations that involve endless amounts of agony and pain.
These are vacations that take you hiking on a forced
march across some glacier or trekking through arid
deserts along the path that Alexander the Great's soldiers
were induced to follow only by threat of death. Or sitting
in some bug-infested rainforest in search of environmental
awareness. Such trips are not fun, but the educated-class
trekkers are not looking for fun. They want to spend their
precious weeks off torturing themselves in ways that will
be intellectually and spiritually enhancing. So travel companies have scouted out these high-status, low-amenity
destinations around the globe. These are the sort of adventure vacations and eco tours that now thrive amongst the
educated class.

For past generations naturalism has meant a renunciation of ambition and social mobility. But Bobo naturalists bring their ambition with them. They don't just sit in
the forest; they trek up a mountain, wade through a rainforest, climb an icy rock, bike up to the Continental Divide. If there's an easy way up the mountain, they'll take

the tougher one. If there's a perfectly good train to some-place, they'll ride a bike on awful roads. They turn nature into an achievement course, a series of ordeals and obsta-cles they can conquer. They go into nature to behave un-naturally. In nature animals flee cold and seek warmth and comfort. But Bobo naturalists flee comfort and seek cold and deprivation. They do it to feel more alive and because their life is a series of aptitude tests, and so an adventure vacation becomes one too.

Corporate executives used to avoid talking about their war experiences. But today's educated executives thrill and then eventually bore you with their high-altitude conquests. A quarter of them seem either to be just back from one of those instant-glacier expeditions or to be deep in the midst of training for one. You'll be minding your own business over the salad at some dinner party when suddenly you will hear the phrases "base camp" and "white-out" wafting ominously across the table. It was all uphill for the one who is speaking, but you know the af-fair will be all downhill for you. "It wasn't just physically demanding. It was mentally demanding," the arduous va-cationer will tell his or her audience of slightly soft dinner companions, who—pathetically—aren't in the habit of going on vacations that require months of training. The tale, which will go on longer than it took Peary to reach the Pole, will be full of accounts of native guides (reposi-tories of native wisdom), discarded gear ("Things were desperate, we had to jettison the three-ounce espresso maker"), frostbitten toes (there is always some other fel-low on the trip who lost a few), and miserable days spent cooped up in tents while the wind whipped by at some un-believable speed, reducing visibility to zero. You get the impression that every spot on earth over 10,000 feet above sea level is packed with magenta-clad millionaires luxuriating in their thin-air hardships.

In the midst of such soliloquies I used to wonder why

these North Face Folks didn't just take their two-week winter vacation and go to Minnesota to join a road crew. If they wanted brutal conditions, a tough challenge, and team camaraderie, at least in Minnesota they could have filled in a few potholes and had something to show for their misery. But, of course, the trekkers aren't lugging their carabiner belts halfway across the world for public service. They want the aesthetics. They want the full in-person IMAX experience. It's not enough to suffer; one must suffer for beauty. One must put oneself through terrible torment—and this can come either on a cold mountain top or in a malarial rainforest—in order to experience the spiritually uplifting magnificence of brutal nature. One must mutilate the body for environmental transcendence.

In that sense these trips represent a fantastically expensive way to renounce the flesh in order to purify the spirit. Instead of fasting or flogging yourself with chains—as past renunciation-of-the-flesh types did—you gather together ten or twenty or sixty thousand dollars, fly across the world to some uninhabitable spot, and torture yourself for the sake of divine transcendence. Those monks who built forbidding monasteries on the rocky outcroppings of Wales must have been seeking the same sort of brutal purity, though of course they lived in their outposts for years, whereas today's trekker can experience a dial-an-ordeal in a week or two and still be back at the corporate campus fresh for work on a Monday morning. But the impulse is the same. From the drug-addled hedonism of Woodstock we have arrived at the asceticism of the educated-class vacation trekker.

Serious Play

And it's not just the expedition types who exemplify this impulse. The rest of us try to affiliate ourselves with the ordeal lifestyle. We're the ones who wear those hiking boots that were constructed for climbing the Himalayas. We're the ones who go out on fall weekends in parkas that were built to withstand −40-degree temperatures. We're the ones who buy our clothing from catalogues like Lands' End, which feature pictures of hikers atop Mount Everest on the cover. I was out at the Microsoft headquarters in Redmond, Washington, recently, and everybody there was dressed for a glacier climb, with boots, rugged khaki pants, and carabiners around their belts with cell phones hanging down. It's like going into a nightclub where everybody is constantly shoving their endurance cleavage in your face.

Then I drove over to the store where these Microsofties buy this sort of gear, the 80,000-square-foot REI emporium in Seattle. It's a store that sells leisure stuff to people who spend their leisure hours strenuously, or at least would like to look like they do.

To get there, I drove my rented minivan to downtown Seattle and parked it amidst the muddied-up sport-utes in the REI garage. I walked past the postage-stamp forest the REI people have landscaped as a place for customers to test-ride their mountain bikes. After a trip up the slate-floored elevator, I was on a large front balcony with huge wooden benches. A plaque on each reassures us that the wood used for the bench was blown down in 1995; no trees were murdered in the making of this rest spot. Up above there are clocks that tell the current time atop Mount Everest and the north face of Eiger in the Swiss Alps, in case you want to make a call there.

I walked through the front door and found myself a few steps in front of the ice-ax section. Out in front of me stretched a great expanse of ordeal-oriented merchandise, aisle upon aisle of snowshoes, crampons, kayaks, tents, and parkas, a daunting profusion of equipment options. I must admit I began feeling as if I were suffering from oxy-

gen deprivation. The goal of reaching the coffee shop upstairs at the store's summit seemed an absurdity. I was like
a character in a Jon Krakauer book. Dazed by this bewil-
dering environment, I knew only that I must somehow
summon the strength to trudge on.

To my right as I entered there was a museum of outdoor gear, so I could enjoy a little edifying foreplay before
I got down to the serious shopping. At the far end of the
museum was the climbing wall, at 65 feet the largest free-
standing climbing structure in the world.

It wasn't the salespeople that made my brain spin. I
knew they'd be products of Seattle's culture of hiking
shorts macho. They bounce around the store displaying
their enormous calves, looking like escapees from the
Norwegian Olympic Team. Nor was it my fellow customers that put me in this state. I was ready for squads of
super-fit software designers with glacier glasses hanging
from Croakies around their necks (because you can never
tell when a 600-foot mountain of ice might suddenly roll
into town, sending off hazardous glare).

The thing that got to me was the load of requirements. If you are going to spend any leisure time with
members of the educated class, you have to prove you are
serious about whatever it is you are doing. "Serious" is
the highest compliment Bobos use to describe their leisure
activities. You want to be a serious skier or a serious ten-
nis player or a serious walker or a serious cross-country
skier or even a serious skateboarder. People engaged in
any of these pastimes are constantly evaluating each other
to see who is serious and who is not. The most accomplished are so serious they never have any fun at all,
whereas if you went out onto some field or trail or court
and acted happy and goofy, you'd be regarded as someone
who is insulting the whole discipline.

Now to be a serious outdoorsperson, you have to
master the complex science of knowing how to equip

yourself, which basically requires joint degrees in chemistry and physics from MIT. For example, up beyond the ice-ax section there's a tank where customers try to test and fathom the differences between a dozen different water filters and purifiers. To traverse that spot, you have to distinguish between purifiers made from iodine resin and tri-iodine resin, glass fiber and pleated glass fiber, a ceramic microstrainer and a structured matrix microstrainer.

And it only gets worse. Every item in the store comes in a mind-boggling number of chemically engineered options that only experienced wilderness geeks could possibly understand. And from each product dangles a thick booklet so packed with high-tech jargon that it makes selecting a computer mainframe seem as simple as picking an apple off a tree. For backpacks, do you want a Sun Tooth Tech pack with 500 x 1000-denier Cordura or a Bitterroot Tech Pack with the 430-denier Hexstop trim? Do you want the semi-rigid 12-point Charlet Moser S-12 Crampon Laniers with the heel-clip in the rear or the Grivel Rambo with the rigid drop-forged points and the step-in bindings? Even something as basic as sandals comes in various high-tech versions, loaded with expedition-class straps and high-performance treads, in case you want to climb to Mount Pinatubo on your way to the Alanis Morissette concert.

I was dimly aware of some code of gear connoisseurship I should be paying attention to. For true nature techies, some things, like boots and sport utility vehicles, should be bought in forms as big as possible. Other things, like stoves and food packs, should be bought as small as possible. And other things, like tents and sleeping bags, should pack up small and open up big.

But the real reason for the REI store is upstairs on the mezzanine level, where the clothing department is. Because while not a lot of people actually go climb glaciers, there are millions and millions who want to dress as if they do. So most of the foot traffic at REI seems to be up on the mezzanine. I went up to the clothing department looking for a respite from all the high-tech mumbo jumbo of the gear section. There were indeed a few soothing racks of all-cotton shirts in muted colors. But I didn't have to walk far before I was assaulted by a blaze of cobalt blue glaring off a vast profusion of polyester. It soon became obvious that while in the seventies the polyester people were low-class disco denizens, now they are high-status strenuous nature types. Between me and the coffee shop at the far end of the mezzanine there remained a treacherous field of artificial-fiber parkas, paddle jackets, zip pants, stretch vests, anoraks, and ponchos. And each of them had ominous-sized booklets hanging down, stuffed with dissertation-level technical detail highlighting the state-of-the-artness of each item. I confess at that moment I lost the will to live. I was content just to sit down and let somebody find my lifeless body there amidst the Gore-Tex mountain bibs.

But an inner voice—which sounded like James Earl Jones's—urged me on, and pretty soon I was slogging through racks and racks of outdoor gear processed from the world's finest chemical labs: Cordura, Polartec, and all the "ex" fabrics—Royalex, spandex, Supplex, and Gore-Tex. There were $400 parkas that advertised their core vent kinetic systems and sleeves with universal radial hinges (I guess that means you can move your arms around). There were heavy-denier parka shells, power stretch tights with microfilaments, expedition-weight leggings, fleece, microfleece, and bipolar fleece (which must be for people on Prozac). My favorite was a titanium Omnitech parka with double-rip-stop nylon supplemented with ceramic particles and polyurethane-coat welded seams. I imagined myself sporting that titanium Omnitech thing and suddenly saying to myself, "Here I am in the middle of the forest and I'm wearing the Starship Enterprise."

Finally I had to puzzle my way through the "performance underwear" section, which was a baffling maze of Capilene and bifaced power-dry polyester, with a few Lycra spandex briefs strengthened with MTS2 polyester. And finally, just as I was about to turn into an underwear Luddite screaming out for a pair of honest white briefs, I spied the coffee shop not more than 50 yards away. I made my way toward the side of the store that has the art gallery, with majestic nature photos, and the lecture hall. I made it through the bookstore and past the park ranger station. And there, finally, was a smiling barista offering me a warm brew and a choice from among a multicultural panoply of sandwich wraps. I settled down amidst the Mission furniture they have strewn up there and finally began to realize how wholesome I was feeling.

I looked around the store and there was nothing but healthy people, educated-class naturalists who seemed to work out regularly, eat carefully, and party moderately. They were evidently well informed about their outdoor-gear options, judging by their boots, packs, and shopping bags. Moreover, as they sat there reading Aldo Leopold's *A Sand County Almanac* and such books purchased from the adjacent bookstore, they radiated environmental concern. Here was a community of good stewards, people who were protecting the earth and themselves. Nature used to mean wildness, abandon, Dionysian lustfulness. But here was a set of people who went out into nature carefully, who didn't want to upset the delicate balance, who studied their options, prepared and trained. If Norman Rockwell were a young man today, he'd head up to this coffee shop to get all this wholesome goodness down on canvas.

• • •

From the careful sadomasochists of the Arizona Power Exchange to the environmentally conscious, technologically informed nature trekkers at REI, the common threads of a Bobo pleasure principle emerge. We are not straitlaced, but we are responsible. We don't go for binges. Instead, we are driven to excel, even in our leisure time. And the final striking thing about all this discipline and self-control is that it is not based on any body of formal rules. Other groups and earlier elites may have submitted to or at least paid homage to divinely inspired moral codes: Masturbation is sinful. Drinking is a vice. But Bobos are uncomfortable with universal moral laws that purport to regulate pleasure. Bobos prefer more prosaic self-control regimes. The things that are forbidden are unhealthy or unsafe. The things that are encouraged are enriching or calorie burning. In other words, we regulate our carnal desires with health codes instead of moral codes.

Bobos don't denounce the evils of demon rum; we warn about the danger of drunk driving. We don't celebrate chastity as a godly virtue, but we do talk about safe sex and emphasize that abstinence is the safest form of safe sex. As the columnist Charles Krauthammer has pointed out, "The core of the modern sexual code is disease prevention." Similarly, the morning television shows would never have a preacher on to talk about how the devil brings sin into your life. But morning after morning they host health and fitness experts who talk about the need for rigorous exercise, self-disciplined eating, getting a full night's sleep, and leading a careful, productive life. These physical regimes are ways to encourage moral behavior through the back door. People who follow them are leading lives of disciplined self-restraint, but they are doing so in the name of their bodies instead of their souls.

Of course, many social critics would say the moral life of the educated class is impoverished if sexuality and leisure are to be evaluated primarily on health, safety, and other utilitarian grounds. If you live in a society like ours, in which people seldom object if they hear someone taking the Lord's name in vain but are outraged if they see a pregnant woman smoking, then you are living in a world that values the worldly more than the divine. You can't really know God if you ignore His laws, especially the ones that regulate the most intimate spheres of life. You may be responsible and healthy, but you will also be shallow and inconsequential.

As usual, Bobos are not blind to this criticism. They have trouble submitting to any set of formal commandments because they value autonomy too much. But they burst with spiritual aspirations and long for transcendence. They don't want to forsake pleasures that seem harmless just because some religious authority says so, but they do want to bring out the spiritual implications of everyday life. And this set of struggles—between autonomy and submission, materialism and spirituality—is the subject of the next chapter.

6

Spiritual Life

I'M SITTING on a rock in the Big Blackfoot River in western Montana. The sun is glistening off the water, and the grasses on the banks are ablaze in their fall glory. The air is crisp and silent, and I'm utterly alone but for the hawk gliding by above and the trout lurking in the water below. This is the spot where Norman Maclean set and Robert Redford filmed *A River Runs Through It,* and I'm sitting here waiting for one of those perfect moments when time stops and I feel myself achieving a mystical communion with nature.

But nothing's happening. I've been hanging around this magnificent setting for 30 minutes and I haven't had one moment of elevated consciousness. The ageless rhythms of creation are happening all around me. The crisp air whispers. The branches sway. The ducks wing by silently. If John Muir were here he'd probably be in rapture. The river would be deep in conversation with

Maclean. Aldo Leopold would be writhing around on the ground in ecstasy over the beauty of some nearby twig. But as for me, not a thing. It occurs to me that maybe it's too late in the season for transcendence.

I never noticed it before, but it always seems to be summertime when those hyperspiritual types come to Montana to explore the deeper harmonies. It's always midsummer when movies like *The Horse Whisperer* are filmed or when jaded urbanites come to Montana to have their souls restored. Now it's October and this state must be spiritually tapped out.

"Eventually all things merge into one, and a river runs through it," Maclean writes. When I read that back in my living room a few months ago, it seemed so profound. Now I can't figure out what the hell it means. The only things merging into one are my fingers into a block of frozen flesh. Frigid conditions always seem inspiring and elemental in the adventure books, but now this brisk wind just makes my extremities hurt. And instead of making me profound, this solitude is just giving me the creeps. The nature writers relish those moments when all of creation reduces down to just the elements: me, the water, the trout. But there probably isn't another human being within 10 miles of here. When I think of the calamities that could befall a person out here—a broken leg, car trouble, allergy attack—I realize there are advantages in seeking inner peace at spots close to a pay phone and an emergency rescue squad. Every twig snap begins to sound like the first hint of an onrushing grizzly. I look at my watch and realize I had better start feeling a serene oneness with God's creation pretty soon. I've got dinner reservations back in Missoula at six.

The Soul Rush

I suppose there are suckers who come in at the end of every rush. The prospectors who went to California in the late 1850s were probably too late to find large gold nuggets just lying around. And these days the Montana Soul Rush has made the competition for transcendence nuggets just as fierce. For Montana has come to occupy an exalted place in the American consciousness. It's become one of those places Where Life Is Honest and True. Back in 1948 Leslie Fiedler wrote an essay in *Partisan Review* called "The Montana Face," jibing Montanans for their romantic attachment to the simple ways of the past. But the future doesn't beckon us as bravely as it did 50 years ago, and it is precisely Montana's simplicity that now attracts us. Montana has emerged as one of the antidotes to our striving lives, as a foil to the grubby ambition of city life and the prefab mediocrity of suburban cul-de-sacs. It is the beautiful place, the forbidding place, the slow, simple place. When the producers of the Robin Williams movie *What Dreams May Come* went looking for a setting for heaven, they chose Montana.

So naturally, business moguls and Hollywood stars have come to Montana by the Lear jet load. It's not only Ted Turner, Jane Fonda, Tom Brokaw, David Letterman, Steven Seagal, and the other big names; it's the compassionate cardiologists from Chicago, the rugged realtors from Atlanta, the naturalist probate lawyers from San Jose. They've all found a place to recharge their batteries, smell the pines, and feel lonely and hard—in the summer months. Two million people voyage up to Glacier National Park alone each year and get all spiritual in the face of its grandeur. Movies like *The Horse Whisperer* serve as fables for the upper middle class: oversophisticated New

York magazine editor comes to Montana, finds simple honest man who communes with horses and helps her rediscover the important things in life. These upscalers have built a part-time, affluent Montana atop the real Montana. Their spiritualized Montana feeds off the idea of Montana and the beauty of Montana while rarely touching the lower-middle-class grind of the actual state.

The Soul Rush started when a few Montanans of a literary bent made a fateful discovery. They discovered they possessed a sense of place. Everybody lives somewhere, of course, but not all places have that spiritual aura that we call "a sense of place." Only places that are inhospitable to ambition have that. We use that phrase only to describe locales that change slowly, that are remote, that are wedded to the old ways more than the new, where opportunities for fame and riches are few. Writers used to call such places stifling backwaters. Ambitious high school students dreamt of getting out. But to members of the educated class, so burdened with opportunities and demands on their time, the changeless places are oases of contentment. People seem, at least to the bicoastal visitor's eye, to die with equanimity in such places.

"Montana's special gift is space," writes local author Glenn Law, "landscape made personal; space that reaches out to the horizon then comes back and gets under your skin. It reaches inward, wraps itself around your soul, incubates and grows." (When people try to capture "placeness" on paper, it tends to sound like a parasitic disease.) The people who actually discovered this "sense of placeness" were the regional authors. Lightly populated though Montana is, the state is packed with landscape poets. It's not only Norman Maclean, Wallace Stegner, Richard Ford, William Kittredge, and Ivan Doig, who have lived in and written about Montana. It's the thousands of less famous authors and freelance writers who are thicker on the ground than the pines. You can scarcely open a national magazine without stumbling across some Bozeman- or Missoula-based wordsmith waxing lyrical about the trees and the trout. "To trace the history of a river, or a raindrop, as John Muir would have done," Gretel Ehrlich writes in *Montana Spaces,* one of the many Montana anthologies that have been published of late, "is also to trace the history of the soul, the history of the mind descending and arising in the body. In both, we constantly seek and stumble on divinity, which, like the cornice feeding the lake and the spring becoming the waterfall, feeds, spills, falls and feeds over itself over and over again."

Pass the beef jerky.

And once it was clear there was a genuine regional literature in Montana, naturally, teams of foundation officials were going to descend on the state looking to stimulate even more Authentic Voices. You'd have the Rockefeller, Ford, and MacArthur types sending out wagon trains across the range looking for raw poets as yet unsullied by literary agents. *TriQuarterly* and other highbrow journals devoted special editions to western writing. The Montana Committee for the Humanities helped corral dozens of the Authentic Voices into one massive anthology—over a thousand pages long—called *The Last Best Place,* a tombstone-size testimony to the spirituality of these Rocky Mountain sages. It's like a great big brick of verbosity all dedicated to the supposedly silent and stoic westerner.

These days in Montana nobody can go to a riverbank without coming back with a basket full of metaphors. You see philosophic fishermen out in the water up to their waders in belles lettres, their fly rod in one hand, their journal in the other. Literary magazines with names like *Northern Lights* have popped up like wildflowers in May, along with the attendant discussion groups, folklore societies, creative-writing programs, and ceramics workshops. Suddenly the air is thick with earnest cause-mongering, and high-minded groups like the Montana Consensus Council and the Montana Land Reliance. There's scarcely a trucker on the interstate, it seems, who's not silently wrestling with his bildungsroman. The region is suddenly dotted with invading potters, independent filmmakers, and telecommuting screenwriters, and of course there are posses of realtors roaming the valleys to scoop the whole carnival of seekers into luxury log cabins and time shares.

The saloons are filled with Rocky Mountain Buddhists and sensitive cowboy sages who come down from their 20-acre spreads in the evening flashing their newly bought belt buckles, ready to drink local beers and listen to country music singers with Ph.D.s. Needless to say, there's been an increase in title rustling. Montana novelists like titles with plain elemental words like *sky, lake, mountain, snow.* So if one writer comes down from the hills to announce he's calling his novella *Bridges of Snow Falling on Mountain Cedars,* the odds are one of the other Big Sky Bellows will have already claimed that stake, and things are likely to get ugly.

I sometimes go to a guest ranch 60 miles south of Bozeman. In the eighties when you took one of the ranch's horses out for a ride, the wrangler would give you a 10-minute safety lecture on how not to get killed while horseback riding. Now, in the heat of the Soul Rush, at the same ranch they sit you down for a 70-minute lecture on the spiritual life of horses, the techniques of horse whispering, the evolutionary secrets of horse psychology, the Zen possibilities that await you on the trail. Now every wrangler has to develop a little Hermann Hesse routine, and every gas station attendant who has a dumb vacant look about him has to pretend that what he's really filled with is deep introspection.

Flexidoxy

There was a story in one of the Montana papers not long ago about Missoula's only Jewish congregation, which is presided over by Rabbi Gershon Winkler. Given the variety of Jews who have come to Missoula from places like Los Angeles and New York, Rabbi Winkler doesn't lead an Orthodox, Conservative, Reform, or Reconstructionist service. He calls his hybrid approach "Flexidoxy."

It's not a bad word to sum up the sort of spiritual pining you see in Montana, the hybrid mixture of freedom and flexibility on the one hand and the longing for rigor and orthodoxy on the other. After all, the Montana mindset has always celebrated flexibility, freedom, and independence. This is a state that until recently didn't have speed limits on its highways, so suspicious are the locals about any authority telling them how to lead their lives. And it is natural that the members of the educated class, who have their own anti-authority impulses, would come up here and find a spiritual home.

But Montana is no loosey-goosey New Age wonderland. It's not Marin County with a timberline. In the first place, the state's harsh climate discourages loose, experimental ways of living. The Montana writers may get humid when talking about the soulfulness of the trout streams, but it's the toughness and discipline of the fisherman they admire. It's the classic traditions of the sport, the endless repetitions, and obedience to the master's forms that evoke their admiration. Norman Maclean and Wallace Stegner are not 1960s or 1970s New Age vaporheads. Montanans are contemptuous of the fuzzy amateurs who come for a few moments of easy communion and then dash back to the cities when the air turns gray. Only about half the people who actually buy vacation homes up here keep them for more than a few years, after they find that the natural grandeur comes at a frigid meteorological price. Native and wannabe native Montanans define themselves against people who don't have real manure on their boots, who haven't been kicked a few times by a horse, who haven't stuck around the state long enough to be painfully lonely. This is still a state mainly of ranchers and pickup truck drivers, not Transcendental Meditation groups. Even the creative-writing instructors who come up here tend to do so because they want to live among regular, practical folk.

And there's another element of the Montana ethos that runs against I'm OK, You're OK sentimentalism. It's most apparent when Montanans start talking about their connection to the land. It's then that you begin to hear how Montana's spirituality is grounded in something tangible. When Montanans begin talking about their sense of place, you hear echoes of the blood and soil nationalism that is more common in Europe than in the States. It's a conservative, even reactionary bond. It's based on the idea that a person's connection to the landscape is deeper than rationality and choice. It is a bond that is earned through years or even generations of suffering, of blood and sweat dropped onto the ground. It's conservative because it is suspicious of change and anything that would alter the landscape or character of the beloved place. Montanans make a point of mentioning how long they have been here and how long their families have been here.

And for Montanans and the high fliers who flock to the state, the whole point of Montana is that it is not cutting edge. It is not California or New York. It is a slow place, tied down by its climate, by its remoteness, and by its traditions. Much of the Montana literature is elegiac in tone, loyal to some earlier age.

As a symbol, Montana stands for depth over breadth. It means doing the same routines year after year, not flitting from one lifestyle to another. It means settling down with a few rituals rather than endlessly sampling a smorgasbord of lifestyles. Living in such a remote place means giving up on certain opportunities—to make money or to lead diverse lives. "Ranching has no corporate ladder," Scott Hibbard writes in the anthology *Montana Spaces.* "The rancher who is owner-operator at age twenty-five will be doing essentially the same things for the same pay at age seventy-five." But Montanans seem to accept the trade-offs, believing that the additional amusements and opportunities that a bicoastal life may bring would not compensate for the permanent and profound connections that are possible in such a rooted place.

So this is why the term Flexidoxy is apt. It suggests the hybrid nature of Montana's spiritual ethic. It starts with flexibility and freedom, with the desire to throw off authority and live autonomously. But it also suggests a second and opposing impulse, an impulse toward orthodoxy, which is to say, a desire to ground spiritual life within tangible reality, ordained rules, and binding connections that are based on deeper ties than rationality and choice.

And isn't this desire to balance freedom with rootedness the essence of the educated class's spiritual quest? This is a class that came of age rebelling against the authority of the preceding elite. Starting in the 1950s, the books and movies that most influenced the educated class have railed against conformism, authoritarianism, and blind obedience. Championing freedom and equality, members of the educated class cultivated a code of expressive individualism. They succeeded in smashing old hierarchies. They cultivated an ethos that celebrates, actually demands, endless innovation, self-expansion, and personal growth. Because of the reforms initiated largely by the educated class, people have more choices. Women have more choices where to work or how to lead their lives. Different ethnic groups have more choices about where they can go to school or which clubs they can join. Freedom and

choice are everywhere triumphant, right down to the
gourmet whole-grain loaf you select at the farmer's market, or the kind of partner you prefer in the bedroom.

But if you look around at the educated class today,
you see a recognition that freedom and choice aren't
everything. Free spirituality can lead to lazy spirituality,
religiosity masquerading as religion, and finally to the narcissism of the New Age movement. The toppling of old
authorities has not led to a glorious new dawn but instead
to an alarming loss of faith in institutions and to spiritual
confusion and social breakdown. So if you look around
the Bobo world, you see people trying to rebuild connections. You see it in Wayne, Pennsylvania, where upscale
consumers shop for farmyard furniture that evokes traditional rituals and simple styles. You see it in Burlington,
Vermont, where educated upscalers have moved in search
of the connections that are possible in small towns. You
see it in the vacation preferences of the educated class, the
way they flock to premeritocratic enclaves where the local
peasantry live stable, traditional lives. And you see it in
places like Montana, where the cosmopolitan class comes
looking for a place to call home.

So progressive in many of their attitudes, the Bobos
are spiritual reactionaries. They spend much of their time
pining for simpler ways of living, looking backward for
the wisdom that people with settled lives seem to possess
but which the peripatetic, opportunity-grasping Bobos
seem to lack.

The question for the educated class is, can you have
your cake and eat it too? Can you have freedom as well as
roots? Because the members of the educated class show little evidence of renouncing freedom and personal choice.
They are not returning to the world of deference and obedience. They are not about to roll back the cultural and
political revolutions of the past decades, which have done
so much to enhance individual freedom. They are going to

try to find new reconciliations. The challenges they face are these: Can you still worship God even if you take it upon yourself to decide that many of the Bible's teachings are wrong? Can you still feel at home in your community even if you know that you'll probably move if a better job opportunity comes along? Can you establish ritual and order in your life if you are driven by an inner imperative to experiment constantly with new things? I've talked about the mighty reconciliations the Bobos make. But these spiritual reconciliations are the most problematic. The Bobos are trying to build a house of obligation on a foundation of choice.

The Limited Life

As members of the educated class have rediscovered the virtues of small-scale local bonds and the vital role deep connections play in a person's spiritual life, there has been an outpouring of books and articles about community and civil society, on how to recreate the mediating structures by which people support one another and find their place. One of the most hardheaded of these books is Alan Ehrenhalt's 1995 work, *The Lost City*. Ehrenhalt went back to describe, fondly but without nostalgia, some of the tight-knit Chicago neighborhoods of the 1950s. These middle- and working-class places were exemplars of the communitarian values that many people long for today. In the St. Nick's parish neighborhood on the Southwest Side of Chicago, for example, children ran freely from house to house, and there were always plenty of adults to watch out for them. On summer evenings everybody hung around outside, talking and joking with their neighbors. Most of the shopping was done at family-owned stores, like Bertucci's meat market. Nick Bertucci knew most of his customers well, and they lingered in his store to trade gossip. Many of the people in the neighborhood had job security at the local Nabisco plant; sometimes two and three generations would be working together there side by side. The vast majority of the neighborhood was Catholic, and most went to mass at St. Nick's on Sundays. Local loyalties were strong. When asked where they were from, people from the parish didn't say Chicago or even the Southwest Side. Instead, they identified individual corners: "I come from 59th and Pulaski." This was, in many ways, a wonderful neighborhood, and the people who lived there look back upon it fondly.

But as Ehrenhalt is quick to point out, there were hardships at the root of all this togetherness. Some were material. People hung out in the street on summer evenings in part because nobody had air conditioning. TV was just becoming popular, so there wasn't much easy entertainment inside anyway. Furthermore, the bungalows the families lived in were tiny, and part of the space the families did have was reserved as a genteel parlor and so was off-limits most of the time. These people didn't have a lot of privacy.

The first chapter in Ehrenhalt's book is called "The Limited Life," and it's clear that the people who lived in St. Nick's parish were restricted in more serious ways as well. The neighborhood was ethnically homogeneous, with all the insularity, parochialism, and prejudice that encourages. There were not many opportunities to get out and thrive in the mainstream American economy, in the high-flying world of State Street and Michigan Avenue. If you lacked the right manners, the right accent, or the right social connections, as most Southwest Siders did, the upper echelons of the corporate world were closed to you. In fact, the whole cosmopolitan whirl of downtown Chicago was remote for many people in the parish. It took three bus rides just to get downtown. Many families went there once a year, to look at the Christmas store windows.

There were other limits. Women had limited career

options, which was good for the local schools but probably not so good for the capable women who might have
aspired to careers other than teaching. Ehrenhalt includes
a photo taken at the school. It shows row upon perfect
row of neat students sitting at meticulously spare desks,
all of them wearing the same uniform and practically the
same expression. It evokes the world of regimented education that was to come under such comprehensive attack in
the following decade.

Furthermore, while the local men had secure jobs at
Nabisco, they were being shortchanged when it came to
salary. Their union was corrupt and cut sweetheart deals
with the company. The workers knew it, but they didn't
have too many other career options. Politics didn't afford
many choices, either. The local government was run by the
machine; local leaders swore fealty to it. Ehrenhalt features a Chicago pol named John G. Fary who spent his
whole life obediently taking orders from Richard J. Daley.
As a reward for long service, Daley sent him to Congress.
Fary told reporters, "For twenty-one years I represented
the mayor in the legislature and he was always right."
That sort of deference to authority exemplifies a mentality
that was not uncommon in the communities in the 1950s
but is alien to most places today. It is a worldview in
which obedience is a virtue, in which authority, order, and
lasting relationships are valued over freedom, creativity,
and perpetual change.

Ehrenhalt has a chapter on religious life in the parish.
St. Nick's had 1,100 seats, and on Sundays they were filled
every hour on the hour for the start of mass. This was pre-
Vatican II, so the mass was conducted in Latin. The priests
stood with their backs to the congregation, facing the
altar. Monsignor Michael J. Fennessy reminded his flock
that the devil is always active, sin and temptation are all
around; the clergy spoke more openly of Satan's active
role in the 1950s than they do today, Ehrenhalt notes.

Spiritual life was as orderly and hierarchical as economic or political life. The way to truth was one, while the paths to error were many, so it was best to stay on the straight and narrow. Christ led you to the true way; Satan tempted you off it. The sins were categorized and enumerated, as were the graces. The parish had a place in the archdiocese, and the archdiocese had its place in the larger structure of the church. The crucial spiritual questions were not the ones we in the educated class tend to ask—"What am I seeking?"—but were more oriented toward authority—"What does God command and love?" The Lord's Prayer, it should be remembered, is spoken in the first person plural—it is spoken together as a community—and its first lines remind us of God's authority and His plan: "Our Father, who art in heaven, hallowed be Thy name. Thy kingdom come, Thy will be done. On earth as it is in heaven." In short, the spiritual universe was as orderly and hierarchical as the physical universe.

And as Ehrenhalt emphasizes, this mode of Catholicism was thriving in the 1950s in Chicago. There were 2 million practicing Catholics, 400 parishes, 2,000 priests, 9,000 nuns, and roughly 300,000 parochial school students. Between 1948 and 1958 the archdiocese opened an average of six new parishes a year. And it was not just in working-class neighborhoods where this attachment to organized religion was so strong. One of the features of life in the 1950s was that higher education correlated with religious observance. People with college and advanced degrees were more likely to be regular church and synagogue goers than were their less educated peers.

The Liberated Life

But, of course, by the 1950s modernity was challenging the ethos of deference and obedience and the whole hierarchical cosmology. The writers and social critics who looked out on that world tended to believe that America had become *too* orderly, *too* passive, *too* group oriented. The general tenor of the social criticism of the 1950s—whether it was *The Organization Man* or *The Lonely Crowd*—was that a smothering spirit of deference had settled over the land. Writers of all stripes attacked conformity, passivity, and deference. William Whyte complained about the prevailing social ethic that emphasized "belongingness" and the "belief in the group as the source of creativity." David Riesman's book was widely interpreted as a critique of "Other Directed Man," of the anxious conformist who is horrified by the thought that he might offend or stick out, who repressed all "knobby or idiosyncratic qualities and vices" in order to better fit in with the group. Protestant theologian Paul Tillich saw an America populated by people who had "an intense desire for security both internal and external, the will to be accepted by the group at any price, an unwillingness to show individual traits, acceptance of a limited happiness without serious risks."

These writers drew from a distinction the philosopher John Dewey had laid down—between "customary" and "reflective" morality. Customary morality is the morality of the tribe, the group, the home, the parental rules that are never challenged. It is based on long-established rules and deference to those eternal maxims. Reflective morality is based on conscious deliberations. It starts when an individual starts thinking through the consequences of various behaviors. It's more experimental and deliberative, as each person questions old rules and draws conclusions. In the 1950s most writers hoped that Americans would mature away from customary morality toward reflective morality. This move from home and religion toward autonomy and psychology, it was assumed, was the way of progress.

So most social critics were calling for a more individualistic form of spiritual life. "We hope for non-conformists among you, for your sake, for the sake of the nation, and for the sake of humanity," Tillich preached to a college audience in 1957. In effect, the writers—whether they were sociologists, Freudians, theologians, or Beat poets—were telling the young to break loose from their communities, groups, and religious orders. Spiritual fulfillment is found when you go your own way.

Among the intellectual class, mores had changed. Writers and academics sought to instill a more individualistic ethos in their children, one that would encourage self-exploration over obedience. Children may have been taught to defer to authority on the Southwest Side, but a few miles toward the lake, in the University of Chicago neighborhood or Hyde Park, the culture was quite different. As Isaac Rosenfeld wrote in a 1957 essay in *Commentary* called "Life in Chicago," "One sure way of telling whether you are visiting an academic or non-academic household is by the behavior of the children, and the extent to which you can make yourself heard above their clatter. If it is still possible to conduct a conversation, you are in a non-academic household."

The dominant trend of social thought in those years was toward individual self-expression and away from the group loyalty and deference that were the ideals in communities like St. Nick's parish. Each person can and must find his or her own course to spiritual fulfillment, the educated-class writers were saying.

Pluralism

It didn't take long for their views to triumph. It is now better to be thought of as unconventional than conventional; it is better to be called a nonconformist than a conformist. It is cooler to be a rebel than an obedient foot soldier. Individualistic pluralism is the foundation of Bobo spiritual life.

The spiritual pluralist believes that the universe cannot be reduced to one natural order, one divine plan. Therefore, there cannot be one path to salvation. There are varieties of happiness, distinct moralities, and different ways to virtue. What's more, no one ever really arrives at a complete answer to the deepest questions or to faith. It is a voyage. We are forever incomplete, making choices, exploring, creating. We are protean.

The proper spiritual posture, therefore, is to be open-minded about new choices and paths, to be empathetic toward new opinions, temperaments, and worldviews. Jane Jacobs opens *The Death and Life of Great American Cities* with a quotation from Oliver Wendell Holmes that celebrates spiritual diversity. "The chief worth of civilization is just that it makes the means of living more complex," Holmes wrote. "Because more complex and intense intellectual efforts mean a fuller and richer life. They mean more life. Life is an end in itself, and the only question as to whether it is worth living is whether you have enough of it." This is a different set of values: diversity, complexity, exploration, self-exploration.

These values are now embraced by millions. In his book *Achieving Our Country,* the philosopher Richard Rorty puts it well. The goal of each society, he writes, is to create "a greater diversity of individuals—larger, fuller, more imaginative and daring individuals." Our efforts, Rorty continues, should be directed toward creating a country in which "the future will widen endlessly. . . . Experiments with new forms of individual and social life will interact and reinforce one another. Individual life will become unthinkably diverse and social life unthinkably free."

This is an optimistic creed. Fulfillment can be sought through perpetual self-expansion. And further, freedom can lead to order. If we give everyone maximum freedom to live their own best lives, the interplay between their efforts will mesh to form a dynamic and complicated harmony. (Remember Jane Jacobs's street.) All that is required is that people of good faith seek their own paths in an open and tolerant manner, without trying to impose their own paths on others.

Spiritual Freedom

Given the opportunity to explore their new-found spiritual freedom, the members of the educated class didn't need to be asked twice. Some of them hightailed away from the rituals and ceremonies of institutionalized religion and set off on individual spiritual quests. Jerry Rubin, whose life became a caricature of the zeitgeist shifts of his age, recalled in his memoir, *Growing (Up) at Thirty-Seven*, "In five years, from 1971 to 1975, I directly experienced est, gestalt therapy, bioenergetics, rolfing, massage, jogging, health foods, tai chi, Esalen, hypnotism, modern dance, meditation, Silva Mind Control, Arica, acupuncture, sex therapy, Reichian therapy and More House—a smorgasbord course in New Consciousness."

The New Age gurus commanded their followers to Love Thyself, and out poured great gushes of spiritual self-absorption, what different writers have called "self-approving joy," "virtuous voluptuousness," or "egoistic hedonism." Of course, not everybody went in for this stuff. America is a complicated place. But there was a moment in the 1970s and early 1980s when people still spoke unironically about the "self," when the therapeutic sensibility seemed everywhere triumphant. This was the apogee of spiritual individualism, the high water mark, at least in the educated class, of the Human Potential movement, the Free to Be You and Me mentality, the whole New Age panoply, which at heart is spirituality without obligation.

By the time Robert Bellah and his research team published *Habits of the Heart* in 1985, they found a nation, or at least an educated class, deep into self-exploration and no longer willing to declare obedience to received spiritual authority. For example, Bellah and his crew interviewed a young nurse named Sheila Larson, who described her faith as "Sheilaism." She had invented her own custom religion, with God defined as whatever fulfilled her needs. "It's just try to love yourself and be gentle with yourself," she said. "You know, I guess, take care of each other."

Habits of the Heart was an important book because it was an early sign the educated class was going to recoil from the more extreme forms of spiritual individualism. The authors wrote:

> We believe that much of the thinking about the self of educated Americans, thinking that has become almost hegemonic in our universities and much of our middle class, is based on inadequate social science, impoverished philosophy, and vacuous theology. There are truths we do not see when we adopt the language of radical individualism. We find ourselves not independently of other people and institutions but through them. We never get to our selves on our own. We discover who we are face to face and side by side with others in work, love, and learning. All of our activity goes on in relationships, groups, associations and communities ordered by institutional structures and interpreted by them.

Bellah and his colleagues were trying to point out the sorts of problems that arise when individualistic spiritual freedom is taken to the extreme. And these basic criticisms have since become the conventional wisdom in Bobo circles. In the first place, maybe there is no "real self" that somehow can be separated from all the external bonds that make up our lives. Maybe people who go deeper and deeper into the self are actually journeying into a void. Second, it is hard for the individualist to construct a pattern of rituals and obligations that give structure to life and make sense of the great transitions in life: birth, marriage, death. Furthermore, the lack of age-old rituals makes it very hard to pass your belief system on to your children. Organized religions have a set of stable ceremonies to guide and cultivate the spiritual lives of kids. Self religions do not. And so even many of the people who were at first most enthusiastic about New Age self-exploration have found themselves returning, sometimes reluctantly, to the institutionalized faiths they rejected—doing so for the sake of their kids.

But the ultimate problem with spiritual freedom is that it never ends. As Rorty points out, it widens endlessly. Freedom means always keeping your options open, so it means you never settle on truth, you never arrive, you can never rest. The accumulation of spiritual peak experiences can become like the greedy person's accumulation of money. The more you get, the more you hunger for more. The life of perpetual choice is a life of perpetual longing as you are prodded by the inextinguishable desire to try the next new thing. But maybe what the soul hungers for is ultimately not a variety of interesting and moving insights but a single universal truth. Dostoyevsky has the Grand Inquisitor say, "For the secret of man's being is not only to live but to have something to live for. Without a stable conception of the object of life, man would not consent to go on living."

Today the Inquisitor might say the Bobos are enslaved by their insatiable desire for freedom and diversity. He might warn that all the Bobos' varied experiences may dissolve into nothingness if they don't surrender to something larger than themselves. The end result of pluralism, he'd say, is an endless moving about in search of more and more lightly held ideas, none of which solves essential questions. The pluralistic ethos is fine for the search, but it makes it difficult to reach the sort of resting place that is offered by less elastic creeds, the sort of tranquillity that is promised, for example, in the book of Samuel: "Moreover, I will appoint a place for my people Israel, and I will plant them, that they may dwell in a place of their own, and move no more."

The Return of Order

The Bobos have surrendered neither their love of individual choice nor their pluralistic mindset. But there is a countercurrent, rarely so obvious as it is now. These days writers and social critics no longer quite so ardently celebrate nonconformism, the way the critics of the 1955–65 period did. They are not so optimistic that maximum personal freedom will automatically produce a dynamic but basically wholesome order. Today few writers argue that Americans are *too* group oriented or *too* orderly. They are not complaining about Organization Man or the other-directed joiners. On the contrary, today most social critics are calling for *more* community, *more* civil society, *more* social cohesion. Today writers tend to try to rein in the individualistic mindset the critics of 40 years ago were busy unleashing. Writers today, by and large, attempt to reestablish the rituals and institutional structures that were all weakened in the great rush of educated-class emancipation.

Over the past decade there has been a mountain of books and articles devoted to the subject of communitarianism, about the importance of "mediating institutions" and neighborly bonds. Hillary Clinton wrote a book called *It Takes a Village*, touting the virtues of stable small-town relations. Colin Powell launched a voluntarism crusade to get more people involved in their communities. Harvard sociologist Robert Putnam made a splash with an essay called "Bowling Alone" in which he maintained that the decline of bowling leagues was a symbol of how Americans were becoming disconnected from each other, becoming less active in the church, the PTA, and other community organizations. Can you imagine a writer in the 1960s choosing bowling leagues as a symbol of healthy community involvement? In those days bowling leagues were considered ridiculous and reactionary by members of the educated class. If they had died out in the 1960s, no intellectual would have shed a tear.

The civil society advocates and the communitarians set out to put some bounds around what they see as the radical individualism that has swept through America. Michael Joyce and William Schambra of the Bradley Foundation, which has supported many civil society efforts, write, "Americans are worried above all about the unraveling of the orderly, coherent, authoritative moral community that they were once able to build around themselves with their strong, local civil institutions." Liberals tend to emphasize that the global marketplace has undermined orderly and coherent moral communities. Conservatives tend to maintain that it is the breakdown of traditional morality. But both sides are interested in moving in the same direction, back to the bonds of local communities and small-scale authority and away from a system that allows individual choice to trump all other values.

Revival, Reconstruction, Return

One of the features of Bobo spirituality that leaps out at you is how backward-looking it is. Some groups seek spiritual fulfillment in some future utopia yet to come, but we Bobos don't look to the future for transcendence. We look to the past, to old traditions, rites, and rituals. The assumption of so much of what we do, of so many of the movies we see and books we read, is that in our efforts to climb upward, we have left something important behind. We have made ourselves so busy that we no longer know and appreciate the essential things. We have become so af-fluent, we have encrusted our lives with superficialities, and we have to look back and rediscover some of the sim-pler and more natural ways of connecting with the world. Maybe now it is time, the Bobo says, to rediscover old val-ues, to reconnect with patient, rooted, and uncluttered realms.

This longing is evident in the way we try to construct our physical environment. Bobos surround themselves with remnants of the small, stable communities that radi-ate spiritual contentment. We saw the style in Chapter 2: the Shaker-inspired tables, rustic pine benches, distressed furniture, archaic farm implements, claw-footed bathtubs, prehistoric crafts, old industrial artifacts, whaling baskets, and on and on—each piece more nobly reactionary than the last. Go again inside the educated-class retail chains, Pottery Barn or Crate & Barrel. These and similar stores try to recapture some long-lost world of stability and order. Restoration Hardware, which is spreading like a home furnishings Starbucks across the nation's upscale malls, caters to its graduate-degreed clientele with old-fashioned ribbed steel flashlights (just like we used to carry in summer camp), hand-forged scissors, old-fashioned ka-zoos, Moon Pies, classic Boston Ranger pencil sharpeners, compartmentalized school lunch trays, and glass and steel Pyrex beakers just like the ones your doctor used to keep tongue depressors in. These are the nostalgic mementos of the communities we left behind. The small towns that were hollowed out by the shopping malls and the global marketplace. The backwaters we left behind us when we went off to college and to big-city job opportunities.

The spiritual quandary of the educated class was in fact beautifully exemplified in a video the Restoration Hardware people produced for potential investors just before they launched their IPO in 1998. The voice-over accompanying this video explains the theology behind the store: "Lurking in our collective unconscious, among images of Ike, Donna Reed and George Bailey, is the very clear sense that things were better made, that they mattered a little more." Images of the forties and fifties fill the video screen. "What happened? Slowly but surely we became a nation obsessed with production and, of course, consumption." At this point we see images of huge suburban developments and large outlet malls. "This was pretty heady and pretty good. We got so proficient at making things we had unlimited choices and an endless array of goods." The "plastics" scene from *The Graduate* comes along. "The retail environment came to reflect this mentality—more square footage, more, more, more. Then, one day, the generation used to having everything recoiled, and became the generation searching for something."

There you have it. The generation that gave itself "unlimited choices" recoiled and found that it was still "searching for something." In so many ways we seem to want to return to some lost age of (supposed) spiritual coherence and structure. We seem to sense the cost of our new-found freedom is a loss of connection to other people and true communities. We want to recreate those meaningful ligatures. And yet, more often than not, we're not willing to actually go back to the age of limits, which would mean cutting off our options.

The Great Pastiche

As a result, you now see a great spiritual pastiche. You see a mixture of autonomy and community. You see younger Bobos especially becoming active in churches and synagogues, but they are not interested in having some external authority—pope, priest, or rabbi—tell them how to lead their lives. Militant secularism is no longer on the march. Now people return to religion, but often they are not content to have just one religion; they dabble in several simultaneously. Princeton sociologist Robert Wuthnow reports on a 26-year-old disabilities counselor, the daughter of a Methodist minister, who describes herself as a "Methodist Taoist Native American Quaker Russian Orthodox Buddhist Jew."

Not everyone has spooned so many helpings from the spiritual buffet table. But even in more traditional circles, when one sees people return to religious participation, one often gets the sense that it is the participation they go for as much as the religion. The *New York Times Magazine* recently ran a special issue on religion that included the astute headline "Religion Makes a Comeback (Belief to Follow)." Francis Fukuyama nicely captured the ethos of Bobo religiosity in his 1999 book, *The Great Disruption:*

> Instead of community arising as a byproduct of rigid belief, people will return to religious belief because of their desire for community. In other words, people will return to religious tradition not necessarily because they accept the truth of revelation, but precisely because the absence of community and the transience of social ties in the secular world makes them hungry for ritual and cultural tradition. They will help the poor or their neighbors not because doctrine tells them they must, but rather because they want to serve their communities and find that faith-based organizations are the most effective ways of doing so. They will repeat ancient prayers and reenact age-old rituals not be-

cause they believe they were handed down by God, but rather because they want their children to have proper values, and because they want to enjoy the comfort of ritual and the sense of shared experience it brings. In a sense they will not be taking religion seriously on its own terms. Religion becomes a source of ritual in a society that has been stripped bare of ceremony, and thus a reasonable extension of the natural desire for social relatedness with which all human beings are born.

This is not to say that Bobo congregants are not rigorous. Often they adhere to dietary restrictions and the like with extraordinary rigor. But somehow it is rigor without submission. Whereas earlier believers felt that, paradoxically, freedom was achieved through a total submission to God's will, blind obedience of that sort is just not in the Bobo mental repertoire. Among Jews, for example, there is a growing movement of young modern Orthodox who know Hebrew, study the Torah, and observe the kosher laws. They are rigorous observers, but they also pick and choose, discarding those ancient rules that don't accord with their modern sensibilities—most any rule that restricts the role of women, for example. Furthermore, they pull back from biblical teachings whenever those teachings clash with pluralism—with any teaching that implies that Judaism is the one true faith and that other faiths are inferior or in error. This is Orthodoxy without obedience—indeed, Flexidoxy.

Organized religion, once dismissed as hopelessly archaic or as a crutch for the weak-minded, now carries with it a certain prestige. Bobos tend to feel a little surge of moral satisfaction if they can drop their church or synagogue attendance into a dinner party conversation. It shows they are not just self-absorbed narcissists but members of a moral community. And yet the religious discourse has been changed. Now sectarian disputes, which took up so much energy for earlier theologians, are considered a bit silly. "I'm not, of course, an expert on religion," Václav Havel writes in *Civilization* magazine, "but it seems to me that the major faiths have much more in common than they are willing to admit. They share a basic point of departure—that this world and our existence are not freaks of chance but rather part of a mysterious, yet integral, act whose sources, direction and purpose are difficult for us to perceive in their entirety. And they share a large complex of moral imperatives that this mysterious act implies. In my view, whatever differences these religions might have are not as important as these fundamental similarities." In other words, the religious impulse is a flexible thing that can take many different forms in different cultures. What's important and good is the essential religious impulse, not the particular strictures of any one particular sect or denomination. So it doesn't hurt to shop around, experiment with a few religions before committing yourself, or maybe even flow between different denominations, depending on your needs and preferences at the moment. Choice reconciled with commitment.

The Grandest Reconciliation

Most people obviously think this reconciliation can work, or at least they are going to give it a shot. And maybe it *can* work. Robert Nisbet, whose 1953 book, *The Quest for Community,* is the forerunner of the current interest in civil society, believed that while the best life was to be found within community, people should not limit themselves to one community. They should experience many communities. "Freedom is to be found in the interstices of authority; it is nourished by competition among authorities," Nisbet wrote. In this way they could enjoy a sense of belonging, but also flexibility and freedom. Nisbet quoted the French writer Pierre-Joseph Proudhon, "Multiply your associations and be free."

But others don't believe that maximum freedom can be so easily reconciled with spiritual fulfillment. They argue that the synthesis the cooperative individualists have created is a phony synthesis. These people talk about tradition, roots, and community, but they are just paying lip service to these virtues. When push comes to shove, they always choose personal choice over other commitments. They move out of communities when a better job comes along. They abandon traditions and rules they find tiresome. They divorce when their marriages become unpleasant. They leave their company when they get bored. They fall away from their church or synagogue when it becomes dull or unrewarding. And this is self-defeating, because at the end of all this movement and freedom and self-exploration, they find they have nothing deep and lasting to hold on to.

Comparing our own lives to those he described in the tight communities of Chicago, Alan Ehrenhalt wrote that we are like the fellow who sits in front of the TV constantly zapping the remote control, that "ultimate weapon of personal choice, proceeding in the course of an hour to select and reject dozens of visual entertainments whose ability to satisfy us for more than a few minutes is crippled by our suspicion that there may be something more stimulating a couple of frequencies further on." Ehrenhalt continues:

> Too many of the things we do in our lives, large and small, have come to resemble channel surfing, marked by a numbing and seemingly endless progression from one option to the next, all without the benefit of a chart, logistical or moral,

because there are simply too many choices and no
one to help sort them out. We have nothing to insu-
late ourselves against the perpetual temptation to
try one more choice, rather than to live with what
is on the screen in front of us.

Ehrenhalt has a point. The thing we are in danger of
losing with our broad, diverse lives is a sense of belonging.
A person who limits himself or herself to one community
or one spouse is going to have deeper bonds to that community or that spouse than the person who experiments
throughout life. A person who surrenders to a single faith
is going to have a deeper commitment to that one faith
than the person who zigzags through in a state of curious
agnosticism. The monk in the monastery does not lead an
experimental life, but perhaps he is able to lead a profound one.

And so we get in Bobo life a world of many options,
but maybe not a life of do-or-die commitments, and
maybe not a life that ever offers access to the profoundest
truths, deepest emotions, or highest aspirations. Maybe in
the end the problem with this attempt to reconcile freedom with commitment, virtue with affluence, autonomy
with community is not that it leads to some catastrophic
crack-up or some picturesque slide into immorality and
decadence, but rather that it leads to too many compromises and spiritual fudges. Maybe people who try to have
endless choices end up with semi-commitments and semi-
freedoms. Maybe they end up leading a life that is moderate but flat. Their souls being colored with shades of gray,
they find nothing heroic, nothing inspiring, nothing that
brings their lives to a point. Some days I look around and
I think we have been able to achieve these reconciliations
only by making ourselves more superficial, by simply ignoring the deeper thoughts and highest ideals that would
torture us if we actually stopped to measure ourselves ac-

cording to them. Sometimes I think we are too easy on ourselves.

The irony of Bobo spiritual life is that it started out with such a bang—the moment of liberation, the throwing off of old constraints, the first delicious experiments with total freedom—but it has ended up with a quietism. The bohemians were appalled by the tepid lives of the bourgeoisie, their shallow contentment and comfortable mores. So they called upon the middle-class burghers to break free from the well-worn paths that had been laid down from time immemorial. Life should be an adventure! Yet if we are to choose our own courses, what are we to make of the people who choose other courses? Life is a diversity of incommensurate values, and every religion has a kernel of virtue, every choice fills a real human need. So the bohemian who goes charging off into a new consciousness filled with heroic dreams quickly stops short and learns to be tolerant of others. Bohemians learn not to be too zealous about their own visions, lest they offend their neighbors, and themselves. The raging bonfire of emancipation quickly turns into the cupped candle of tolerance and moderation.

Members of the educated class are suspicious of vehemence and fearful of people who communicate their views furiously or without compromise. They are suspicious of people who radiate certitude, who are intolerant of people not like themselves. Bobos pull back from fire and brimstone. They recoil from those who try to "impose" their views or their lifestyles on others. They prefer tolerance and civility instead. Bobos are epistemologically modest, believing that no one can know the full truth and so it's best to try to communicate across disagreements and find some common ground. Be moderate in your own faith because you probably don't have the complete answers, and don't try to push your faith onto others.

There is something humane about this mentality.

Bobos are pleasant to be around, which is no small thing. But, as always, there are trade-offs. Nietzsche once wrote, "Nobody will very readily regard a doctrine as true merely because it makes people happy or virtuous." After all, prophets and saints didn't believe what they believed because it made them happy. Many of them were turned into martyrs precisely because they clung to truth regardless of its earthly consequences. But Bobos are more utilitarian. Maybe that sort of surrender and heroism is beyond the reach of Bobo spirituality.

The sociologist Alan Wolfe calls the morality of the upper middle class "small scale morality." For his 1998 book, *One Nation, After All,* Wolfe interviewed 200 members of the middle and upper middle class in suburbs spread across America, a demographic sample that overlaps reasonably well with the educated class. Wolfe's group included some people who are orthodox believers and some whose faith is highly individualist, including a woman who spoke about finding her own individual God within, in the same terms as Sheila did in Robert Bellah's *Habits of the Heart* 13 years earlier. Wolfe's general finding was that upper-middle-class Americans value religion but are unwilling to allow it precedence over pluralism. "Americans take their religion seriously," Wolfe writes, "but very few of them take it so seriously that they believe that religion should be the sole, or even the most important, guide for establishing rules about how *other* people should live." The italics are Wolfe's. One hundred sixty of his respondents agreed or strongly agreed with the proposition "There is such a thing as being too religious," an apparent critique of those who use their religious creed to judge or evangelize others.

This tolerance and respect for diversity, Wolfe found, leads to a style of faith that is radically anticontentious. The people he spoke to shy away from judgmentalism of almost any sort. These upper-middle-class Americans prefer, he concluded, a morality "modest in its ambitions and quiet in its proclamations, not seeking to transform the entire world but to make a difference where it can." That means, Wolfe writes, that members of the upper middle class think of morality in personal terms. They think of establishing moral relationships with those close to them but do not worry about formal moral rules for all mankind. They offer moral advice tentatively. They have "either given up finding timeless morality or would be unwilling to bring its principles down to earth, if, by chance, they came across it." They draw moral guidance from a variety of sources, from the Bible to the movies, and improvise a flexible set of guideposts. They make moral distinctions but are quick to amend them as circumstances warrant. When faced with moral claims that inescapably conflict, they try to blur those too: "Ambivalence—call it confusion if you want—can be described as the default position for the American middle class; everything else being equal, people simply cannot make up their mind."

This is a morality, in other words, that doesn't try to perch atop the high ground of divine revelation. Nor does it attempt to scale the heights of romantic transcendence. Instead, it is content with the workable and peaceful oases on the lower ground. It follows the path of least resistance between the two hills.

Let's try to weigh the pros and cons of Bobo spirituality. It is more a temperament than a creed. Bobo moralists are not heroic, but they are responsible. They prefer the familiar to the unknown, the concrete to the abstract, the modest to the ardent, civility and moderation to conflict and turmoil. They like comforting religious rituals, but not inflexible moral codes. They like spiritual participation but are cautious of moral crusades and religious enthusiasms. They savor spiritual sentiments, so long as they are flexible, and theological discussions, so long as they are full of praise rather than blame.

They have an ability to not react; to accept what doesn't directly concern them. They tolerate a little lifestyle experimentation, so long as it is done safely and moderately. They are offended by concrete wrongs, like cruelty and racial injustice, but are relatively unmoved by lies or transgressions that don't seem to do anyone obvious harm. They prize good intentions and are willing to tolerate a lot from people whose hearts are in the right place. They aim for decency, not saintliness, prosaic goodness, not heroic grandeur, fairness, not profundity. In short, they prefer a moral style that doesn't shake things up, but that protects the status quo where it is good, and gently tries to forgive and reform the things that are not so good. This is a good morality for building a decent society, but maybe not one for people interested in things in the next world, like eternal salvation, for example.

Bobo Heaven

Given this moderate, small-scale morality, it's hard to imagine what will happen to us Bobos when the world finally comes to an end. It's hard to imagine some fiery Last Judgment, some awful moment when the God of the Educated Class separates the saved—those who bundled their newspapers for the recycling bin—from the damned, those who did not. Bobo morality is so gentle and forgiving. Dwelling as it does in the moral temperate zone, Bobo morality doesn't seem compatible with the unrelenting horror of hell. On the other hand, Bobo morality doesn't seem compatible with something as final and complete as heaven either. Maybe instead of a Last Judgment, there will just be a Last Discussion.

Or maybe, as in that Robin Williams movie *What Dreams May Come,* Montana is the closest we get to heaven. Maybe our heaven isn't some grand place far above earth and its reality. After all, we are a group who seem to get our spiritual charges from tangible things, from spiritual places and evocative objects. Maybe if we walked around with a coherent moral order built into our head, we would feel at home in the supernatural realm. But lacking that faith in that next world, we tend to experience our spiritual epiphanies while communing with the physical environment in this one. We Bobos are more likely to try to discover great truths in particulars, the wonder of a leaf or the shape of a child's ear, than in a divine vision. With our tendency to seek peace in serene places, maybe a second home on some beautiful mountainside really is as close as we can come to experiencing paradise. Maybe our heaven is grounded in a piece of realty.

Picture a saintly Bobo woman pausing on her Montana hilltop at dusk, with thoughts of her law practice or mutual funds or teaching load far away. The air is still and fragrant, and even her dogs, Caleb and George, pause to savor the silence. As the breeze comes up, she pulls her FoxFibre shirt close around her neck. Lights are coming on in the distant houses across the valley, where former urban professionals have moved to start their own specialty food companies—Uncle Dave's Pestos is just on the far ridge to the north, Sally's Sauces is over to the west, and Yesterday's Chutney is on a few hundred acres south of that. She looks out over the tangle of wildflowers on the field that was junk strewn when she and her partner bought this "ranch," and she gazes lovingly upon the old pine she hired a tree surgeon to preserve.

Someone once said the essence of American history is the conversion of Eden into money. But with a little income, effort, and the right contractors, the educated person can spend money to build Eden. For hundreds of miles around, content couples are just settling into the creaky divans of their B&Bs and cracking open books by writers who have moved to Provence, novels that are like pornography to the overstressed. And so the Bobo decides to head down the path toward her second home. She is careful not to compact the soil over the tree roots and remembers a wonderful phrase by Steinbeck about a gentle person who "steps high over bugs." She passes under the arbor she attempted to cultivate last season and the pond she and her partner installed as a skinny-dipping space—they're much more sensual up here, though they wouldn't do anything that might alarm the hawks. As she approaches the house, she can hear the soundtrack of a Merchant-Ivory film wafting up to greet her; the melodies echo off the walls of the outbuildings that now serve as guest cottages.

The biggest thing they had to do when they moved in to this place was to triple the size of all the windows. They wanted to meld the interior and exterior elements of the home and so live more fully within nature. How sweet it is to wake up in a bedroom with one wall made entirely out of glass, allowing yourself a quiet hour to observe the sunrise (it helps if you own the surrounding 150 acres so there will be no neighbor observing you observing the sunrise). As she approaches the house, she slows to admire the sophisticated mosses that now grow along the walkway to the front door. She smells the aroma of the native grasses they planted around the house, and then she bounds lightly onto the wraparound porch, gently patting the aspen woodpile stacked neatly by the door. They don't burn this wood. But they've become devotees of the woodpile aesthetic, feeling that its form and texture complete a place such as this. As she pushes open the maple door that was flown in from New England, she hears her partner working away in his studio. This property has allowed him to take up the activities he never had time for. Aside from his new hobby as a narrator of environmental documentaries, he's playing the violin again, reading the novels of women writers of the Asian subcontinent, and doing community work—he's now treasurer of the local preservation society.

The living room is large but spare. The broad floor planks appear to glow and set off the redwood mantelpiece that sits amidst their massive stone fireplace. The redwood tree blew down nearly three years ago, and the stones they found a few years further back while hiking in Colorado. The furniture is rustic but comfortable. There are three of those massive curl-up chairs, each the size of a comfy Volkswagen. They're so much nicer than all those wingback chairs of her parents' generation. In the wingbacks you had to sit up straight. But in these wide shabby-chic chairs you can bend around into all sorts of relaxed positions.

The Bobo glances at the wooden ladles she has been collecting. She is taken by their slender curves, and prizes them more than any of the other objects she has harvested during her counter-connoisseur browsings. On the big wall she has displayed some old tortoiseshells and Cambodian statuettes. Her favorite statue is of the Bodhisattva, the spiritual entity who achieved enlightenment but delays entry into Nirvana in order to help others get there.

And just as she is feeling delicious tranquillity wafting over her, she notices there in the doorway to the kitchen stands the Angel of Death, the one especially delegated for the Bobos. He looks radiant in an old tweed jacket, and he must have been waiting for her for some time, for he has found one of the supersize ceramic mugs she bought at the crafts fair in Santa Fe the previous spring. The Angel of Death is full of questions about the renovations they did last year. She tells him that they decided to build the new kitchen wing using a Nordic technique called straw bale construction, which does not require the depletion of any timberland. Then they filled in the walls with rammed earth, which involves taking raw dirt and compacting it with such awesome force that it forms sturdy walls, caramel in color and radiating a woodsy aroma. The new doors were made from reclaimed wood from an old mission house in Arizona and squeak intentionally when opened. Nonapparent technology controls the heating and air conditioning and turns off the lights after everybody has left a room. The Angel of Death is enchanted by how they have tripled the original size of the ranch home and yet still preserved its original integrity. He informs her that she has just died but he doesn't plan to take her anywhere. She just gets to exist forever amidst all this glorious materiality. The only thing he requests is that she redo the floor tiles in the hall, which didn't really work out as nicely as she had hoped anyway. This final resting spot doesn't offer the bliss of salvation. But this is a sensitive, New Age eternity, and every radio frequency is filled with National Public Radio. She thanks the Angel of Death, and after a final sip of hazelnut, he fades into the distance, taking her Range Rover with him as he goes.

7

Politics and Beyond

IF YOU SIT DOWN and read through a series of books or essays with titles like "The Spirit of the Age," you'll discover that no matter when they were written, they almost always contain a sentence that says, "We are living in an age of transition." Whether it is the 1780s or the 1850s or the 1970s, people tend to feel themselves surrounded by flux. The old labels and ways of doing things seem obsolete. New modes and ideas seem as yet unformed.

We must be special. We are not living in an age of transition. We are living just after an age of transition. We are living just after the culture war that roiled American life for a generation. Between the 1960s and the 1980s the forces of bohemia and the forces of the bourgeoisie launched their final offensives. Bohemian counterculturalists attacked the establishment, the suburbs, and later the Reagan eighties. Conservative politicians and writers attacked the sixties and blamed that decade for much that was wrong in American life. Each force on the bohemian left—from the student radicals to the feminist activists—awakened a reaction in the bourgeois right, from the Moral Majority to the Supply Siders. This last spasm in the long conflict was a bumpy time, with protests, riots, mass movements, and a real breakdown in social order.

But out of that climactic turmoil a new reconciliation has been forged. A new order and a new establishment have settled into place, which I have tried to describe. And the members of this new and amorphous establishment have absorbed both sides of the culture war. They have learned from both "the sixties" and "the eighties." They have created a new balance of bourgeois and bohemian values. This balance has enabled us to restore some of the social peace that was lost during the decades of destruction and transition.

The Politics of Beyondism

The politicians who succeed in this new era have blended the bohemian 1960s and the bourgeois 1980s and reconciled the bourgeois and bohemian value systems. These politicians do not engage in the old culture war rhetoric. They are not podium-pounding "conviction politicians" of the sort that thrived during the age of confrontation. Instead, they weave together different approaches. They triangulate. They reconcile. They know they have to appeal to diverse groups. They seek a Third Way beyond the old categories of left and right. They march under reconciling banners such as compassionate conservatism, practical idealism, sustainable development, smart growth, prosperity with a purpose.

Whatever its other features, the Clinton/Gore administration embodied the spirit of compromise that is at the heart of the Bobo enterprise. In the first place, the Clintons were both 1960s antiwar protesters and 1980s futures traders. They came to the White House well stocked with bohemian ideals and bourgeois ambitions. They campaigned against the "tired old labels of left and right." In 1997 Bill Clinton effectively summarized his policy approach in a speech to the Democratic Leadership Council: "We had to go area by area to abandon those old false choices, the sterile debate about whether you would take the liberal or conservative positions, that only succeeded in dividing America and holding us back."

Confronted with a culture war that pitted traditional values against liberationist values, the Clinton administration merged, blurred, and reconciled. The Clintonites chose three key words—"Opportunity, Responsibility, and Community"—as their perpetual campaign themes, rarely pausing over whether there might be tensions between them. They embraced school uniforms and other traditional-sounding gestures, as well as condoms in schools and other liberal-sounding measures. Clinton triangulated above the hard-edged warriors on left and right and presented a soft and comfortable synthesis. He could, he declared, balance the budget without painful budget cuts, reform welfare without meanness, mend affirmative action but not end it, toughen the drug war while spending more on rehabilitation, preserve public schools while championing charter school alternatives. Battered early in the administration with a culture war skirmish over gays in the military, the Clintonites settled on "Don't Ask, Don't Tell." If ever there was a slogan that captures the Third Way efforts to find a peaceful middle ground, that was it.

Many of Clinton's attempts to reconcile opposing policies were unworkable. Nonetheless, the Clinton administration does leave behind an approach to politics that is enormously influential and is consonant with the Bobo age. This Third Way approach, neither neatly liberal nor conservative, neither a crusading counterculturalist nor a staid bourgeois, is a perpetual balancing act. And now if you look across the industrialized world, you see Third Way triangulators perched atop government after government. A few decades ago theorists predicted that members of the New Class would be *more* ideological than previous classes, *more* likely to be moved by utopian visions and abstract concepts. In fact, when the children of the 1960s achieved power, they produced a style of governance that was centrist, muddled, and if anything, anti-ideological.

They have settled on this style of politics because this is what appeals to the affluent suburbanites and to the sorts of people who control the money, media, and culture in American society today. Today there are about nine million households with incomes over $100,000, the most vocal and active portion of the population. And this new establishment, which exerts its hegemony over both major American political parties, has moved to soften ideological edges and damp down doctrinal fervor. Bobo Democrats sometimes work for investment houses like Lazard Frères. Bobo Republicans sometimes listen to the Grateful Dead. They don't want profound culture-war-type confrontations over first principles or polarizing presidential campaigns.

Whereas the old Protestant Establishment was largely conservative Republican, the new Bobo establishment tends to be centrist and independent. In 1998 the *National Journal* studied the voting patterns of America's 261 richest towns and discovered that they are moving to the center. The Democratic vote in those communities has risen in every election over the past two decades as members of the educated class have flooded into tony places like Wayne, Pennsylvania. The Democrats won 25 percent of the rich vote in 1980 and 41 percent in 1996. In that year

Bill Clinton carried 13 of the 17 most affluent congressional districts.

The affluent suburbs send moderate Republicans or moderate Democrats to Capitol Hill. These politicians spend much of their time in Congress complaining about the radicalism of their colleagues from less affluent districts. They can't understand why their liberal and conservative brethren seem addicted to strife. The less affluent polarizers rant and rave on *Crossfire*. They are perpetually coming up with radical and loopy ideas—destroy the IRS, nationalize health care. They seem to feel best about themselves when they are alienating others. All of this is foreign to the politicians from the Range Rover and Lexus districts. Like their Bobo constituents, they are more interested in consensus than conquest, civility than strife.

Indeed, in the Bobo age disputes within parties are more striking than conflict between parties. That's because, as University of Chicago philosopher Mark Lilla has pointed out, the central disagreement today is not the sixties versus the eighties. It is between those who have fused the sixties and the eighties on one side and those who reject the fusion on the other. In the Republican Party, moderates and modern conservatives do battle with the conservatives who want to refight the 1960s. On the Democratic side, the New Democrats do battle with those who have not come to terms with the Thatcher-Reagan reforms of the 1980s.

The people of the left and right who long for radical and heroic politics are driven absolutely batty by tepid Bobo politics. They see large problems in society, and they cry out for radical change. This new centrist establishment frustrates or stifles their radical ideas, and yet they find it hard to confront this power elite head-on. The Bobo establishment seems to have no there there. It never presents a coherent opposition. It never presents its opponents with a set of consistent ideas that can be argued and refuted. Instead, it co-opts and it embraces. Whether you are liberal or conservative, Bobo politicians adopt your rhetoric and your policy suggestions while somehow sucking all the radicalism out of them. They sometimes tilt to the left and sometimes to the right. They never rise up for a fight. They just go along their merry way, blurring, reconciling, merging, and being happy. While those on left and right hunger for confrontation and change, the Bobos seem to be following the advice on their throw pillows: "Living Well Is the Best Revenge."

The Project

But this does not mean that Bobo politics lacks direction. In fact the Bobos do have a project that will shape politics in the years to come. Their political project is to correct the excesses of the two social revolutions that brought them to power.

The bohemian sixties and the bourgeois eighties were polar opposites in many ways. But they did share two fundamental values: individualism and freedom. Writers in both decades paid lip service to community action and neighborhood institutions, but the main effort was to liberate individuals. The bohemian revolt in the sixties was about cultural freedom. It was about free expression, freedom of thought, sexual freedom. It was an effort to throw off social strictures and conformist attitudes, to escape from the stultifying effects of large bureaucracies and overbearing authority figures. The bourgeois resurgence of the 1980s, on the other hand, expanded economic and political freedom. The economy was deregulated and privatized in order to unleash entrepreneurial energies. The nanny state was attacked and in some cases rolled back. Cozy corporatist arrangements were ended. Large bureaucracies were cut. Even as late as 1994, the congressional Republicans swept into power calling themselves the Leave Us Alone Coalition. They wanted to get government off people's backs in order to maximize individual freedom.

Many of the people who led the social and political movements of the sixties and the eighties naively assumed that once old restrictions were removed and individuals liberated, then better ways of living would automatically blossom. But life isn't that easy. If you start up-ending obsolete social norms, pretty soon you'll notice that valuable ones, like civility and manners, get weakened too. If you start dissolving social ties in order to unleash individual self-expression, pretty soon you'll notice that valuable community bonds are eroded as well. Efforts to weaken oppressive authority end up corroding all authority. The stature of teachers, parents, and democratic institutions gets diluted along with that of bureaucratic despots and uptight busybodies. The economic dynamism that brought such great wealth also threatened the small communities and the social stability that many people cherish. In the nineties Americans increasingly felt there needed to be a correction. If the sixties and the eighties were about expanding freedom and individualism, the Bobos are now left to cope with excessive freedom and excessive individualism.

That's why the two crucial words in the Bobo political project these days, as we began to see in the last chapter, are *community* and *control*. Across American society one sees effort after effort to restore social cohesion, reassert authority, and basically get a grip on the energies that have been unleashed over the past quarter century. So we see universities reasserting their *in loco parentis* authority, reimposing curfews as well as rules on cohabitation, drinking, unsupervised parties, fraternity hazing, and sexual conduct. Colin Powell has led an upsurge in volunteerism as millions of people donate their time supervising latchkey kids, setting up adult-organized activities, and cleaning up and thereby bringing a little order back into anarchic neighborhoods. In legislatures across the country, there have been efforts to control Internet smut, control guns, control tobacco advertising, and control, or at least label, violent television programming and video games. The country has seen a historic wave of welfare reform in which local, state, and federal agencies have imposed more rules and restrictions on welfare recipients. Cities across the nation have reimposed controls on panhandling, vagrancy, public drinking, and even littering. Community policing programs have given the police more day-to-day authority in high-crime areas.

And, of course, politicians have learned to adopt a new language. Republicans no longer talk so aggressively about getting government off our backs. "My first goal is to usher in the responsibility era," George W. Bush said in announcing his campaign for the presidency. A few months later Bush attacked "the destructive mindset: the idea that if government would only get out of way, all our problems would be solved. An approach with no higher goal, no nobler purpose than 'leave us alone.' " Meanwhile, Al Gore also sought to distance himself from some of the antiauthority impulses that had once influenced his party. "It is our lives we must master if we are to have the moral authority to guide our children," he said in announcing his candidacy. "The ultimate outcome does not rest in the hands of any President, but with all our people— taking responsibility for themselves and for each other."

Some of the most dramatic efforts to reassert authority have been in the home and in the neighborhood. Back in the 1960s a man named A. S. Neill ran a school in Britain called Summerhill, which had virtually no rules except those that were set by the children themselves. Neill's book on his Summerhill method sold well over two million copies in the United States, part of a broad movement at that time to give children maximum freedom to explore, create, and otherwise develop "naturally." Any of us who were in school in those days can point to programs and progressive reforms that were designed to enhance student freedom and so encourage greater individualism—schools without walls, open classrooms, open campuses. There were even smoking rooms in public high schools, despite the fact that underage smoking was illegal.

But these days the ethos has entirely flipped. Now leading politicians from both parties advocate the return of uniforms in public schools. Now children are monitored and supervised, enshrouded with rules and devices. Now, for example, there is unprecedented concern with children's safety, part of our fumbling efforts to protect and regulate our kids. Bicycle manufacturers have noticed a drop-off in sales as parents become less likely to allow their children to spend their days roaming their neighborhoods on bikes. Today's children spend their days awash in moral instruction to an extent unprecedented even at the height of the Victorian era: children's television shows preach incessantly on subjects ranging from recycling to racism; teachers are asked to give homilies as well as instruction, on everything from drugs to civility. After the shootings in Littleton, Colorado, in 1999, there was a tidal wave of commentary. But on one subject there was total agreement: parents need to exercise more authority over their kids. The days of Rousseauistic liberation are over.

Equally striking are the efforts, especially by the residents of upscale towns, to gain control over neighborhood growth and development. The Reaganites may have preached the virtues of laissez-faire, but that approach is decidedly out of fashion in most Bobo suburbs today. If you go into a Bobo neighborhood, you will find a powerful group of citizens promoting stricter zoning requirements, opposing new commercial development, and fighting tear-downs (when an owner tears down a house on his or her property and erects a larger one) and other "improvements." Rather than being progressive and forward-looking, upscale neighborhoods seem to be looking back, seeking to preserve their stable and orderly past or at least to create the sorts of communities that hew to the patterns of what seem to have been stable and orderly pasts. Bobos spend more time restoring lost treasures, renovating old structures, or preserving old buildings than they do creating new and experimental institutions. Every third Bobo automobile seems to have a bumper sticker on it that implores, "Save the _____." Bobos are saving old theaters, old neighborhoods, old factories and warehouses, or even historically significant diners. When they do allow new building, these mostly affluent activists will insist that the new construction adhere to the patterns of the past. They will talk about preserving local character, fighting sprawl, combating unregulated growth, and enhancing "livability" and "quality of life." Here, too, they are trying to preserve order and stability and restore community control.

Intimate Authority

The main thrust of Bobo politics is the effort to restore the bonds of *intimate* authority. Bobos are not much interested in grand efforts to assert large-scale authority. One hundred years ago Herbert Croly gave voice to the Progressive Era's desire to create a national community with a powerful national government guided by technocratic experts who would organize and rationalize American life. That was an era of consolidation, when small entities seemed to be drawn ineluctably together to form big entities—big trusts, big bureaucracies, big cities. But we no longer feel we are living in an age of consolidation;

on the contrary, deconsolidation seems to be the order of the day. So upscale Americans, like most Americans, show little desire to launch a new set of massive political enterprises, whether it is another liberal War on Poverty or a grand conservative War on Cultural Decay. They tend to distrust formal hierarchies that are imposed from above and Olympian lawgivers who would presume to govern from glorious heights. They are generally disenchanted with national politics. They tend not to see it as a glorious or capital R Romantic field of endeavor, the way so many people did earlier in the century. Utopianism of that sort is practically extinct. Instead, they are more likely to see politics as a series of humble improvisations enacted with cautious hopes and some anxiety.

Instead, they think most highly of political action that is conducted on the local level, where communication can be face to face and where debate tends to be less ideological. When confronted with thorny national problems like poverty and education, Bobos tend to favor devolution, decentralizing power to the lowest possible level. This way each person or community can discover its own pragmatic solution without having to engage in seemingly futile debates over first principles.

Intimate authority is imparted, not imposed. It is the sort of constant, gentle pressure that good parents and neighbors provide: be polite when you are introduced to someone, don't litter in the park, don't tell fibs, help people with their packages when they are burdened, comfort them when they are grieving, and reassure them when they are uncertain. Intimate authority isn't mainly about writing down formal codes and laws; it is about setting up patterns, instilling habits, and creating contexts so that people are most likely to exercise individual responsibility. It means setting up welcome wagons so that new people feel part of an interdependent community. It means volunteering at the youth center so teenagers will have a place to go and be minded. It can be as trivial as the penny jar near the cash register so that the next person will have a penny handy if it's needed. Or it can be as pervasive as residential projects along the lines of the New Urbanism movement, which are designed to make sure there are eyes on the street, people watching out for each other and subtly upholding community standards of behavior and decency.

In true reconciling fashion, intimate authority is a Third Way between excessive individualism on the one hand and imposed formal authority on the other. This is not authority as physics—one powerful body exerting pressure on a smaller body. It is authority as biology, with all the members of the ecosystem exerting a gradual and subtle pressure on the others so the whole network can thrive.

It was just this sort of constant pressure that the old bohemians found so stifling. It is why they fled small towns for the anonymity and freedom of the big city. But today most Bobos seek community and control more than liberation and release. They have become conservatives.

Blue Jean Conservatives

I don't mean that members of the educated class are overwhelmingly conservative in the sense that the Republican Party uses the term, meaning in favor of tax cuts, less intrusive government, and larger defense budgets (although certainly many Bobos support these things). Rather, the ethos that unites most Bobos is an older meaning of conservatism, a meaning that describes a temperament rather than an ideology.

Edmund Burke called the great property owners of his day the "ballast in the vessel of the commonwealth." And in many regards that is true of today's upper-middle-class property owners. Today's Bobos seek to conserve the world they have created, the world that reconciles the bourgeois and the bohemian. As a result, they treasure civility and abhor partisanship, which roils the waters. They seek to preserve the simple things that have stood the test of time. They seek to restore gentle authority. They treasure religion so long as it is conducted in a spirit of moderation rather than zeal. They appreciate good manners and cherish little customs and traditions. They value what Burke called the "little platoon," the small intermediating institutions that make up a neighborhood and town. They seek to restore order, not foment radical change.

A 19th-century conservative, Walter Bagehot, wrote, "It is of immense importance that there should be among the more opulent and comfortable classes a large number of minds trained by early discipline to this habit of restraint and sobriety." And these days it is certainly true that Bobos have learned restraint and sobriety, albeit the Bobo code of sobriety owes more to the American Medical Association than Victorian rigor.

Conservative in temperament, Bobos almost always reject grand rationalistic planning, feeling that the world is far too complicated to be altered effectively by some person's scheme to reshape reality. Though they are an elite based above all on education, they are not overwhelmingly impressed by the power of expertise. Instead, they seem acutely aware of how little even the best minds know about the world and how complicated reality is compared to our understanding. They know, thanks to events like the war in Vietnam, that technocratic decision making can produce horrible results when it doesn't take into account the variability of local contexts. They are aware, thanks to the failure of the planned economies of eastern Europe, that complex systems cannot be run from the center. In other words, they are epistemologically modest, the way such conservatives as Burke and

Oakeshott would have wanted them to be. They are more interested in preserving the imperfect institutions that have already proved some usefulness than they are in taking a flyer on some as yet untested vision of the future. They have learned that revolutions usually backfire and that, when it comes to social change, steady reform is best. Many Bobos would fight like hell against being labeled conservatives, but often the ones in the hemp clogs and ponytails are the most temperamentally conservative of all. If you go to places like Berkeley and Burlington, Vermont, you see that this kind of conservatism can emerge directly out of liberalism.

The Bobo Achievement

Thanks in large part to the influence of the Bobo establishment, we are living in an era of relative social peace. The political parties, at least at the top, have drifted toward the center. For the first time since the 1950s, it is possible to say that there aren't huge ideological differences between the parties. One begins to see the old 1950s joke resurface, that presidential contests have once again become races between Tweedledum and Tweedledumber. Meanwhile, the college campuses are not aflame with angry protests. Intellectual life is diverse, but you wouldn't say that radicalism of the left or right is exactly on the march. Passions are muted. Washington is a little dull. (I know. I live there.) The past 30 years have brought wrenching social changes. A little tranquillity may be just what the country needs so that new social norms can form and harden, so that the new Bobo consensus can settle into place.

So far it seems to be working. Many of the social problems that grew at epidemic ferocity during the 1960s and 1970s have begun to ease, if unevenly. Crime rates have come down, and so have divorce rates, abortion rates, cocaine use, teenage drinking, teenage promiscuity. Meanwhile, the nation's economy, which is not unrelated to the nation's culture, has gone from strength to strength.

Bobos have reason to feel proud of the contributions they have made to their country. Wherever they have settled, they have life more enjoyable (for those who can afford it). Shops are more interesting. The food in the grocery stores and restaurants is immeasurably better and more diverse. Communities are now dotted with gathering places and meeting grounds. Homes are less formal and more comfortable. Moreover, Bobos have done wonderful things to the world of American capitalism. Bobo businesspeople have created a corporate style attuned to the information age, with its emphasis on creativity, flat hierarchies, flexibility, and open expression. It's simply impossible to argue with the unparalleled success of America's information age industries over the past decade.

On balance, intellectual life has been improved as well. Sure, some of the intellectual intensity is gone. Fewer people seem to live for ideas, the way the old *Partisan Review* crowd did. But that rarefied world was insular (in spite of the fact that its members thought they were fighting for the working class). They were cut off from daily political and social realities. Today's careerist intellectuals have a foot in the world of 401(k) plans and social mobility and so have more immediate experience with life as it is lived by most of their countrymen. This grounding means that intellectuals have fewer loony ideas than did intellectuals in the past. Few of them fall for visions of, say, Marxist utopias. Fewer idolize Che Guevara–style revolutionaries. On balance, it's better to have a reasonable and worldly intellectual class than an intense but destructive one.

Leisure has also improved. Any survey of ecological tours of the rainforest or meritocratic slumming in Tuscan peasant towns will yield a rich harvest of mockery. But the impulse to seek edifying experiences is basically an admirable one. Moreover, Bobos have achieved a reasonably decent balance between mindless sexuality and uptight Puritanism. They have domesticated many sensual activities so they can be enjoyed without posing much of a threat to the social order. That's no small achievement, either.

As we turn around and look back at the range of Bobo manners and morals, we find a bit that's risible, a bit that is too precious by half, but a lot that is wonderful. Bobos have begun to create a set of standards and mores that work in the new century. It's good to live in a Bobo world.

This New Age of Complacency

I don't want to close with a paean of praise for everything Bobo. Spiritual life is tepid and undemanding. (Indeed, it's possible to imagine a coming generation that will grow bored of our reconciliations, our pragmatic ambivalence, our tendency to lead lives half one thing and half another. They may long for a little cleansing purity, a little zeal in place of our materialism, demanding orthodoxy in place of our small-scale morality.)

Moreover, while the relative tranquillity we have achieved is not to be sneezed at, given the alternatives, it is also possible to be tranquil to a fault. In preferring politicians who are soggy synthesizers and in withdrawing from great national and ideological disputes for the sake of local and community pragmatism, we may be losing touch with the soaring ideals and high ambitions that have always separated America from other nations. I mentioned in the introduction to this book that I spent four and a half years in Europe in the early nineties. I came back warning my friends, only half-jokingly, of the Menace of Belgian Cultural Hegemony. I was trying to describe the temptations that accompany affluence. We may become a nation that enjoys the comforts of private and local life but has lost any sense of national union and any sense of a unique historical mission. The fear is that America will decline not because it overstretches, but because it enervates as its leading citizens decide that the pleasures of an oversized kitchen are more satisfying than the conflicts and challenges of patriotic service. It could have been something like this that alarmed Tocqueville as he speculated about the future of America. "What worries me most," he wrote in *Democracy in America,* "is the danger that, amid all the constant trivial preoccupations of private life, ambition may lose both its force and its greatness, that human passions may grow gentler and at the same time baser, with the result that the progress of the body social may become daily quieter and less aspiring."

This is no longer a prediction for the future. Tocqueville's scenario has come to pass. These days most of us don't want to get too involved in national politics because it seems so partisan and ugly. And as a result, most Americans citizens have become detached from public life and have come to look on everything that does not immediately touch them with an indifference that is laced with contempt. We have allowed our political views to be corroded with an easy pseudo-cynicism that holds that all politicians are crooks and all public endeavor is a sham. As the public opinion polls demonstrate with utmost clarity, we have lost faith in public institutions and many private ones. We have turned a healthy skepticism about government action into a corrosive negativism, which makes us passive even as we stare at political practices and policies that make us ashamed. In short, our national life has become compressed, our public spirit corroded by cynicism, our ability to achieve great things weakened by inaction. We are threatened with a new age of complacency, which may be just as menacing to our dreams for America as imperial overstretch or defeat in war.

The Bobo task is to rebuild some sense of a united polity, some sense of national cohesion, without crushing the individual freedoms we have won over the past generation or the bonds of intimate authority that are being restored today. That is to say, we have to consolidate the gains we have made as individuals and communities while at the same time re-energizing national politics. In that famous passage when Burke praised the "little platoons" of family and community life, he went on to make an equally important but much less often quoted observation. Local affection, he argued, "is the first link in the series by which we proceed toward a love of country and to mankind." Healthy families and healthy communities are insufficient if the nation is in decay. Healthy self-interest becomes self-absorption if it is detached from larger national and universal ideals.

That suggests a course of action that is reform at home and activism abroad. Reform of those institutions and practices that no longer make us proud: the campaign finance system, which has become a corrupting bog, the tax code, which has become complex and alienating, the welfare state, which needs to be debureaucratized. And at the same time on an international sphere, it means picking up the obligations that fall to the world's lead nation: promoting democracy and human rights everywhere and exercising American might in a way that reflects American ideals.

For Americans to become engaged once again in public life and proud of their public institutions, something else has to happen to the Bobos. They have to assume a leadership role. They are the best-educated segment of society and among the most affluent, and yet by and large they have not devoted their energies to national life. Obviously, Bobos work in government and politics, but the public arena hasn't become a focus of attention for the educated class as a whole. This has left a gaping hole in public life. Filling this hole means doing what the postwar ruling class did. It means developing a public service ethos, concluding, as people like Dean Acheson, John McCloy, George C. Marshall, and Dwight Eisenhower did, that to those who are blessed much is expected, and that public service is the highest secular service a person can perform. When we look back on the postwar ruling class, we see some mistakes and some hubris. But we also see a group of men and women who made genuine commitments to America that sometimes overrode their individual self-interest. Which of us doesn't long for an updated version of that sense of service, of that sober patriotism? And which of us doubts that the Bobos, with all their brains and good intentions, can make the same sorts of contributions if they direct their energies in the right direction?

The Bobos are a young elite, only dimly aware of themselves as an elite and unaware as yet of their capacities. This is a class of people who grew up with the word *potential* hanging around their necks, and in many ways still, their potential is more striking than their accomplishments. They have been trained, nurtured, and educated. They have been freed of some old restrictions and they have forged some new bonds. They are largely unscarred by economic depression and war. They can be silly a lot of the time. But if they raise their sights and ask the biggest questions, they have the ability to go down in history as the class that led America into another golden age.

Acknowledgments

I WROTE SEVERAL magazine articles about upscale culture before I realized they pointed to a single thesis that could be the basis for a book. I wrote about Status Income Disequilibrium, countercultural capitalists, Latte Towns, and Cell Phone Naturalists for the *Weekly Standard,* and chunks of those pieces have been adapted in these pages. I'm grateful to Bill Kristol, Fred Barnes, and John Podhoretz for encouraging me to do those pieces. This is also a good place to say how grateful I am to them for starting the *Standard* and for asking me and so many of my friends to work there. The hours we spend every week schmoozing at the office are among the great pleasures of my life.

There are other editors to thank. The section on the *New York Times* weddings pages is adapted from an essay I wrote early on for the *City Journal,* and I'm grateful to Myron Magnet for his help on that. My first foray into the realm of the affluent was done for Brian Kelly and Steve

Luxenberg of the *Washington Post* "Outlook" section. I'd also like to thank Henry Finder and Susan Morrison of the *New Yorker*. I began writing pieces on commercial culture for them relatively late in the game, when I thought I knew my subject pretty well. But their off-the-cuff insights were intimidating, since they knew so many things I didn't and had observed patterns that never occurred to me. The paragraphs on Restoration Hardware are drawn from work I did for them.

Many other people helped me along the way. First mention has to go to Erich Eichman, Dan Casse, and John Podhoretz, who read the manuscript and offered valuable advice. Michael Kinsley and Jack Shafer helped me understand the Seattle culture, and Mike even took me camping. John Baden gave me valuable suggestions about what to do and see in Montana. Irving Kristol led me to César Graña's book *Bohemian versus Bourgeois,* which helped crystallize my thinking. Tori Ritchie of *San Francisco Magazine* helped me appreciate the full cultural import of the kitchen. My agents, Glen Hartley and Lynn Chu, have been friends for over a decade; their labors on my behalf have been above and beyond the call of duty. Marion Maneker was the editor who acquired this book for Simon & Schuster; his skills are formidable. After Marion left for HarperCollins, I was honored to have Alice Mayhew take on the project. A writer couldn't hope for a more responsive editor. She seemed to ponder every word in this manuscript, and her comments improved it in ways great and small.

Finally, there is my family. My parents moved to Wayne, Pennsylvania, because Lewis Mumford said pre–World War I suburbs are the best places to live in the United States. Going to high school there, I thought the place was bourgeois and reactionary, which it was. But now it's changed and I've changed and I realize what a wonderful community it is. I'm grateful to my parents and my brother, Daniel, for our happy life there. And I'm more grateful than I can say to my wife, Jane, and our kids, Joshua, Naomi, and Aaron, for their sacrifices as I reported, researched, and squirreled away in the basement writing this book.

Index

About the Author

DAVID BROOKS is a political journalist and "comic sociologist" who writes a biweekly Op-Ed column for *The New York Times*. He appears regularly on PBS' *The NewsHour with Jim Lehrer* and NPR's *All Things Considered*. Formerly a senior editor at *The Weekly Standard*, his articles have also appeared in *The Atlantic Monthly, Newsweek, Reader's Digest, Men's Health*, and other publications. He lives in Bethesda, Maryland.

Also available by David Brooks

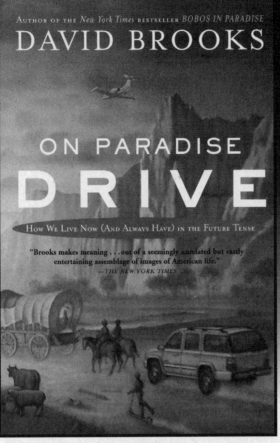

0-7432-2739-5

Take a look at Americans in their natural habitat: guys shopping for barbecue grills, doing that special walk American men do when in the presence of lumber; super-efficient übermoms who chair school auctions, organize the PTAs, and weigh less than their kids. Many around the world see us as the great bimbo. Sure, Americans work hard and are energetic, but that is because they are money-hungry and don't know how to relax.

But if you probe deeper, you find that we behave the way we do because we live under the spell of paradise. We are the inheritors of a sense of limitless possibilities, raised to think in the future tense and to strive toward imagined happiness, fulfillment of our dreams.

SIMON & SCHUSTER
PAPERBACKS
A VIACOM COMPANY

www.simonsays.com